Scribe Publications
THE SECRETS OF THE ANZACS

For Maurice Buckley, Albert Crozier, Ernest Dunbar,
Harold Glading, and Richard Waltham

THE
SECRETS OF THE ANZACS

**the untold story of
venereal disease in the
Australian army,
1914–1919**

RADEN DUNBAR

SCRIBE
Melbourne • London

Scribe Publications
18–20 Edward St, Brunswick, Victoria 3056, Australia
2 John St, Clerkenwell, London, WC1N 2ES, United Kingdom

First published by Scribe 2014

Typeset in Minion 11/15.25pt by J&M Typesetting
Indexed by Richard McGregor
Printed and bound in Australia by Griffin Press

 The paper this book is printed on is certified against the Forest Stewardship
Council® Standards. Griffin Press holds FSC chain of custody certification
SGS-COC-005088. FSC promotes environmentally responsible, socially
beneficial and economically viable management of the world's forests.

National Library of Australia
Cataloguing-in-Publication data

Dunbar, Raden, author.

The Secrets of the Anzacs: the untold story of venereal disease in the Australian Army,
1914–1919 / Raden Dunbar.

9781925106169 (AUS edition)
9781925228007 (UK edition)
9781925113402 (e-book)

1. Australia–Army. 2. Australian and New Zealand Army Corps–History.
3. World War, 1914-1918–Health aspects–Australia. 4. Sexually transmitted diseases.
5. War–Health aspects.

616.951

This project has been assisted by the Australian
government through the Australia Council for
the Arts, its arts funding and advisory body.

Australian Government

scribepublications.com.au
scribepublications.co.uk

CONTENTS

PREFACE AND ACKNOWLEDGEMENTS

During World War I, millions of soldiers and women from all combatant nations became infected with venereal diseases during an unprecedented outbreak of wartime sexual promiscuity. Included were at least 60,000 Australian soldiers, who were treated by army doctors for venereal infections between 1914 and 1919 in Egypt, the United Kingdom, and France, and in Australia.

This is a subject that, although rarely described by historians, is so big that a single book like this one could never adequately cover it. It has numerous aspects, and there are voluminous Australian and overseas original archival and other resources about it. These include thousands of individual service and military records, and hundreds of documents, newspaper, and journal articles, and some books from the time. Although the VD infections of so many soldiers was an important part of Australia's war experience, and, although during the war and immediately after, there was considerable public discussion about it, the subject seems to have later become almost unmentionable, even by historians.

This book tells the stories of a number of individuals in the Australian Imperial Force whose lives were affected by the outbreak of VD that began in Cairo in 1914. Some of these men were the senior army commanders who had to deal with the problem using policies that were progressively adjusted until 1919. Others were Australian Army Medical Corps officers in Egypt, Australia, and England who had to devise the medical methods to try to prevent and to cure the diseases. Included are stories about the army venereal-disease isolation barracks at Abbassia in Cairo and at Langwarrin near Melbourne, and about the troopship voyages carrying infected men from Abbassia to Langwarrin. In particular, this book tells the stories of five young soldiers who became infected in Egypt in 1915, were returned to Australia in disgrace on the troopship A18 *Wiltshire*, and had to deal with the consequences for the rest of their lives.

My interest in the fates of these soldiers began with the knowledge that my great-uncle Ernest Dunbar had an unusual record of service in the First World War. Soon, I began to look in more detail at the *Wiltshire*'s voyage and her young passengers. Reading through hundreds of century-old AIF service files, it became obvious that, for each soldier, a few moments of sexual gratification had led to a series of personal disasters. Documents and letters revealed the harsh lessons in life that had begun after each prodigal's VD infection was discovered in Egypt, and how long those lessons had gone on for.

Although my research led me in many directions, this single book, however, cannot provide all the stories of such a big topic as venereal disease in the Australian army during the war. For example, the plight, circumstances, and fates of women and girls trafficked into the brothels of Egypt and elsewhere could not be included. Also not included is detailed analysis of why wartime promiscuity on such a large scale occurred, what the Allied powers did to try to control it, or why so many Australians became infected with VD.

Although the wonderful story of the New Zealand wartime safe-sex campaigner Ettie Rout is mentioned briefly, far more space is given to her Australian collaborator James Barrett. Rout's story has already been told in a book by her compatriot Jane Tolerton.

Nor could the full story of the 1st Australian Dermatological Hospital at Bulford in England be included, although it is frequently mentioned. Bulford was the largest Australian VD hospital during the war, and is a story in itself. This book mentions many ordinary soldiers who were admitted to Bulford between 1916 and 1919, including decorated war heroes, but space precluded accounts of the commissioned officers who were treated there and at other hospitals, or their unusual circumstances.

Other important topics that could not be included are the general post-war consequences of wartime VD for soldiers who were infected overseas and eventually repatriated, purportedly cured; and the consequences for their wives, their families, and Australian society during the decades after the war. In the space available, it was not possible to fully explain why wartime VD became such a sensitive post-war topic — readers can draw their own conclusions about that. Finally, although speculation is included about the long-term health consequences for soldiers treated during the war with toxic anti-VD drugs containing heavy metals, this subject could not be given the thorough attention it deserves.

I would like to acknowledge and thank a number of individuals who assisted me in researching and writing this book. In particular, I acknowledge assistance given at the very beginning by Dr Milton Lewis, a medical historian at the University of Sydney. He introduced me to the historian Brendan O'Keefe, who, among other accomplishments, has written extensively about venereal disease in the Australian army. Brendan conducted considerable archival research on my behalf, which provided the basis for much in the book.

Robin Brown was the first reader of early drafts, and provided considerable advice about the language I should use in writing the stories. I would also like to thank Professor Peter Stanley of the University of NSW, at the Australian Defence Force Academy in Canberra, for his encouragement and help. Among many others consulted, a number of individuals formed a readers' panel to go through the first full draft manuscript and provide comment and criticism. Some are former or still-serving officers of the Australian Defence Force; others, colleagues of mine in the Australian Civilian Corps. They are Phil Bennett, Kerry Clifford, Bob Kyle, Alan Moore, John Peachey, Beth Pearce, and Dr Mark Weston Wall. Very early in the project, I was able to explain my intentions to Australian expatriates of the Capricorn Society in Jakarta, and from them received encouragement and advice.

During the course of research, I had the pleasure of contacting and, in some cases, meeting with a number of enthusiastic amateur historians, including two Hunter Valley men: the indomitable Harry Willey of Scone, and David Harrower of Cessnock. I also met with members of a number of local historical societies.

I wish to praise the National Library of Australia for developing the Trove integrated database of numerous archival resources. I also commend the National Archives of Australia, the Australian War Memorial, the AIF Project, and many libraries and museums in Australia and overseas that provide online research facilities. These valuable research tools have made the task of historians immeasurably easier.

Acknowledgement is given to archives organisations for granting permission and licences to reproduce images in this book, and, in several instances, for waiving all or part of the usual fees. They are the Australian National University Archives, the Australian War Memorial, Discover Mornington Peninsula, Fairfax Syndication, the Library of Congress, Melbourne University Archives, Musee du Louvre/RMN, Museums Victoria, the National Library of Australia, PrenticeNet, the Public Records Office of Victoria, the State Library of NSW, and the State Library of Victoria.

Finally, I would also like to thank Henry Rosenbloom and David Golding of Scribe for their kind advice for improving the manuscript, and throughout the production stages. Their many superb skills in writing and publishing contributed to bringing this long project to successful fruition.

ABBREVIATIONS

1AGH	1st Australian General Hospital
AAMC	Australian Army Medical Corps
AIF	Australian Imperial Force
ANZAC	Australian and New Zealand Army Corps
AWL	Absent Without Leave
Btn	Battalion
CMG	Companion of the Order of St Michael and St George
DCM	Distinguished Conduct Medal
DSO	Distinguished Service Order
GP	General Practitioner
HMAT	His Majesty's Australian Transport
HMS	His Majesty's Ship
MC	Military Cross
NCO	Non-Commissioned Officer
NSW	New South Wales
POW	Prisoner of War
RAMC	Royal Army Medical Corps
RSL	Returned and Services League
RSSILA	Returned Sailors and Soldiers Imperial League of Australia
VC	Victoria Cross
VD	Venereal Disease
YMCA	Young Men's Christian Association

Egypt 1915

a military, medical, and moral problem

At sea near the southern entrance to the Suez Canal, one evening late in August 1915, hundreds of soldiers of the Australian Imperial Force stood in cooling breezes at the deck rails and portholes of a troopship, the A18 *Wiltshire*. Thick plumes of black coal-smoke whirled away from the vessel's large funnel as she gathered way to the south, into the Gulf of Suez night, heading away from Egypt and towards Australia. As the sweltering heat of the day faded, the men on board watched the bright lights of Port Suez slowly disappear over the sea.

Until early that morning, all of them had been prisoners in a hot and crowded detention barracks at Abbassia in the city of Cairo. They had been moved from there that morning, under guard, to Suez and onto the *Wiltshire*, thence to be conveyed to another detention barracks far away at Langwarrin, near Melbourne. The 8,000-nautical-mile voyage on which they had embarked would take about a month, across the Indian Ocean via Aden and Colombo to Fremantle, then through the Great Australian Bight to Port Melbourne. When the *Wiltshire* departed from Egypt, it was late summer, but she would be greeted at her destination by a fine Melbourne spring.

The men on the *Wiltshire* had been banished from Egypt by the army. Very recently, in various AIF camps, each man had discovered he had a

HMAT A18 *Wiltshire*, an Australian troopship
from 1914 until 1919. *(SLV)*

venereal disease. It was an offence in the army to conceal this, so each
had revealed his condition to an army doctor, and had in turn been sent
to the Abbassia barracks. It was crowded with hundreds of infected men
being given painful VD treatments — repeatedly injecting and syringing
them with toxic drugs. Every few weeks, when space was available on a
troopship returning to Australia, a few hundred men were selected to be
sent to Langwarrin.

The army had decided that each man in Abbassia was guilty of
misconduct. Because of that, each had been abruptly removed from his
battalion or regiment, and those who were non-commissioned officers
were reduced to the ranks. As well, the army pay of each man was
stopped for the duration of his VD cure, which could take months. The
stoppage also meant that if a man had allotted part of his pay to a family
member in Australia, that was also stopped — and without explanation.
Before men were sent to Australia, they were told that, probably after
their arrival in Melbourne, they would be discharged from the army for
misconduct.

This was what the 275 infected soldiers on the *Wiltshire* could look forward to: their pay had been stopped indefinitely, they were going to have daily injections and syringing all the way back to Australia, and then they might be discharged. What worried most of them, however, was the thought of having to explain all of this to those at home who cared about them. All privately knew that the journey they were taking might have to be kept secret forever.

The problems with the diseases they had acquired lay partly in the micro-organisms that caused them: in 1915, no reliable method had been developed to stop these troublesome bacteria from being transmitted during sexual intercourse; nor were there any guaranteed cures. But there was also a problem due to the victims' perceived lack of morals, and that was perhaps worse. People with VD could have only been infected through pre-marital or extra-marital sex, and, in respectable Australian society, this was immoral. Even worse, the men in Egypt had become infected by having sex with prostitutes; this was doubly immoral and also foolish. Churches in Australia preached that venereal diseases were God's punishment for sinners, and this certainly felt like the case to the infected men. Because of the heavy social stigma, those with VD tried to keep it a secret, and implored the doctors who attempted to cure them to keep the secret as well.

The men on the *Wiltshire* with VD were unusual: most AIF troops who passed through Egypt from the end of 1914 until mid-1916 did not become infected with venereal diseases. About 10,000 men, however, were treated at army hospitals for them during this period; and, because of unusual circumstances in 1915, 1,344 were sent to Langwarrin. Most had been infected in the brothels of Egypt, but some had been infected in Australia before they had left, and others at ports of call on the way.

Egypt had been a world-famous centre for vice long before the Australians arrived, and things were made worse when 40,000 British soldiers had landed in Egypt in the 1880s and stayed permanently. They were an irresistible target for local sex-industry operators, and for traffickers of women and girls. To try to control the contagious VD that

3

Considered pornography in Australia, risqué postcards like this were
freely available in Egypt for soldiers to buy. Pictures of semi-nude
Moorish serving maids holding an amphora of wine were very popular.

inevitably followed, the British made laws that had the effect of making
prostitution tolerated. Districts in cities such as Cairo and Alexandria
became fleshpots with bars, brothels, and sex shows for foreigners, and
these even became tourist attractions.

How, then, was it possible for large numbers of young Australian
soldiers to be sent to this infamous centre of vice and venereal disease?

Before the war began in August 1914, the Australian government
offered to send 20,000 men to any destination desired by the British
government, in anticipation of a possible conflict. The AIF was formed
hastily, and troopships left Australia in October, heading for England via
the Suez Canal in Egypt. A few days from Suez, however, the commander
of the AIF, Major General William Bridges, received orders to disembark
his force there and to continue the journey to England later. Accordingly,
in December 1914, the Australians set up their camps close to Cairo
— one just over the River Nile at Mena, and another at Maadi — and

Australian troops lining the deck rails of the *Wiltshire* at Port Suez.
On this occasion, it was December 1914, and the troopship was
arriving in Egypt with the first AIF contingent from Australia. *(AWM)*

troopships from Australia continued arriving, bringing more men. For
the next 18 months, thousands of well-paid Australian boys lived very
close to the famous brothels of Cairo, and very far from their moral
guardians at home.

The AIF's troubles with venereal disease started just after the first
contingent arrived from Australia before Christmas 1914. Plentiful leave
was granted, and men made straight for the dance halls, brothels, sex
shows, and bars in the Wasa'a — a cluster of crowded tenement buildings,
shacks, and narrow alleys. These dizzy experiences were not available at
home; and for the 'Wozza', the boys had money and freedom. There were
brazen 'tarts' everywhere, and most were not wearing much clothing.
The men barely noticed how shabby and filthy the place was, let alone its
pervasive foul odours.

In this fabulous place, there was a very clear danger: the Wasa'a was
well known for venereal diseases. The Australian soldiers who so eagerly

Cairo, Clot Bey Street.

شارع كوت بك

This innocent-looking postcard of Clot Bey Street in the centre
of the Wasa'a district of Cairo was sent by many AIF soldiers to
families at home. It was actually where prostitutes lived and worked,
and at night was transformed into the world-famous brothel quarter.

queued in droves at the brothels were inevitably going to be infected
with the common venereal diseases of the time: gonorrhoea (the clap),
syphilis (the pox), and the genital sores of chancroid. In 1915, there was
no reliable way for a soldier to protect himself against these, other than
by abstaining from sex.

If a man could not abstain, and bothered to be careful, he might use
some prophylactic ointments that needed care to prepare, but were better
than nothing. He could apply to his genitals a thick film of antiseptic
ointments: Calomel, an anti-syphilitic that contained mercury; and
Argyrol or Nargol, anti-gonorrhoeals that contained silver. If he followed
exactly the elaborate instructions for using them, the bacteria might be
killed. This was the method privately recommended by some Australian
Army Medical Corps doctors to troops in their care, but was the subject

of much disagreement. Vulcanised rubber condoms, called sheaths, were also available, but they were uncomfortable, easily damaged, and unreliable, and were not commonly used by sexually active soldiers in 1915. All of these prophylactics were morally controversial, and their use was disapproved of by the AIF commanders in 1915.

The worst part, however, was that, when obvious signs of infection appeared shortly after sex, there was no sure way of killing the bacteria that had entered the body. Gonorrhoea, syphilis, and chancroid were then known by doctors as diseases difficult to cure, either perfectly or quickly. The antibiotic penicillin, the first fast-acting and reliable anti-gonorrhoeal and anti-syphilitic drug, would not appear for another 27 years; and erythromycin, a fast antibiotic cure for chancroid, would be available in 37 years' time. In 1915, the only medical treatments for the three diseases were lengthy, brutal, and uncertain.

Most venereal-disease drugs used at the time contained small amounts of the heavy metals mercury, arsenic, and silver, but other toxins as well. The usual cures for gonorrhoea involved introducing fluids to a patient's body — containing silver in a drug called Protargol, or potassium permanganate, or sandalwood oil. These were repeatedly inserted into a male patient by syringing or douching through a nozzle placed in his urethra. The usual cures for syphilis were low doses of mercury in a drug called Hydrargyrum, or of arsenic in drugs with names like Salvarsan or Arsenobenzol, which were repeatedly injected into muscles and veins using hypodermic needles. The skin surface lesions and buboes of syphilis and chancroid were destroyed by repeatedly applying mercury in lotions and ointments. Mercury and sandalwood oil were also given orally, with patients consuming considerable quantities in a typical course. All of these toxic substances might kill the bacteria, but with many doses and over much time.

During the course of a cure, testing was done to gauge its effectiveness — especially after the visible symptoms disappeared. Simple testing to confirm if a man still had gonorrhoea was done by looking for pus threads in a sample of his urine. If laboratory facilities were available, testing for the presence of *Neisseria gonorrhoeae* was done using Pappenheim's staining method, where a sample of pus in a microscope slide turned bright pink if gonorrhoea was still present. Another test was the Leszynsky method, which turned the *Neisseria gonorrhoeae* black. Testing for the presence of the syphilis bacteria *Treponema pallidum pallidum* was frequently done during a cure using the Wassermann antibody test on samples of blood.

The courses of treatment were not short — typically at least a month for gonorrhoea and a few weeks for syphilis and chancroid, but far longer if the infections had really taken hold or if multiple diseases were present, as was often the case. The toxicity of the drugs created unpleasant side effects in patients, so that the cures might feel worse than the diseases. There were also obstinate long-term venereal-disease complications for male patients, including gonococcal arthritis, gleet, urethritis, prostatitis, and orchitis. Men could still carry these side-afflictions long after the original disease had been apparently cured.

If treatment for gonorrhoea was not begun soon after infection, the unpleasant symptoms became worse, and the chances of obtaining a complete cure were reduced. Syphilis had to be treated in its very early stages, when symptoms were visible; after the signs of infection disappeared, syphilis could develop undetected to its dangerous latent stages. If a man with syphilis was not treated at all, or treated incorrectly, he could suffer serious long-term health consequences, including heart, organ, and brain diseases, and premature death. A man with venereal disease could easily infect others during sexual intercourse — perhaps his wife and, through her, his innocent children. In Australia, many children living in institutions for the blind, deaf, and disfigured had been infected before birth with the venereal disease of a parent.

By February 1915, the epidemic of venereal infections among Australian troops who had been in the Wasa'a was alarming their commanders. That month, a conference in Cairo of army doctors was told that about 1,000 men were in hospital with venereal disease every day. Despite the powerful stigma attached to the diseases, and general knowledge among soldiers in Egypt of the dangers, it was difficult to prevent many from becoming infected.

Soldiers who succumbed found themselves condemned by people of influence in Australia and Egypt who were united on military, medical, and moral grounds, and some of the infected men were sent back to Australia. Then, after the Gallipoli landing in April, and the very high number of casualties that had to be evacuated to Egypt, attitudes hardened towards men with VD. They were now unwanted occupants of AIF hospitals struggling to accommodate the Gallipoli wounded. An order was given that all venereal cases were to be banished from Egypt and sent to Australia. Thus began, in May 1915, a procession of shiploads of infected men from Suez Canal ports to Port Melbourne, from where the men were taken to Langwarrin.

This was to be the destination of our poor wretches on the A18 *Wiltshire*, now far out in the Red Sea night as the ship rolled and pitched in the long ocean swells. Would they be discharged from the army at Langwarrin? What would they have to do to get back to the war, if indeed they wanted to do that at all? How could they keep their secret from those at home, and conceal what had happened to bring such shame?

But, before answering those questions, we first need to understand the opinions held by senior officers and army doctors in Egypt about soldiers who caught venereal disease. We also need to know about the decisions they made in 1915 that led to the making of the *Wiltshire*'s voyage.

CHAPTER ONE

William Birdwood, William Bridges, and Charles Bean

sodden with drink or rotten from women

The Australian soldiers becoming infected with VD in Cairo were clearly unaware that the British generals who commanded them did not tolerate sexual misconduct at all. Their supreme commander was General Herbert Kitchener: Lord Kitchener of Khartoum, the secretary of state for war in London. He was a puritan, and his acerbic opinions about soldiers who caught venereal disease were very well known in the British army, but not yet to the AIF troops. Kitchener's views were fully understood by Lieutenant General Sir William Birdwood, who had been handpicked by him to command the Australians, and who had been close to Kitchener for years. When the VD problem started in Cairo, Birdwood ordered Major General Bridges to stop it by taking on methods used by Kitchener for the British army. To do parts of this work, Bridges sought the assistance of Captain Charles Bean, the newspaper correspondent accompanying the AIF.

Before the First World War, at the height of the British Empire, Lord Kitchener had been one of the standard-bearers of a movement to affirm the virtues of British masculinity — believing that imperial success was assured only if Englishmen were morally of good character, and

Lord Kitchener in 1915. *(Bain News Service; Library of Congress)*

physically pure and strong. Kitchener set the example in his personal life by living austerely, following a daily routine of Spartan rigour, and controlling sexual urges.

General Birdwood was an authentic *puk'ka sa'hib* officer of the Indian army: genteel, decent, charmingly correct, and definitely superior. He served the empire in India for 15 years until 1899, when, at the outbreak of the Boer War, he was sent to South Africa and became General Kitchener's military secretary. Kitchener was also an Indian-army man, and, after the Boer War, he and Birdwood returned to India, and their close association continued. After Kitchener became commander-in-chief of the Indian army in 1902, Birdwood enjoyed a rapid rise to the rank of major general.

In the Indian army, Kitchener's puritanism had put him at odds with other generals, who could be more forgiving if officers and men became profligates during their postings. Many men became unfit for military duty because of drunkenness and venereal disease, and VD outbreaks in the Indian army had, on occasions, seriously depleted its fighting fitness.

Lieutenant General Sir William Birdwood. *(SLV)*

During the 1890s, the percentage of men admitted to hospitals in India with gonorrhoea and syphilis had reached the staggering proportion of over 50 per cent of all troops. There was a parliamentary inquiry in London, and methods were devised to deal with the problem, including tolerating the use of regulated brothels. But when Lord Kitchener became commander-in-chief, he could not approve of such tolerance. He exhorted his troops to be abstinent and to live healthily like him; men who could not might be punished, and would certainly be denounced. After the outbreak of the First World War, the British army published a pamphlet about avoidance of VD that was based on Kitchener's ascetic views, and contained a message from him:

> It is discreditable and even dishonest, that by contracting through self-indulgence a disease which he can avoid, a man should render himself incapable of doing that work for his Country which he enlisted to do.

So when, in November 1914, Kitchener gave command to Birdwood of the military forces of Australia and New Zealand, it was going to be impossible for sexual misconduct to proceed unnoticed and unpunished. In early December 1914, Birdwood left India with the temporary rank of lieutenant general; he arrived in Cairo a few days before Christmas, shortly after General Bridges and the Australians had arrived.

Charles Bean had also recently arrived with the AIF's first contingent. He had been a journalist on the *Sydney Morning Herald* until September 1914, when he was chosen to be Australia's sole official war correspondent. For this new job, he was given the honorary rank of captain and was attached to the headquarters of the 1st AIF Division. Although Bean had been born in Australia, he had for 15 of his formative years lived and been educated in England, where he had become very respectful of British traditions, and impressed by the ideals of the imperial way.

In Cairo with the AIF in December 1914, and although young and a mere captain, Bean discovered he had unrivalled access to the senior British and Australian officers of the imperial force. He got to know General Birdwood, General Bridges, General Sir John Maxwell, who commanded all British forces in Egypt, and especially Colonel Cyril Brudenell White, who was chief of staff of the AIF division. From his written descriptions of them, it is apparent Bean was in awe of these very senior men. He began regularly dining with some, travelling with others to inspect military activities outside Cairo, and frequently consulting them about the kinds of stories they might approve of his sending away. With their blessing, he cabled innocuous, informative news stories to Australia, which were published in many newspapers. On Christmas Day 1914, he cabled a story about dinners given for the men, how mail from home had arrived, and how soldiers had climbed the pyramids and engaged in sports. Bean also reported that 'many of them spent the afternoon and evening in Cairo'.

On New Year's Eve, Bean cabled a story about a march that day of Australian troops at the Mena camp, and quoted General Maxwell

Captain Charles Bean in France in 1919. *(NLA)*

describing this 'splendid sight', and Birdwood saying that it was 'quite first class'. But, in truth, what had really happened during this period, and could not be reported by Bean for Australian newspapers, was that, before Christmas, some of the Australian and New Zealand troops had discovered the Wasa'a district in Cairo. On Christmas Day, when all of them had been given a holiday, swarms had descended upon the area. So began night after night of absences without leave, riotous binge-drinking sessions, and visits to brothels — and the first symptoms of gonorrhoea, syphilis, and chancroid infections that appeared on hundreds of soldiers after they eventually drifted back to the AIF camps.

As this outbreak of mass misconduct unfolded, Bean began recording in his diary his aghast observations of what was occurring, each day filling page after page:

There was a time about Christmas when the sights in the streets of Cairo were anything but pleasant for an Australian who had any regard to the good name of Australia. There was a great deal of drunkenness &

Major General William Bridges. *(Falk Studios; SLNSW)*

I can't not help noticing that what people in Cairo said was true — the Australians were responsible for most of it.

For Bean, and evidently for Birdwood and Bridges as well, outrageous behaviour like this should not have been happening at all. Men sent to the war by Australia were meant to be her best — a demonstration to the world that the new nation should be admired. Recruitment standards were supposed to have been deliberately high, and recruiters were expected to select men of good character. Soon, when describing to the Australians in Egypt what they were meant to be upholding, Bean wrote:

Amongst [the Egyptians] we have a great reputation for high principles and manliness, and even the humblest Britisher here in the East carries that reputation in his keeping ... The one thing the natives have come to know about British troops ... was that the British soldier never interfered with their women and never interfered with their religion. There is a third point in our reputation. Throughout this country the phrase for 'truth' or 'good faith' is 'word of an Englishman'. Is not that something for our whole race to be proud of?[1]

General Birdwood decided the misconduct was a result of the rush to form the AIF from scratch a few months earlier. There had been few opportunities since then to instil the standard of discipline needed to make good soldiers. Until that could be done, he decided to make the entire city of Cairo out of bounds for Australian and New Zealand troops, and issued the necessary orders. As it happened, the bounds were repeatedly broken, and the rampage went on. Bean then noted in his diary a dramatic action taken by Birdwood to stop it:

> When I got back from Cairo the other night General Bridges had a letter from General Birdwood and he would show it to me. From what he said I take it that he would not take it amiss if I sent a letter & a wire to give people in Australia some idea of how things are; we shall probably be getting rid of a few of these old hard heads — sending them back to Australia.

The agitation of General Bridges, and his discussion with Bean about getting rid of troublemakers, was caused by the alarming contents of Birdwood's lengthy letter, which, in a most courteous way, ordered Bridges to stop the misconduct. Written in late December 1914, when Birdwood had clearly lost patience, his letter said that Sir John Maxwell had complained about the Australians, and it contained a number of criticisms of them, including that 'men seemed to think they have come here for a huge picnic'. It also said, in words reminiscent of Lord Kitchener's, that the Australian government was relying on the AIF to uphold Australia's good name:

> But there is no possibility whatever of our doing ourselves full justice unless we are every one of us absolutely physically fit, and this no man can possibly be if he allows his body to become sodden with drink or rotten from women, and unless he is doing his best to keep himself

efficient he is swindling the Government which has sent him to represent it and fight for it.[2]

The letter ended by informing Bridges how Lord Kitchener was 'following every movement of ours with unfailing interest, and surely we will never risk disappointing him by allowing a few of our men to give us a bad name'.

Birdwood seemed to think that only a hard core of the men was involved; his letter referred only to a 'very small proportion of our contingents in Cairo'. Within weeks of him writing to Bridges, however, there would be about 1,000 venereally infected men in hospital every day. Bean began making diary notes about the extraordinary numbers:

> There was a great deal of disease amongst our men, which they brought on themselves by their indulgences in Cairo. The disease is simply deplorable, but apparently quite unpreventable. Cairo is a hotbed of it — in particularly serious forms & some of the cases are simply tragic; young soldiers, really fine clean simple boys who have been drinking & have found themselves with a disease which may ruin them for life. In one case which I heard of, the youngster was said to have been made drunk by two older soldiers.
>
> Some of our commanding officers have had boys come to them — bright decent youngsters who in Australia would have been ashamed to do or think of the things, or go near the places into which they have been led here — the youngsters have come to them almost in tears bitterly ashamed & half horrified with themselves.

Birdwood knew exactly what Kitchener would want him to do. AIF men should be diverted from vice, and those who continued to catch VD should be dealt with severely. He proposed to Bridges that far more attention should be given to improving the physical fitness and self-pride of the troops, and to developing healthy recreational diversions for them. General Bridges then arranged to intensify physical training — including long route marches in the desert, competitive sports and athletics carnivals, and especially wrestling and boxing tournaments. The Red Cross and the YMCA were invited to open attractive recreation halls in the AIF camps, and dry canteens in Cairo, to lure men from the Wasa'a. As well, battalion and medical officers, and especially army chaplains, were directed to give regular talks to their troops about the perils of strong drink and promiscuity. This included straight talk for newly arrived troops even before they had disembarked from the troopships. A medical officer addressed troopers of a Light Horse regiment, and told them about the diseases in a straightforward way:

> When men who were badly affected in this way married, their children were a terrible disgrace to them. He [told] the Light Horsemen of the appalling mortality rate amongst those venereally affected. Barring Port Said, Cairo was about the worst city in the world, and full of women of bad reputation, with whom he advised and urged the men to have nothing whatever to do; it would be highly dangerous.[3]

The physical training, healthy recreations, and practical talks by medical officers probably did reduce the appeal of the Wasa'a for some, but the use in Egypt of army chaplains to give church-parade sermons about the diseases was not so successful. During parades, men might be invited to make pledges of sobriety and Christian chastity, and join rousing prayers for protection from the 'God of Battles'; they were encouraged to sing popular hymns for soldiers like 'Where Is My Wandering Boy, To-night?' AIF chaplains preached that venereal disease was a moral problem, and that only men of virtue could be protected from it by God. The chaplaincy service would persist through the war with a morals campaign that the official medical historian would later describe as 'worse than useless' for stopping VD.

Notwithstanding the medical lectures, and in spite of the sermons, the misconduct and infecting of soldiers continued. So, in accordance with

Lord Kitchener's known views, Birdwood and Bridges began invoking sections of the army regulations that provided punishments for men who caught VD. At the time, most regulations for the Australian army were copied from the King's regulations for the British army. Under these, catching VD was not a crime in itself; but because the usual instinct of an infected soldier was to keep it a secret, there was a regulation that forced him to reveal it, under threat of punishment if he did not. Since a soldier might be reluctant to co-operate for VD treatment, he could be ordered to submit, and the regulations provided punishments if orders were disobeyed.

Another method provided in the regulations was a rule enabling a soldier to be discharged from the army because of medical unfitness caused by misconduct. That possibility was contained in an AIF circular signed by General Birdwood in February 1915, part of which read:

Warning to Soldiers respecting Venereal Disease

Venereal diseases are very prevalent in Egypt. They are already responsible for a material lessening of the efficiency of the Australian Imperial Forces, since those who are severely infected are no longer fit to serve. A considerable number of soldiers so infected are now being returned to Australia invalided, and in disgrace. One death from syphilis has already occurred.

Intercourse with public women is almost certain to be followed by disaster. The soldier is therefore asked to consider the matter from several points of view. In the first place if he is infected he will not be efficient and he may be discharged. But the evil does not cease with the termination of his military career, for he is liable to infect his future wife and children.[4]

Another regulation allowed the stopping of a soldier's pay while he was in hospital with a disease not incurred as a result of military duty. This was, originally, not intended to be a punishment, but, in practice, became one for men with VD. In January 1915, General Bridges cabled

Senator George Pearce. *(NLA)*

the minister for defence, Senator George Pearce, with a request for him to approve stopping the pay of AIF soldiers catching VD. Pearce quickly obliged, and the approval he gave was backdated to December 1914 to include soldiers already infected. Within days, Bridges issued Divisional Order 398, which stated: 'No pay will be issued while abroad for any period of absence from duty on account of venereal disease.' The order exempted officers, warrant officers, and non-commissioned officers, but it also stipulated that wages allotted by a soldier to his family were also forfeited, and would have to be made up after he was cured before he could again receive pay.

Australian soldiers in Egypt were paid generous wages compared with those of other imperial troops. They were each on a daily rate of at least six shillings — more than three times the pay of a British soldier — and this was a reason that Australians had so much money for indulgences in

Cairo. The high AIF pay had attracted recruits: there was unemployment in Australia, soldiering seemed like a lucrative job, and some were financially supporting wives and parents at home by having allotted pay for them. The stopping of allotments by the army was deliberately intended to expose an infected soldier's moral sin to those close to him — 'a kind of prophylactic blackmail', as it was later described.

Presumably, the drastic order to withhold pay and allotments must have stopped men from visiting brothels, and must have reduced infection rates. What is known is that, when army paymasters began doing this, soldiers who lost their pay were very upset. They had not expected it, and felt it was unfair, because the duration of a VD treatment was something over which they had little control, and could go on for months.

To further intensify the punitive campaign against men who became infected, it was initially arranged for them to be isolated at a camp near the aerodrome at Mena. The barbed-wire enclosure for men with VD was arranged with particular rigour: they were closely supervised by sentries who were instructed to be unfriendly, they were made to wear a white armband, they could not receive food or articles from outside, and, if mates came to visit them, these visitors could be arrested. Soon after the camp was opened, a medical officer who was sent to inspect it reported that

> The men in the camp suffering from venereal disease are deprived of pay, they know they are in disgrace, and many of them are sullen and in an attitude of almost aggressive insurgence. Some of them would I believe respond to sympathetic treatment, and efforts could be made to arouse in them some human interest. Those who are positively objectionable should in my judgment be punished with severity. I do not think many punishments would be necessary.[5]

From December 1914, there were also discussions among senior AIF officers about the possibility of sending the worst of the misbehavers, drunks, and 'venereals' back to Australia. They realised that the Australian public might be surprised if this were to happen, and might need forewarning. To do this, General Bridges enlisted the help of Charles Bean to cable an explanatory story to newspaper readers at home. At the same time, Bean obtained the general's approval to write a guidebook to Egypt for Australian soldiers, which was to include warnings about alcohol and venereal diseases. Both of these writing projects were well meaning in intent and thoroughly prepared, but the first was to backfire spectacularly for Bean.

His long and quite cautious article began appearing in Australian newspapers in late-January 1915. It mostly comprised praise for the troops of the AIF, and spoke admiringly of them. But it included criticism of 'only a small percentage — possibly 1 or 2 per cent ... a certain number of men who are not fit to be sent abroad to represent Australia'. To Bean's later regret, editors all over Australia reworked the story and published it under sensational headlines, such as 'WASTERS IN THE FORCE — SOME NOT FIT TO BE SOLDIERS' and 'TOO MUCH LIQUOR'. The treatment was in response to Bean having not just described misconduct and drinking, but also men who had 'contracted certain diseases by which, after all the trouble and months of training and of the sea voyage, they have unfitted themselves to do the work for which they enlisted'.

There was a horrified reaction by readers, many of whom had husbands and sons in Egypt. Anxious to play down the hitherto-hidden problem now revealed by Captain Bean, Australia's wartime leaders had to step in. The prime minister, William Morris Hughes, issued a statement saying, 'It is no doubt a very serious matter, but I should be more concerned if I believed such conduct fairly reflected the code of the Expeditionary Force generally. I don't believe it does for a moment.' Senator Pearce had this to say in response to the Bean story:

> It is to be remembered that these forces were very hurriedly got together,
> that men were unknown to the officers in a great number of cases, and that

it takes some trouble and time to try out any body of men and discover the 'wasters'. The officers have any amount of power to punish offenders, but the best means of dealing with them — and what will be the greatest punishment and disgrace — will be to send them home again.[6]

Within days of the senator's comment, the sending home of men was ordered by General Bridges. On 3 February 1915, the A55 *Kyarra*, then an Australian hospital ship, departed from Suez carrying 341 men to Australia, including 'invalids and [those] unfit for service' and 132 VD patients. The army had declared that each of these was 'Unlikely to become an Efficient Soldier' and that they were to be 'Discharged– Services No Longer Required' on arrival in Australia. Their publicised removal from Egypt was meant to send a strong warning to others. The *Kyarra* thus became the first of a series of homeward-bound ships that left Egypt during 1915 carrying the rejects of the AIF.

Publication of Charles Bean's article began the first controversy of the war for Australia, and it spawned much discussion. Letters were sent to Egypt seeking re-assurance from soldiers there; back came replies angrily denying that such things were occurring. Anger was also directed at Bean for making his allegations: he was threatened with tarring and feathering, was told he would 'stop a bullet' sooner or later, and became the target of a witty mock-doggerel poem of ten verses that was published in a Cairo newspaper. This asked him to

> Cease your wowseristic whining,
> Tell the truth and play the game,
> And we only ask fair dinkum
> How we keep Australia's name.

Bean's discovery that other Australians so strongly objected to what he thought was a morally principled story shook his self-confidence. In a conversation with himself in his diary, he said he could not understand the reaction, and referred to how General Bridges had asked him to write the article, and saw nothing objectionable in it. There was one AIF officer, however, who thought the article was very offensive. Colonel John Monash was commander of the 4th Infantry Brigade, and had also led the convoy carrying the second AIF contingent to Egypt. He mistakenly took Bean's article to be criticism of himself and his men. In March 1915, he wrote to Senator Pearce to complain about the 'lurid stories' of 'drunken and immoral orgies', and appealed to the senator 'that for the sake of our parents, our wives and our children, you will not allow our good name to be tarnished in Australia'.[7]

Bean made amends for starting the furore by publishing the booklet *What To Know in Egypt: a guide for Australasian soldiers*. This contained a short history of Egypt and the Nile River delta, and descriptions of the people, religions, and antiquities of Cairo. There was practical advice about diet, distances, and currency, and useful phrases in Arabic and French. In 'A Few Short Rules — Women', he wrote that 'Men must be careful to avoid any attempts at familiarity with native women; because if they are respectable they will get into trouble; and if they are not, venereal disease will probably be contracted.' In a long section about 'Health in Egypt (what is unsafe — and the reasons why)', Bean covered sanitation, typhoid, and dysentery. Under the heading 'A hot bed of disease', he elaborated on the subject of VD:

> Modern Cairo with its mixture of women from all nations, East and West has long been noted for particularly virulent forms of disease. Almost every village contains syphilis. And if a man will not steer altogether clear of the risk by exercising a little restraint, his only sane course is to provide himself with certain prophylactics beforehand to lessen the chances of a disastrous result.

By mentioning prophylactics, Bean was touching on an acutely sensitive subject. Even though educating soldiers about prophylactics, let alone providing them, were obvious measures for reducing VD, no senior officer wished to be associated with such activities at this early stage of the war. Some believed it would be condoning immorality; others, who felt that prophylaxis was unreliable, feared it might result in more infections. In early 1915, General Birdwood was asked by an Australian medical officer, Major James Barrett, to seriously consider issuing prophylactics to men going to brothel areas, but Birdwood refused.

Following the reaction to his newspaper article, Charles Bean never again wrote stories that could be construed as criticism of Australian soldiers. Even though the drunkenness in Cairo continued until early April 1915, when most ANZAC troops left for the Dardanelles, and the daily rate of men being treated for VD barely declined, there was not another article from him about it. As an example, just before departing from Cairo, the soldiers were granted short pre-embarkation leave. That evening, many went to the Wasa'a district and ransacked the brothels and drinking halls, setting some on fire. A number of reasons were given then, and have been since, for this famous act of vandalism, but it seems the main cause was a desire to wreak vengeance on a place that so many had previously been eager to visit. That night, Charles Bean inspected the wreckage, and wrote a diary account of what had happened. A few months before, he might have condemned the Australians, but this time he wrote, 'I have known rows of exactly the same sort at Oxford & Cambridge, carried through in precisely the same spirit, & people only called it light-heartedness there.'

Bean accompanied the AIF to Gallipoli; during his absence from Egypt, and after his return, the misconduct and venereal infections continued, well into 1916, until the AIF moved from Egypt to France. There and in England, drunkenness, crime, frequent absences without leave, and a high rate of VD became a permanent part of AIF life, but there would be hardly a word about it reported by Bean.

Throughout the Dardanelles campaign, General Birdwood continued to command the ANZAC forces, and also became the AIF commander after General Bridges was mortally wounded at Gallipoli. Following the end of that campaign, Birdwood oversaw a doubling in size of the AIF in Egypt during 1916. It was here that, in March, VD infection rates reached record levels. The Australian surgeon-general, Colonel R. H. J. Fetherston, wrote to Birdwood, imploring him to bring an end to it:

> I now have over two thousand of your troops under treatment for venereal disease. It is with diffidence that I again call your attention to mitigate this growing evil. Would it be possible to place the streets [in Cairo] where the principal brothels are located out of bounds?[8]

Birdwood then led the AIF from Egypt to Europe, and through all the campaigns in France and Belgium, until May 1918, when he handed command of the Australian Corps to John Monash, now a lieutenant general. During his long period with the AIF, Birdwood saw the dismantling of almost every measure introduced in Egypt to stop venereal disease. The first to go was the mandatory return of infected men to Australia, when, in October 1915, a decision was made in Melbourne to keep troops who became infected well away from home.

Then, beginning in mid-1916, it was realised by AIF medical officers that wartime conditions in Europe had produced moral standards quite different from those the pre-war world had regarded as civilised. There was also a loss of the ability, or even the willingness, of civil, religious, and military leaders to prevent wartime promiscuity. These conditions were perfect for the spread of venereal infections, which became far worse than anything experienced by the AIF in Egypt. During the war in Europe, millions of men and women became infected with VD — mostly during the last two years of hostilities, when the war entered a most intense and destructive phase. In the British and dominion armies alone, there were over 400,000 admissions for venereal diseases to military hospitals.

The mass slaughter of Australian soldiers started in Europe in mid-1916 during the long campaign at Pozieres and at Fromelles. Very high casualties caused a constant need for more manpower, and the AIF could not exacerbate this problem by leaving large numbers of troops out of

Lieutenant Colonel Graham Butler in 1916. *(AWM)*

action due to VD. Because of this, the policy for handling it underwent a series of pragmatic changes, and the use of punishments as the only form of cure began to be supplemented before being mainly replaced by medical methods. The reason was explained by Lieutenant Colonel Graham Butler, an AIF medical officer, at a conference in Paris arranged by the Allied Powers to discuss VD. He said that

> The Australian at home is not a loose-living man; but it was obvious that very systematic and definite measures would be required to avert a serious interference, by venereal disease, with military efficiency and also a danger to the future of the race.

An event that might have helped General Birdwood accept this reality was the removal in June 1916 of the powerful influence of Lord Kitchener, who was drowned after the British armoured cruiser HMS

Hampshire, on which he was travelling to Russia, struck a German mine and sank in the North Sea.

In the scheme of preventive and curative medicine for VD that was introduced by the AIF in 1916 and perfected on a large scale by 1917, the only retained part of the old methods was to continue the health-education campaign devised in early 1915 in Egypt. Apart from describing to the troops the nature of the diseases and the contributory effect of drinking alcohol in spreading them, the essence of the new education campaign was, in Colonel Butler's words, 'denunciation of the idea that continence is ever harmful, and that incontinence is an essential attribute of manliness'.

In Egypt in early 1915, any proposal for the AIF to issue prophylactic kits had been rejected by General Birdwood on moral grounds. In Europe, that position was completely abandoned: prophylaxis was deliberately adopted as AIF policy. Huge quantities of Calomel and Nargol were procured and packed into what were variously called Blue Light, Blue Label, or 'dreadnought' kits, and these were freely available for men going on leave to use immediately before and after sexual intercourse. Hundreds of thousands of the kits were issued free of charge at AIF depots in Europe and England, and condoms were made available for sale. As well, there was free provision of 'preventive early treatment' at medical-corps preventive-medicine sections in every army unit, called Blue Light depots. Early treatment involved a medical examination immediately after a soldier might have been exposed to VD, and precautionary use of Calomel and Nargol. Hundreds of thousands of inspections were made.

To deal with cases when early-treatment inspections showed definite signs of disease, there was free provision of what was called 'abortive treatment'. This was an attempt to kill VD bacteria at the very early stages of infection, in the hope of avoiding having to send men to a hospital for much longer treatment. About 20,000 infected men received abortive treatment, and about 15,000 were cured.

If the use of prophylactics, early preventive treatment, or abortive treatment failed, and an infection developed beyond the stage where it

This Blue Light prophylactic kit is similar to those issued in the AIF from 1916. One of the tubes contains Calomel ointment; the other contains Nargol jelly. *(Museums Victoria)*

was quickly treatable, men were admitted to hospital. This was usually to the AIF venereal-disease hospital at Bulford in England, but some were also treated at hospitals in France. Bulford operated from 1916 until 1919, and had about 30,000 admissions — many for soldiers with multiple infections, and many being repeat visits.

Since early 1915, the main measure used by the AIF as a deterrent and as a punishment had been full stoppage of pay. In Europe, the regulation had been re-affirmed in December 1916, with officers, warrant officers, and non-commissioned officers now included. This was the last of the measures introduced in Egypt to be discarded in Europe, and the change was approved by General Birdwood himself. In January 1918, his AIF Order 1282 relaxed the regulation, and, from that time, men in hospital with VD would only forfeit one-third of their pay.

In Cairo in early 1915, long before all the VD rules were relaxed, General Birdwood, General Bridges, and Captain Bean had the confidence, which came from knowing they were right, to take principled

CHAPTER TWO

James Barrett
and John Brady Nash

the isolation-detention barracks at Abbassia

In early 1915, the doctors of the Australian Army Medical Corps in Cairo knew their main duty was to prepare for the casualties of battles the AIF might soon be engaged in. Most arrived *en masse* in mid-January on the *Kyarra*, the first hospital ship to arrive from Australia. This was the same vessel that would shortly carry back to Australia the first group of men with venereal infections. The *Kyarra* brought a number of complete hospitals, and each was dispatched by rail to its assigned camp at Cairo. Some were established in tents and marquees; others, in permanent buildings in the city.

Another duty of the AAMC doctors was trying to protect the troops from infectious diseases. In the dusty and fly-ridden Cairo camps, close attention was given to hygiene and sanitation to prevent infections from local bacteria and viruses. With so many men crowded together, the doctors were especially alert for predictable contagious diseases spread by personal contact — such as chickenpox, influenza, measles, mumps, and meningitis — and isolation wards were prepared in case of outbreaks.

The spectacular Heliopolis Palace Hotel in Cairo, which was
occupied by the 1st Australian General Hospital from January 1915.
(Barrett and Deane (1918))

Within weeks of their arrival, however, the surprised doctors found
themselves confronted with thousands of soldiers suffering from
contagious diseases that had not been predicted on such a large scale,
and for which they were not equipped to prevent or cure. Although
some cases of venereal disease had been expected, as in any army, what
the doctors faced was an epidemic. For instance, soon after the 520-bed
1st Australian General Hospital was established at the Heliopolis Palace
Hotel in Cairo, the number of venereal patients became so great that
another 500 beds were added. The 300-bed 2nd Australian Stationary
Hospital at the Mena camp was, by the end of January, completely filled
with venereal patients, with 150 more waiting to be admitted. To the
AAMC doctors this was astonishing, because these were contagious
diseases that were entirely avoidable. Catching gonorrhoea, syphilis,
and chancroid involved a deliberate exposure to infection from a sexual
partner, but here were thousands of men becoming diseased entirely
through their own actions.

On 17 February 1915, a conference of senior AAMC officers was
arranged at the 1st Australian General Hospital at the Heliopolis Palace
Hotel.[9] The meeting was asked to 'devise an efficient means of combating
venereal disease in the Australian Imperial Force'. All the men who
attended had until recently been prominent doctors, surgeons, or

medical specialists in Australia, with the exception of Colonel William Williams, the surgeon-general and director-general of medical services for the AIF, who had been the army's only full-time doctor when the war started. As respected senior members of Australia's medical profession, all enjoyed great social status and substantial incomes. Some had already been rewarded with high royal honours, and others would be knighted as the war progressed.

A number had offered their services on a *pro bono* basis as a patriotic duty. Some had taught in medical faculties at the universities, where they were esteemed, and all were active in Australian branches of the British Medical Association and other bodies for the advancement of medical science. Most had experience with military medicine in the militia, and a few had been medical officers in past wars. Some had also been professional rivals in Australia, and had brought their rivalries, and substantial egos, to Egypt, where they would engage in behind-the-scenes struggles and power plays.

The gathering in February 1915 at the Heliopolis Palace Hotel could be portrayed as a mighty medical brains trust, brought together to solve a major medical problem for the AIF. The records give the impression, however, that not all the doctors in attendance wanted to become overly involved. Such esteemed medicos might have felt reluctant to develop a too-close association with these medically difficult and morally controversial diseases. Their disdain for the venereal diseases, and the infected men, too, reflected attitudes held within the medical profession more generally; venereology was considered to be particularly unglamorous.

But there were two prominent doctors at the conference who would become deeply involved with resolving the AIF's VD problem in Egypt — one in a most committed way, the other reluctantly — and they would become remembered for this. We shall return to these two in due course.

Those at the conference included the three most senior Australian medical officers in Egypt: Colonel William Williams, Colonel Charles Ryan, and Colonel Neville Howse. Colonel Williams had served as a medical officer in Sudan and South Africa, and in 1902 had been appointed surgeon-general of the army. In August 1914, he had been chosen by General Bridges to prepare the medical corps for its role with the expeditionary force. He had only recently arrived in Egypt when the VD problem was suddenly thrust upon him. In early 1915, Williams was perceived to be at the end of his career; he was 58, had advanced cardiac disease, and was becoming medically unfit.

He opened the conference proceedings by noting that

> It was estimated that about 1,000 men of the 1st and 2nd Australian Divisions are suffering from Venereal Disease at any one day, and of these a large number are incapacitated from working. The proportions seemed to be much greater than those of other forces, such as the Territorials in Egypt. The displacement of so large a proportion of men, and the ultimate consequences of numerous infections, rendered it necessary to take a comprehensive view of the position, and to endeavour to take some action to minimise the damage done.

The conference launched into discussing the problem under five subjects: 'Military assistance', which was stricter control over men in brothel areas, and punishments for those who became infected; 'Use of prophylaxis', the possible provision by the army of prophylactics for soldiers; 'Treatment — general and special', the medical methods to be used to cure the diseases; 'Establishment of convalescent depots', the removal of VD cases from general hospitals to isolation facilities; and 'Ultimate destination of affected men', which considered the advantages and disadvantages of treating patients in Egypt or sending them to Australia.

The agenda was arranged to facilitate open discussion about the clear military and medical aspects of the disease outbreak. There was also an important item not on the published agenda — one more difficult to deal with, and which could not be openly spoken of. This concerned the immorality of soldiers engaging in sexual activities and deliberately exposing themselves to contagious disease. Some doctors at the conference had strong, privately held opinions about this that could not be easily separated from purely military or medical aspects.

At this point, it is important to know there was an influential guiding mind behind the Heliopolis conference, a person who was its secretary and was recording the proceedings. This was Major James Barrett, the registrar of the 1st Australian General Hospital, where the conference was being held. In Melbourne, he was an eminent ophthalmologist, surgeon, medical researcher, and lecturer; well-known, well-connected, and wealthy, with a magnificent home in Toorak, and the recipient of an appointment by King George V as a Companion of the Order of St Michael and St George.

Barrett had joined the AIF without military experience, and offered his considerable talents to the army *pro bono*. Upon arriving in Egypt, he had acquired a number of roles, each of which was a challenging job in itself: consulting oculist to the AIF, registrar of the hospital, and executive officer of the regional Australian Red Cross. Because of this last job, he spent much time in Cairo cultivating relationships with senior AIF leaders, diplomats, and influential members of the local British ruling class. To his AAMC colleagues, Barrett seemed to have an opinion about everything and a finger in every pie, and soon — and almost certainly unwittingly — he made himself the subject of unkind jokes. He also promoted an unpopular opinion that venereal diseases were, first and foremost, medical problems, to be controlled using all the tools of preventive medicine, including prophylaxis.

Colonel Charles Ryan had been, until the war, a surgeon at Melbourne Hospital and at the Children's Hospital in Carlton. In August 1914, he had become assistant director of medical services for the AIF, and, after he arrived in Egypt, he had been assigned to ANZAC headquarters. At the Heliopolis in 1915, Colonel Ryan made only a modest contribution to the discussion. He suggested it would be difficult to place the brothels out of bounds because they would move to other areas, and instead thought that venereal cases should be isolated, and that men with syphilis should be sent home.

Colonel Neville Howse was a well-known military hero who had been awarded a Victoria Cross in the Boer War. He was now the assistant director of medical services for the AIF, and during the Heliopolis conference had plenty to say. He said military police could not control brothel areas in Cairo, since they had no power under the law. He noted that some officers had tried to get soldiers to take VD precautions, and none had been taken. He thought that issuing circulars about VD to arriving troops was 'a waste of time', pointedly noting that those given circulars by Major Barrett ended up having a greater chance of being infected than those who received none. Howse played down the VD problem, and also suggested it was partly the fault of medical officers in Australia sending to Egypt men who were already diseased. He agreed with Colonel Ryan that syphilis cases should be sent home.

Apart from Williams, Barrett, Ryan, and Howse, there were seven other doctors at the Heliopolis conference, but only a few made contributions of note. There was general agreement that syphilis cases should go to Australia, and that hospitals should not be filled with gonorrhoea patients who 'required little more than rest'. One doctor raised the problem of choosing which venereal cases should be returned to Australia, observing that 'officers had also to recollect that the future of these soldiers was to be considered and the part they would play in civil life'. Others noted that an 'outstanding feature' of the venereal-case statistics was the comparative absence of syphilis.

However, consensus was reached about three practical actions that should be taken, and these set the standard for how venereal cases would be managed from then on. The first was to remove all venereal patients to isolation hospitals, and it was suggested these could be in ships moored off the Egyptian coast. The second was to send syphilitics, and perhaps all venereal cases, back to Australia for more effective care there. The troopships used could be temporary isolation hospitals, with treatments continued during voyages. The third recommended action was to continue the education program about the diseases that had been started

Sir James Barrett in Melbourne in 1919. He is wearing a KBE, CB,
CMG, Order of the Nile, and war decorations and medals. *(UMA
Lafayette)*

Colonel Neville Howse, VC, in Cairo. *(NLA)*

by Major Barrett. He could distribute a new pamphlet about venereal disease and arrange regular lectures by medical officers.

Inevitably, when the delicate question of prophylactics arose, there was a division of opinion. Howse was sceptical, while some others were mildly supportive. Barrett's was the only voice heard that was strongly in favour; he argued that prophylactics 'had been absolutely proved to be of value' when he had run a public-health campaign in Victoria to combat VD. To the Heliopolis conference, he made a radical proposal: special depots for soldiers on leave in Cairo should be established, 'because at many of the brothels there were no conveniences for obtaining personal cleanliness'. Without spelling it out, he was recommending that Calomel ointment and Argyrol jelly be made freely available to men visiting brothels; he had already been handing them out to staff at his hospital. The Heliopolis conference could not, of course, reach agreement about this, but it was suggested that, when the doctors returned to their hospitals, further research could be made by those interested.

The day after, Barrett arranged for a parade to be held of everyone working at his hospital, during which they were medically examined. Only one was subsequently suspected to have VD. In a report sent to Colonel Howse that afternoon, Barrett revealed that staff at the hospital had been warned about brothels, but, if they insisted on going, they were to take Calomel and Argyrol provided by him free of charge. He reported that the results of the parade confirmed that their use had practically eliminated venereal disease from his unit.

Lieutenant Colonel Arthur White, commandant of the 2nd Australian Stationary Hospital, also arranged research about prophylactics after the conference. In February 1915, White's hospital was treating hundreds of venereal cases, so he had 540 infected men interviewed. The results showed that only in 51 cases had men not used protection at all. The majority had unsuccessfully used a variety of prophylactics, including Calomel ointment and syringing. Only four infected men had used rubber condoms: three had burst during intercourse, and, although the other had not, the man had become infected with gonorrhoea, anyway.

Major Barrett continued to argue that Calomel and Argyrol were effective if used exactly according to the detailed instructions meant to be given. However, the Australian army in Egypt in 1915 could not seriously countenance any plan to issue kits and instructions, even though hospital admission rates remained high well into 1916 — when they substantially increased. Prevention was an idea before its time, and could only be adopted later, when the AIF was in Europe. The revolutionary changes that occurred there were introduced by Neville Howse himself, who by then was director of medical services for the AIF and a major general. Under his policy, Blue Light kits were freely issued, along with educational pamphlets that, in 1915, Howse had called 'a waste of time'.

We now come to a doctor at the Heliopolis conference who was not recorded as having said anything, but who was about to become chosen, apparently reluctantly, as the officer who would select the infected soldiers to be sent to Australia. This was Lieutenant Colonel John Brady Nash, second-in-charge at the 2nd Australian General Hospital and a prominent medical practitioner, surgeon, and politician from New South Wales.

He had been a doctor and surgeon in the Newcastle area, and also a major figure in the affairs of the Catholic and Irish-Australian communities in New South Wales. He had moved to Sydney in 1900 after being appointed to the NSW Legislative Council. A major in the 4th Irish Regiment of the militia at the outbreak of war, he had decided, at 57 years of age, to take a year off from his political duties to become an AIF medical officer. He had been appointed a lieutenant colonel, and arrived in Egypt on the *Kyarra* with the 2nd Australian General Hospital. When Brady Nash attended the Heliopolis venereal-disease conference the following month, where he managed to avoid appearing over-interested, he could not possibly have expected that, a few months later, he would be intimately involved with the problem. This came about as a direct consequence of the landings at Gallipoli on 25 April 1915.

Although preparations for military action had been underway since March, the final orders given on 1 April to mobilise the ANZAC force for the Dardanelles campaign caused a re-arrangement of AAMC hospitals in Egypt. It was decided that some would be relocated with the troops to the Dardanelles area, including to Lemnos and Imbros islands, and to Gallipoli to support the Australian attack, while others would remain in Egypt to await casualties.

At this time, with 30,000 AIF troops on the move in Egypt, the recommendations made at the venereal-disease conference at the Heliopolis Palace Hotel were only partly accomplished. There was a plan to remove venereal cases to special isolation facilities, and to send some or all back to Australia. The first had been done, with venereal patients now in isolation wards at a number of hospitals. The second had been started, with some hundreds of infected men sent to Australia and some to Malta. There were still many VD patients in Egypt, and no decisions had been made about them.

However, no one in the AIF or the British army had anticipated the very high casualty rates after the fighting began. On 25 April,

A portrait of Dr John Brady Nash made in 1907. *(SLNSW)*

the disastrous first day at Gallipoli, 2,000 Australians were killed or wounded as they went ashore and attempted to scale the hills. Over the next weeks, many thousands of British and Australian casualties were sent from the Dardanelles back to Egypt, and this was far more than had been prepared for. Then, at Gallipoli, many soldiers began falling ill with dysentery, influenza, and typhoid, and were also evacuated to Egypt. During May and June 1915, an urgent re-organisation of the hospitals in Egypt was undertaken to vastly increase the number of beds, and all kinds of buildings in Cairo were requisitioned to be turned into hospitals. For example, the 1st Australian General Hospital, which in January had opened at the Heliopolis Palace Hotel with 520 beds, was, by the end of May, a 10,600-bed hospital occupying 11 buildings in the city.

Three members of the NSW parliament on active service with
the AIF in early 1915: Sergeant Edward Larkin (left); Lieutenant
Colonel George Braund (mounted on the donkey); and Lieutenant
Colonel John Brady Nash. *(SLNSW)*

The time had arrived to remove venereal patients from Egypt. Two
days after the landings at Gallipoli, and amid much decision-making in
Melbourne brought on by the crisis, Senator Pearce agreed to a request
from Cairo that 'all cases of venereal should be transferred to Australia,
since it was urgently necessary to relieve hospital pressure'.[10] The
'venereals' were to be concentrated at a newly formed isolation-detention
barracks at Abbassia in Cairo, and then shipped back to Australia. The
barracks was to be an independent command within the 1st Australian
General Hospital, located in an old British army building, and guarded
by armed sentries. Up to 2,000 beds would be made available, mainly
for Australians, but also for infected New Zealand and British soldiers.
The Australians were to be given whatever medical treatment they
needed before being sent away. Their destination was an old army camp

at Langwarrin, south of Melbourne, part of which had already been converted into a small detention barracks for the VD-infected soldiers sent earlier in 1915.

Now a sufficiently senior medical officer had to be found to command Abbassia. When some of the Cairo hospitals had been relocated to be closer to the fighting, Lieutenant Colonel Brady Nash had not been sent with them. Two days after the Gallipoli landings, he received a letter from the surgeon-general of the British army in Egypt, which politely ordered Brady Nash to take charge at Abbassia.

Few Australian doctors or patients associated with venereal diseases in Egypt in 1915 recorded their experiences in writing for posterity. Of the patients, some later wrote to the army, sometimes to complain about mistreatment and sometimes to request secrecy, and their letters are preserved. Of the doctors, apart from Barrett, who wrote copiously on the subject, only Brady Nash has left us with written impressions of his time at Abbassia, in a meticulous diary — the daily entries barely legible, written in his atrocious doctor's scrawl. He also wrote letters, some to *The Medical Journal of Australia*, about his experiences. In a report published in September 1915, his appointment to Abbassia was recalled:

> The Director of Medical Services called upon [Brady Nash] to take charge
> of this hospital. Although he felt that this duty was not one for which he
> was specially suited, he obeyed without murmur, merely pointing out
> that 'It is not my job, sir; but if you desire it my best efforts will be put
> forth to run the show'.

On his first day at Abbassia, at the beginning of May 1915, Brady Nash discovered that he was the sole doctor there. He had no particular training or expertise in diagnosing and treating VD, but had to decide on the methods he would use. For gonorrhoea cases, the patients would be given urethral irrigations of colloidal silver or sandalwood oil. The syphilis cases would receive intravenous injections of Arsenobenzol, and intramuscular injections of Grey Oil, a solution of mercury. The progress of syphilis cases would be monitored using Wassermann blood tests. The lesions, buboes, and sores of syphilis and chancroid on patients' genitalia were to be destroyed using mercury-chloride ointment, mercury-oxide lotion, or diluted mercury-nitrate acid.

Although he was the officer in charge of a 2,000-bed hospital, Brady Nash was initially allocated just three staff to assist him: a warrant officer, a staff-sergeant quartermaster, and a staff-sergeant dispenser. He discovered that his patients would carry out the treatments on themselves, and that they would also be his medical orderlies. Fortunately, the expected influx of infected men took some time. Elsewhere in Cairo, the first 261 infected men to be sent to Australia following Senator Pearce's approval were being collected directly from hospitals and taken by train to the Suez Canal, where they were loaded onto the troopship *Ceramic*. On the day that Brady Nash started at Abbassia, the *Ceramic* left Egypt for Melbourne.

Two days later, the first two patients were admitted to Abbassia; from then, the number of admissions rapidly grew to hundreds. It was discovered that many men being admitted had just arrived from Australia — they had been infected shortly before they embarked, or shortly after they arrived. Over the following months, a hospital population crisis was averted by discharging patients who showed signs of having been cured, or by sending large batches of Australians to Melbourne. Despite the sweeping plan Senator Pearce had approved, not all the Australians admitted to Abbassia would be automatically shipped away; some were discovered to not be infected, and others were cured. It also turned out that stories inmates had heard about their being sent home in disgrace as a punishment were not entirely true; the decision to send a man home would be based mostly on an assessment of his likelihood of recovery.

In May, Brady Nash was joined at Abbassia by a young doctor who would be his principal assistant. Captain Harold Plant was young and single, and had been a resident doctor at the Brisbane Children's Hospital when he joined the AIF in 1914. Assigned to the 1st Australian General

Tents pitched for patients staying at the VD detention barracks at
Abbassia in Cairo. The immense daytime heat of the Egyptian
summer in 1915 made these very uncomfortable to live in.
(Barrett and Deane (1918))

Hospital, he had left Brisbane on the *Kyarra*. He hadn't been sent to
Gallipoli, and was still with the hospital in Cairo when ordered to help
Brady Nash.

A month after Abbassia opened, Brady Nash had to select the first
group of patients to go to Melbourne. The Australians in Abbassia wanted
to get out, but not to be sent to Australia; and, when selections were
underway, some men pleaded to not be sent, or attempted to escape.
Brady Nash decided that his judgments would be based on an assessment
of the severity of a man's infection, especially if multiple diseases were
present. Some of the men had been carrying their infections for weeks,
even months, before treatment had commenced, and their diseases had
developed to an advanced state. If a cure could not be achieved in a
reasonable time, the man was to go to Langwarrin.

For the first selection, Brady Nash chose 111 men. They were taken to
Suez, under guard, on 9 June 1915 to be loaded aboard the *Kyarra*, which
was about to make another of its homeward journeys, this time carrying
hundreds of Gallipoli invalids, with a medical team to care for them during

the voyage. At Suez, the Abbassia medical records for each VD man were transferred to the ship's senior medical officer, to be kept up to date during the voyage and eventually delivered to medical staff at Langwarrin.

When Brady Nash wrote to *The Medical Journal of Australia* at the end of June, he was caring for almost 500 Australian patients. He described how most 'are placed on verandahs, while extra accommodation is found in tents pitched on the sands. Of the eight wards, one is reserved for men who are acutely ill. This ward contains beds, while all the others have but mattresses on the floor.' He also explained that almost 200 of the Australians then in Abbassia had fought at Gallipoli, and expressed his admiration for them in spite of the fact that they were 'under his care for the results of their folly'.

In late June, Brady Nash had to make a second selection of those who would be going to Langwarrin. On 5 July, he sent 131 to Suez when the A70 *Ballarat* called there from Alexandria with 500 Gallipoli invalids on board. During the following weeks, the number of Australians at Abbassia rose to 550, then 609, and then 658. In early August, when he had nearly 700 patients, Brady Nash selected 414 to go to Langwarrin. This large group was taken to Suez and loaded onto the A17 *Port Lincoln*, which had just arrived, almost empty, from Alexandria. Brady Nash wrote in his diary that the men he sent 'were amenable to discipline and gave no trouble'.

On 23 August, he wrote this series of questions in his diary:

> Ramsay Smith relieved of his command. Why? Barrett relieved of all his military duties and ordered to confine his energies to Red Cross work. Why? Jane Bell the matron formerly of 1AGH is to return to Australia. Why? A real convulsion. I fear some dirty bad work.

The answers lay in the general troubles at the 1st Australian General Hospital, which had become unmanageable. Complaints were made, some from the doctors, and this came to a head with a storm in a teacup when Lieutenant Colonel William Ramsay Smith, the medical officer in charge of the hospital, had a dispute with his head of nursing, Matron Jane Bell, over nurses' rosters. Ramsay Smith and Bell were recalled to Australia, and Barrett was also blamed. He also came under fierce public attack for alleged mismanagement of the Australian Red Cross in Egypt. Barrett was also recalled to Australia, but then told he could stay to continue his Red Cross work. He immediately went on sick leave to London, and arranged to be transferred to the British army. In early 1916, he returned to Egypt as a lieutenant colonel in the Royal Army Medical Corps, and worked with it there for the rest of the war.

In late August at Abbassia, Brady Nash made his fourth selection of men to be sent to Australia. On 31 August, he wrote in his diary that '300' infected men left the barracks at eight o'clock in the morning for the trip to Port Suez. There, they boarded the A18 *Wiltshire*, and after their arrival at Langwarrin at the end of September, these fellows became known as the 'boys ex-*Wiltshire*' — including the five subjects of Part Two of this book.

A month later, Brady Nash dispatched the last shipload of VD men to be sent to Australia in 1915, this time from Suez and again on the *Ceramic*. This was one of his last duties at Abbassia, because it had been arranged for him to go to the Dardanelles. Thus began for him a very interesting two months of adventures at AIF hospitals on Greek islands and at Gallipoli. In December — and back in Cairo, with his year at the war almost ended — he received orders to take on the position of senior medical officer on the A32 *Themistocles*, which was about to take Gallipoli invalids to Australia. A few days later, he left Suez, and arrived back in Sydney early in January 1916.

During 1915, 1,344 infected men were returned to Australia from Egypt, and Brady Nash was the doctor who had selected most of those sent. He could not have known as he sent them away that there would be a number of unfortunate incidents involving his former patients on the ships, at Australian ports, and at their destination, Langwarrin. Serious questions would be raised about the risks of sending venereal cases back, particularly after the hospital-accommodation crisis in

The staff of the 1st Australian Dermatological Hospital,
photographed at Abbassia in 1916 — all were male. *(SLNSW)*

Egypt was resolved. All of this led to a decision in October 1915 by the Department of Defence, made on the recommendation of the surgeon-general, Colonel Fetherston, to expand the army's VD-treatment facilities in Egypt and handle all cases there.

The 1st Australian Dermatological Hospital, a new AAMC medical unit specifically for venereal cases, was hastily raised in Sydney. This was commanded by Major William Grigor, a young, newly commissioned medical officer who had been a dermatologist in Macquarie Street. The seven doctors and 100 other ranks of the hospital embarked for Egypt from Sydney on the A61 *Kanowna* just before Christmas 1915, and, after they arrived in Cairo, took over the detention barracks at Abbassia, which was converted into a proper hospital.

The dermatological hospital remained at Abbassia until August 1916, and, during its first months, the daily totals of patients under treatment far surpassed those during 1915. At the peak of the infections, in March 1916, a record daily average of 1,500 men was being treated. Then, as the re-organised AIF progressively moved its battalions to Europe, the numbers at Abbassia began to decline. By June 1916, there were about 700; in July, 240; and in August, only 100. That month, Major Grigor received orders to pack up the hospital and follow the AIF to Europe.

The dermatological hospital arrived in England in September 1916. It moved into an existing hospital at the British army camp at Bulford on the Salisbury plain in Wiltshire. Over the next three years, there were about 30,000 admissions, and the hospital was still admitting and discharging AIF soldiers until November 1919, a year after the war had ended. Despite Bulford being the largest of the Australian venereal-disease hospitals, it developed a reputation as a place where medical staff who had made mistakes elsewhere in Europe were sent to work without recognition or thanks. It was also never a happy place for the officers and soldiers who were treated there — some for multiple admissions, some for months at a time. The much smaller AIF venereal-disease hospital at Langwarrin became a place of light and learning, and provided positive experiences for patients, but apparently that never happened at Bulford.

The last words in this chapter are mainly about James Barrett. As we shall see, he would have many last words in the coming post-war revelations and debates about VD in the AIF. After he left the AIF in Egypt, Barrett became an assistant director of medical services for the RAMC there, and, in February 1916 he met Ettie Rout, who had recently arrived from New Zealand, leading the New Zealand Volunteer Sisterhood, a group of women to care for New Zealand soldiers.

Rout immediately noticed the large number of soldiers infected with VD, and began a vigorous campaign, first in Egypt and then in France and England, for Allied armies to treat the diseases as a medical problem, and not a moral one. She urged that all available preventive measures be used, including properly supervised brothels, and she invented prophylactic kits to be given to soldiers. Rout became famous for her work, and popular among ANZAC soldiers; but, in New Zealand, she was disapproved of, and her name was unmentionable. After she arrived in Egypt, Rout discovered that James Barrett held similar ideas to her own, and the two collaborated. He became the medical expert who helped guide Rout's safe-sex campaigns, and he also arranged introductions for her to important British officers in Cairo and London, and sometimes to their influential wives as well.

In March 1916, Rout made an inspection visit to the Wasa'a prostitution quarter. This was when venereal infections in Australian troops reached record levels, and, after her inspection, Ettie explained why this was happening in a report that was circulated to senior Australian and New Zealand officers, and eventually to the Australian prime minister. Even though it was now over a year since General Birdwood had become upset about it, and the AAMC doctors had met at Heliopolis to discuss the problem, nothing much had changed in the Wasa'a:

> The streets and alleys were filthy with offal and the stenches abominable, but they were crowded with men in Khaki. There were several drinking shops and dancing halls quite open to the streets, and hundreds of soldiers were in these. Outside notorious brothels long queues of soldiers waited their turn. One open door revealed a stairway with lines of soldiers going up and down — in and out. Soliciting and enticing was quite openly carried on. Bedizened and lustful women thronged the streets and doorways, many of them being embraced by soldiers. Doors were open and soldiers could be seen inside the rooms sitting on women's laps and vice versa.[11]

For a long time after the war, Barrett re-fought the old battles of 1915 about venereal-disease prophylaxis. He wrote letters to editors, and articles for newspapers and medical journals, and he occasionally spoke at medical conferences. In 1940, he was unapologetic after writing that, during the First World War, the British army was overrun during the German spring offensive in early 1918 because so many British soldiers were in hospital with VD.

A 1917 photograph of the New Zealand social reformer Ettie Rout.
She is wearing the badge of the New Zealand Volunteer Sisterhood,
which she founded in 1915. *(Jane Tolerton)*

In 1916 and 1918, Barrett was mentioned in dispatches for his work
in Egypt with the RAMC, and, in 1916, he was awarded the Order of the
Nile. In 1918, his wartime service was recognised by King George V: he
was appointed a Knight Commander of the Order of the British Empire,
and a Companion of the Order of the Bath. With the widespread use of

prophylactics and other preventive measures having been approved in the AIF and other armies from 1916, Sir James could now be satisfied that his advocacy of these methods since early 1915 had been proven correct.

CHAPTER THREE

The Voyage of the *Wiltshire*

la nef des fous

In late 1918, in the last months of the First World War, when it was clear the German army was losing the struggle and would soon leave France, a French art collector, Camille Benoit, gave a number of valuable paintings from his private collection to the Musee du Louvre in Paris. To protect its treasures, the Louvre had been closed during the war, but it re-opened in February 1919. Soon to be put on public display for the first time, one of the gifts of Monsieur Benoit was the central panel of a triptych tableau made in the last decade of the 15th century by a Flemish painter, Jheronimus van Aken. He is today usually known by the alternative form of his name, Hieronymus Bosch, and is famous for his remarkable religious and moral allegories, some with themes that parodied the drunkenness, licentiousness, and venereal disease of his time. His painting in the Louvre is usually called *La Nef des fous*, the ship of fools, and is a caricature of the prodigality of mankind. It depicts a curious little sailboat filled with men and women thoroughly obsessed with sinful pleasures, but unaware of where the vessel is taking them.

It is unlikely that many of the men of the AIF who, during 1915, were sent back to Australia in disgrace with venereal disease would have known of Bosch or *La Nef des fous*, but they might have hotly resented being characterised as fools. Each tended to think of himself as a victim, carrying a damned infection received through pure bad luck — no fault of his. But what better word than fools could be used to describe those who had ignored the loud warnings of the AIF's leaders and doctors, and had become infected anyway? Most of the AIF men who passed through Egypt in 1915 were not so foolish and did give a wide berth to the brothels. Those who became infected and got sent home were the odd men out who, by their unusual behaviour, brought upon themselves the deepest of trouble.

But it does seem that, privately, some of the prodigals returning to Australia on the *Wiltshire* in September 1915 did know they had wasted their chance, and felt like fools. We know this because we are aware of how profoundly some would later regret their moment of folly in Egypt; and we also know the efforts some later made to conceal what they had done from those who loved them and cared about them. But at this stage, like the voyagers in *La Nef des fous*, the men on the *Wiltshire* were still barely aware of the consequences in their future lives from bad choices made in Egypt.

Men with venereal disease began to be sent back to Australia from February 1915. As noted above, the minister for defence had made a threat that this would happen, and General Bridges had quickly arranged for some of the 'wasters' of the AIF, including venereal-disease cases, to be sent home. In February 1915, the first group of unwanted men, including 132 VD patients, departed on the A55 *Kyarra* from Port Suez. On 15 March, the New Zealand ship *Moloia* sailed with another mixed group of disciplinary and medical cases; to be followed, on 20 March, by 300 on the A38 *Ulysses*. The standard procedure followed for transporting venereal cases on troopships returning to Australia was to continue their isolation from other troops while they were being moved from an isolation barracks in Egypt to another in Australia. The orders covering this stated that 'A corner of a hammock deck is set aside and bulk-headed off for venereal disease. Separate lavatories and messing are provided, and apparatus and drugs for treatment'. In this way, on board the ships, infected men were treated like pariahs.

The Ship of Fools, or the Satire of the Debauched Revelers, an oil-on-wood painting made by Hieronymus Bosch. *(RMN; Martine Beck-Coppola; Musee du Louvre)*

When the *Kyarra* arrived at Port Melbourne in March 1915, the Melbourne *Argus* reported that, although a large crowd of curious citizens had gathered at the pier, the ship remained anchored offshore and the troops remained aboard. The report described men on the ship as

> not casualties of battle. They are the cases which inevitably occur in camp. Men will get kicked by horses, will, if there are pyramids to climb, fall off them, and will find innumerable ways to damage themselves. And many of these cases are the results of the mens' own folly.

The following day, *The Argus* published a statement by the Department of Defence 'regarding the soldiers who have returned from Egypt by the Kyarra'. Headed 'A Cruel Slander', this statement played down the VD issue:

> The Minister for Defence wishes to correct an impression which appears to have gained ground among the public that a large proportion of the men of the Australian Imperial Force returned invalided by the Kyarra are suffering from venereal disease. The Minister is in receipt of a report from the acting director of the Commonwealth Army Medical Services in which that officer states that the rumour is a cruel slander upon the troops. For the number of men sent from Australia the percentage of venereal cases is small. Adequate steps are being taken to deal with the small number of venereal cases which do exist among the returned men.

The following month saw the landings at Gallipoli, and Senator Pearce's consequent approval to clear the hospitals in Egypt of venereal cases. When repatriation began shortly after, the first ship to transport a group of infected men also carried soldiers being invalided home with other infectious diseases. Thus, in early May 1915, the A40 *Ceramic* sailed from Suez carrying over 400 men to Melbourne, including 261 VD cases collected hurriedly from hospitals in Cairo.

We know that many of the men with venereal disease sent to Australia intended to cut and run, to 'do a bolter' at the first opportunity after their ship reached an Australian port. These fellows had no intention of going through the humiliation of arriving as marked men. They would jump ship, if necessary by swimming ashore, and 'take to the tall timber'. There would be many of these escapes after ships carrying 'venereals' reached Australia.

In July 1915, the *Kyarra* arrived at Fremantle after her second voyage from Egypt, this time with a mixed group of 330 men wounded at Gallipoli and over 100 VD cases selected at Abbassia by Colonel Brady Nash. The local authorities had arranged 'welcoming entertainments' for the returning heroes; but, to the disappointment of the welcoming party, no one on board was permitted ashore. However, a number of the men with venereal disease did manage to get ashore by sliding down mooring ropes, and they soon disappeared into the town. One of the escapees, Charles Rudolph, who had become infected with VD in May, was arrested a few days later after he was discovered on a street haranguing startled bystanders. Under the headline 'Deserter's Language — Hope Germans Will Win', his fate was reported in a newspaper:

A returned South Australian soldier named Charles Rudolph, who deserted from the Kyarra, appeared at the Fremantle Police Court yesterday charged with disorderly conduct and with having used obscene language. Sergeant Pilmer said that on Saturday week Rudolph was standing on the corner of High and Market streets holding forth to a crowd. He was not drunk, but was using most obscene and seditious language. The language complained of was 'They treat us like dogs. I hope the Germans win right through, and that all the Australians at the Dardanelles will be shot'. Rudolph, who had no defence to offer to the charge, was imprisoned for three months.[12]

Complaints were made in the Australian parliament about the 'maltreatment' of men on the *Kyarra* after she docked at Port Melbourne.

It was found that, at the very end of the voyage, more of the venereal cases had escaped.

> ... no attempt was made to distinguish between soldiers returned for disciplinary reasons and those who had been rendered unfit for further service by reason of wounds received in action. The Minister for Defence promised to enquire into these [complaints]. It is understood that one phase of Kyarra's arrival which will come within the scope of the official enquiry is the debarkation and entraining of the venereal disease cases. Provision had been made for the conveyance of these men by special train to Langwarrin. It is stated, however, that 40 of these men managed to break away, and, mixing with the medical and wounded cases ... left Melbourne. [13]

Permitting venereally infected men to mix with the wounded and ill when ships arrived at Australian ports had other unintended consequences. At the ports of arrival, misunderstandings arose among relatives and wellwishers there to greet invalid soldiers. Sometimes, the venereal cases also received enthusiastic 'welcomes home' by mistake; other times, non-venereal cases were regarded with suspicion because they had been on a ship that had carried venereal patients.

Another unintended consequence arose at this time when returned Gallipoli invalids and men with venereal disease were discharged from the army because of medical unfitness. Because of publicity surrounding the return of infected men, suspicions were aroused that any man who was discharged unfit might have VD. A public announcement by the Department of Defence explained how this was to be rectified:

> In view of the fact that an impression exists amongst the public that men who are discharged from the Australian Imperial Force, and whose cause of discharge is stated on the discharge certificate as 'being medically unfit for further service' or 'medical unfitness' are men who have been rendered unfit through the contraction of venereal disease. It

has been decided that in future the cause of the discharge of men who are medically unfit through a cause not due to misconduct is to be stated on the discharge certificate as follows: 'Being medically unfit not due to misconduct'.[14]

For the men returning on ships, it was decided to handle the venereal cases separately so their arrivals could be managed without controversy. Initially, this still involved loading, in Egypt, venereal and non-venereal cases on board a returning ship, but managing them quite differently on arrival in Australia. A troopship that carried men to be separated in this way was the A70 *Ballarat*, which left Alexandria in June 1915 carrying a group of 500 amputees, and men deafened and blinded at Gallipoli. After passage through the canal, on 5 July, the *Ballarat* stopped at Suez to take on 131 venereal cases, the second group selected by Brady Nash at Abbassia. For the voyage, they were regarded as disciplinary cases; so, after boarding, they were isolated from the Gallipoli invalids behind a bulkhead in the front of the ship. During the trip to Western Australia, however, they made their presence known by riotous behaviour.

The ship made its Australian landfall at Albany, but no men were permitted to go ashore, apart from the Western Australian invalids on board. This was a difficult restriction for the wounded and infected men alike, and, in the middle of the night, while the *Ballarat* lay at anchor, about 40 invalids and VD men commandeered lifeboats and rowed away. Some got only to a coal barge moored nearby, while others made it to shore and disappeared into the town. Within a day, all had been rounded up, detained, and then sent to Melbourne on a following ship, the *Indarra*. Later, some of the escapees said they left the ship to 'find a good feed' in Albany, because meals served during the voyage from Egypt were appalling. Meanwhile, the venereal patients who remained on the *Ballarat* continued to be nuisances. After the ship left Albany, they smashed fittings in their section of the ship, and started fires to keep themselves warm.

When the *Ballarat* arrived with her crippled heroes at Port Melbourne, a newspaper described the welcome given, under bold headlines: 'BACK FROM THE FRONT', 'WOUNDED MEN AT MELBOURNE', 'AN ENTHUSIASTIC WELCOME'.

The majority of the men who returned to-day by the Ballarat had sufficiently recovered from their wounds to enjoy to the full their hearty reception. They shouted back greetings to men, waved their hands to girls, and shook hands all round when a temporary stoppage occurred on the long line of motor cars. The enthusiasm was intense, the people it would appear, being anxious to make up for the scanty welcome given to soldiers who came home on an earlier hospital ship. A triumphal arch was erected over the entrance gates to the Port Melbourne town pier, and immediately inside the gate a band played lively airs as the soldiers came through.[15]

But what was the welcome given to the venereal cases that had also arrived with the ship? The same article tells us:

There was no danger today of the wrong men being cheered. Disciplinary and venereal cases, numbering about 130, were transferred to a launch while the Ballarat was lying in the bay and taken direct to Langwarrin.

In fact, special arrangements had been made to ensure the venereal cases could not land at Port Melbourne. Before the *Ballarat* arrived there, she briefly stopped further south in Port Phillip Bay, near the Mornington jetty, and the 'venereals' were offloaded onto launches for a short trip to shore. From Mornington station, they were taken by train directly to the isolation barracks, escorted by armed militia guards.

Because of the escapes and arrival embarrassments, it was decided in July 1915 that wounded Gallipoli men would be provided with troopships for their exclusive use, and, when empty returning ships were available, venereal cases would be transported separately on them.

The A17 *Port Lincoln* was the first ship from Egypt to take only venereal cases to Australia, and carried the large group of 414 infected men sent by Brady Nash. There is an interesting side story attached to this voyage.

General Bridges was shot at Gallipoli in May 1915. The bullet went through the femoral artery in his thigh, and he later died on the ship evacuating him to Egypt. After the arrival of his body at Alexandria, he was buried in a cemetery used for Australian dead. The Australian government arranged for him to receive a posthumous knighthood, and then, in June, announced that his remains would be repatriated for a ceremonial re-burial at the Duntroon Military College in Canberra, where Bridges had been the first commandant. His body was exhumed at the Alexandria cemetery and placed in a lead-lined coffin, and this was loaded onto the *Port Lincoln*, which happened to be in Alexandria, empty and on the verge of departing — first to Port Suez and then to Melbourne.

The *Port Lincoln* left from Alexandria with only the general's coffin on board. At this point, an AIF embarkation officer, a Major McLeod, was suddenly told that the *Port Lincoln* intended at Port Suez to take on the venereal cases from Abbassia. It had been our old friend James Barrett in Cairo who had taken it upon himself to inform McLeod that a disaster was about to happen. It would be an outrage for Lady Bridges, and a public scandal, if the remains of Australia's first general arrived at Melbourne escorted by 400 venereally diseased men! However, neither McLeod nor Barrett evidently knew that senior Australian officers in Cairo were aware of the impending situation, and had already made a plan to offload the general's coffin at Port Suez and transfer it to another ship before the 'venereals' appeared. In his ignorance of this, McLeod took it upon himself to also arrange to offload the coffin at Suez. In addition, he sent a cabled report to Senator Pearce in Australia, eagerly advising what he had done to stop a serious embarrassment from occurring.

Accordingly, at Suez, after a number of misunderstandings, the coffin was ceremoniously transferred by launch from the *Port Lincoln* to the P&O steamer *Arabia*, which was loading wounded Gallipoli men for repatriation. Reacting to McLeod's report, Senator Pearce cabled to Cairo demanding an explanation for the purported bungle, and wanting to know who was responsible. A reply was sent to the senator, by a weary, irritated officer, which explained that there had been no mistake made, that McLeod had acted hastily, and that his last-minute intervention had caused the only embarrassments in the affair.[16]

The *Arabia* departed from Suez just before the *Port Lincoln*, and arrived at Port Melbourne on 1 September. The general's coffin was moved ashore with great reverence and taken to the city, where a state funeral service was held the following day at St Paul's Cathedral. After the service, the coffin was placed on a horse-drawn gun carriage draped with a Union flag, then escorted in a solemn procession through hushed crowds to Spencer Street station. From here, it was taken by train, accompanied by the official mourning party, to Canberra for burial at Duntroon.

Also arriving at Port Melbourne on 1 September, late in the evening, the *Port Lincoln* docked with her 414 infected men. Their arrival was discreetly reported by *The Argus* on the next day, without mentioning the diseases with which they were afflicted, or the name of the ship:

> Another big contingent of Australian soldiers, numbering 414 in all, arrived in Hobson's Bay at about 9 o'clock last night by a transport from Suez. It is stated that all the men on the vessel are described as medically unfit, none of them being wounded. The whole batch will be landed at Port Melbourne, it having been arranged that the transport shall berth beside the Railway Pier early this morning.

In late August 1915, four big troopships began departing from Suez to return to Australia, carrying large numbers of Gallipoli invalids, but with no venereal cases. In the fashionable style of the time, each of the four had been named by its owners after a famous ancient Greek. Thus the A32 *Themistocles*, the A14 *Euripides*, the A38 *Ulysses*, and the

The funeral procession for Major General William Bridges, moving along Flinders Street. *(SLV)*

A11 *Ascanius* all steamed down the Red Sea to Aden, then to Colombo and across the Indian Ocean to Fremantle. When they began arriving, their progress was telegraphed to eastern Australia and enthusiastically reported in newspapers. Under the headline 'RETURNING HEROES', the Adelaide *Advertiser* reported that 'the ships have been practically racing each other across the Bight', and provided extensive details about the public receptions and ceremonies being arranged for the heroes.

However, there was a fifth big troopship that had sailed from Suez at the same time as the *Themistocles*, *Euripides*, *Ulysses*, and *Ascanius*, which overtook them, and was the first of the five to reach Port Melbourne. Although also carrying many invalided soldiers, the ship's details, faster progress, and purpose were not reported in the Australian press.

This was our *nef des fous*, HMAT A18 *Wiltshire*, named, more prosaically, after a county in England (where, coincidentally, the 1st

Australian Dermatological Hospital would later be based). She had departed from Port Suez on 31 August with 295 troops on board: 20 medical staff and escorts, and the '300' — actually 275 — infected men sent by Colonel Brady Nash from Abbassia to Langwarrin. The transport's quiet arrival at Port Melbourne on 24 September 1915 was blandly reported in *The Argus* the following morning: 'A transport arrived at Port Melbourne yesterday with 275 soldiers on board. The men will be removed to the camp at Langwarrin to-day.'

The *Wiltshire* was a modern, beautifully proportioned large steel steamer, one of the newest and fastest of the fleet of British passenger and cargo vessels that, before the war, had plied the vast distances of the route from the United Kingdom to Australia and New Zealand. She had been built in 1912 in Scotland, and in 1914 became the property of the Commonwealth and Dominion Line of London. At the outbreak of war, she had been lying at anchor in Brisbane, and was immediately leased for use as a troopship for Australia.

Her first wartime service occurred in October 1914, when, code-numbered A18 for Australian duties, the *Wiltshire* became part of the convoy carrying the first AIF contingent to Egypt. She returned to Australia, and in April 1915 left for Egypt with reinforcements, arriving in June. Her return voyage to Port Melbourne was to carry exclusively the fourth shipload of venereally infected men sent by Brady Nash. After unloading the patients, the *Wiltshire* returned to Egypt in November 1915, taking more reinforcements. In 1916, she became the property of the Cunard Steamship Company, but continued to be used as an Australian troopship until 1919.

For her voyage from Port Suez to Australia in August and September 1915, the ship was under the command of Captain William Prentice, a longstanding employee of the Commonwealth and Dominion Line. He became captain of the *Wiltshire* in January 1914, and remained in command after she became an Australian troopship. In early 1916, during the *Wiltshire*'s third wartime voyage to Egypt, he died aboard of heart failure, near Western Australia, and was buried at sea.

The troopship A18 *Wiltshire*, moored at Port Melbourne in 1915.
(Allan C. Green; SLV)

When used to carry AIF contingents to Egypt, the *Wiltshire* had been crammed with soldiers, horses, carriages, carts, and military stores. Every available space had been used, and the ship had teemed with activity during its voyages to ports along the Suez Canal. However, for the August–September 1915 trip back to Australia, the cavernous ship was almost empty. Apart from the crew, there were only 20 working passengers on board: two medical officers, six medical orderlies, and 12 AIF soldiers acting as guards. The guards were particularly vigilant when the ship entered Australian waters, and, because of this, there were no 'bolters' from the *Wiltshire*: the 275 who had embarked at Suez were delivered without incident at Port Melbourne.

The senior medical officer on board was Captain Herbert Alsop, who was in civilian life a medical practitioner in Bowral, south of Sydney. He had been a reservist in the AAMC, became a ship's doctor for the AIF, and his first voyage to Egypt, in June 1915, was with the *Wiltshire*. Following successful delivery of his 275 patients to Port Melbourne, he re-embarked there on the *Wiltshire* in November 1915, and shortly after was involved in attempts to save the life of Captain Prentice at sea off Western Australia.

In late September 1915, as the ship approached Port Melbourne, Captain Alsop wrote his *Report on health of Troops on board the above Steamer, during voyage from Suez to Melbourne*, and, from this, we learn he was caring for 229 cases of gonorrhoea, one case of gonorrhoea and paratyphoid, one case of gonorrhoea and measles, and 44 cases of syphilis. With the voyage about to end, Captain Alsop was able to report that 'of the gonorrhoea cases, 70 are now free from any indication of disease. The Paratyphoid and Measles have both recovered from those conditions', but the syphilis cases had not been cured.

The members of the guard escort were all invalids being sent home, including the NCOs in charge, Sergeant Albert Tiegs and Sergeant Thomas Keane, although later they would go back to the war. Corporal Ernest Edgar was being returned to Australia because of persistent intestinal complaints, and he would be discharged as medically unfit in December 1915. Private William Dilley had been shot at Gallipoli and would also be discharged as medically unfit after arrival in Melbourne.

Other members of the *Wiltshire*'s guard might have also been VD patients. In January 1915, Corporal Terence O'Neill had been admitted to the isolation hospital at Mena with signs of VD. The doctors had been uncertain of the diagnosis; but, when he was released from hospital, his papers were marked 'disability–VD', anyway. O'Neill was sent to Australia on the *Wiltshire*, and, after his arrival in Melbourne, would eventually be discharged from the army 'medically unfit not due to misconduct'. Private Albert Pritchard had been evacuated with influenza from Gallipoli, and, in Egypt, had been discovered to also have an infection that might have been related to VD. He was to be discharged very soon after the *Wiltshire* arrived. Private Jack Haddon had been evacuated from Gallipoli because of cardiac strain; afterwards, it had been decided he also had traces of chancre. He had been sent as an escort on the *Wiltshire*, and was to be discharged in May 1916 because of medical unfitness.

As we shall soon see, the distinction between who were the guards and who were the patients became progressively blurred as the voyage continued to Australia. However, in the army record of each member of the guard party on the *Wiltshire*, it was clearly marked that each was 'on duty' as an escort for the voyage. By contrast, in the record of each man on board sent from Abbassia, it was marked that he was being returned to Australia 'VD' or 'venereal' — in most cases, with the name of his disease described. For some, there was also a note saying they were 'for discharge' from the army.

The infected men on the *Wiltshire* were a varied lot, but had much in common apart from VD. Most were very young, between 18 and 22, although one fellow was only 17 — he had used his older brother's identity when he enlisted, aged 16. Only a few were over 30, with the oldest being 44. They were all private soldiers, for the few who had been NCOs in Egypt had been reduced to the ranks before being sent to Abbassia. All men on board were also penniless, because each man's army pay had been stopped. The forced removal of the sense of independence that came with having money was an especially grievous 'injustice', and they did not know when they would have that sense again. Most had enlisted in New South Wales and Victoria, but there were others from Queensland, South Australia, Western Australia, and Tasmania. They came from the bush and from cities, from respectable middle-class homes and from working-class backgrounds. Many were immigrants from England, Scotland, or Ireland, or their parents were immigrants from those places. They were in all branches of the AIF, mostly from the infantry battalions and Light Horse regiments, with some from the artillery and base-support units.

The infected men on the *Wiltshire* fell into two general categories. The first category comprised about one-third of them, the men who had taken part in the Gallipoli landings. Most had been evacuated to Egypt with battle wounds or sickness to hospitals in Cairo and Alexandria. While convalescing and on leave, they had caught VD in July and August 1915. The rest in this category had become infected just before embarkation to the Dardanelles, and had carried their diseases to

Gallipoli. Their secret had been revealed there, usually after they were wounded or fell ill. One of the Gallipoli men had been infected with VD and cured before the landings, where he was shot; he had then been re-infected after his evacuation to Egypt. Notwithstanding their special status as battle veterans, the fates of all the Gallipoli men on the *Wiltshire* had been sealed by the defence minister's April 1915 decision to banish all venereal cases from Egypt, and by their selection at Abbassia to be sent to Langwarrin.

The other, much larger, category of men on board the *Wiltshire* comprised those who had not been at Gallipoli. They were mostly reinforcements who had arrived in Egypt to join their battalions and regiments in the months immediately after the first landings. Most had only recently volunteered at recruiting stations in Australia during the surge of national pride that followed the sensational news from the Dardanelles. In May and June, these fellows had left Australian ports, cheered off to the war in scenes of great excitement and with expectations of heroic deeds. A few weeks later, in July and August 1915, they had arrived at the AIF camps near Cairo. From these they were meant to have gone to Gallipoli, but instead had caught VD shortly after arrival. Judging from the number who must have become infected within days of disembarkation at Suez Canal ports, many had made a visit to the Wasa'a something very high on their list of priorities on arrival. Now, before firing a shot in battle, they were being sent straight back to Australia in disgrace.

Also on the *Wiltshire* were a number of fellows who had just arrived in Egypt but with a VD infection from Australia, and who had been immediately sent back. A handful of other men who had not been at Gallipoli had arrived in Egypt before the landings in April, but their military duties as drivers and clerks had exclusively been as 'base wallahs' in the camps around Cairo.

Only about one in ten of the men on board the *Wiltshire* had been married at the date of enlistment, although that proportion might have risen by the time of their departure from Australia. Also, only a relatively small number had allotted part of their pay to a family member during their service abroad. Most had not arranged allotments at all; in Egypt, they had their entire 'six bob a day' army pay available for personal spending. Thus, only some of the men were affected by the army regulation to stop family allotments. It was these who had a puzzled relative in Australia knowing something was amiss when a regular payment to them was cut off with no explanation by the army.

On board the *Wiltshire*, as she ploughed through the ocean to Port Melbourne, Captain Alsop's small medical team continued the gruesome treatments for gonorrhoea, syphilis, and chancroid that Colonel Brady Nash and Captain Plant had begun at Abbassia. Many of the patients, eager to be rid of disease, appear to have earnestly co-operated in these unpleasant episodes. They did not want to return still carrying an infection and be 'discharged–medically unfit–VD'. These proud fellows had no intention of being dumped in Australia and having to make awkward explanations to those at home. They were fully committed to return to the war as soon as possible, using whatever means necessary, without anyone knowing about their premature return on the *Wiltshire*.

It appears, however, that some of the patients resisted the VD treatments, and resented the army for causing their troubles. They were sullen and unco-operative, and did not care what the army did to them on arrival in Melbourne, even if they were discharged. Indeed, it seems likely that some hoped this might happen. As soon as an opportunity presented, many of these rebels intended to 'discharge themselves' anyway, by 'doing a bunk'. These characters did not care at all to return to the war, or explain anything to anybody.

We can safely assume then that, during this voyage, the private thoughts of each man and the conversations among the men revolved around one main question: how would each handle his predicament after he arrived in Melbourne? Rightly or wrongly, most believed that they were being sent home for sexual misconduct and that their career in the army, which was definitely uncertain, might end unpleasantly. The men who had agreed to allot part of their pay to a family member had a particularly heavy burden: they could expect questioning about why the flow of funds had suddenly ceased. Men who had stopped writing home after being sent to Abbassia must have known that the lack of news from them would be causing concern. Unbeknown to the men, the army was already receiving anxious letters of enquiry from parents and wives about this silence, and some letter writers had already been informed by the army that their man was returning to Australia for undisclosed medical reasons.

From what we know of the behaviour of the men of the *Wiltshire* in the months and years ahead, each had already decided that his foolishness in Egypt would be kept as a secret forever. Each had devised a story for concealing the truth about his inexplicable return. The Gallipoli men on board already had that story: all had been wounded or became ill during the battle, and Australians knew that invalided Gallipoli heroes were being sent home. The Gallipoli men on the *Wiltshire* were, if not quite in fact, also wounded heroes. They would say they were 'invalided to hospital in Melbourne' because of the wound, injury, or illness they had genuinely received at Gallipoli, and some had the scars to offer as proof.

Those who had not fought at Gallipoli had a difficult predicament. They had no easily invented story for being sent home so soon after those cheering farewells a few months before. For some, to avoid having to explain anything at all, plans for drastic action were forming in their imaginations. If their difficulties became too hard to handle, they would escape into the civilian population of Australia, travel as far away as they could manage with no money, and start their lives anew. They would do this, cured or not.

There was, of course, for all the men on board, a very attractive and plausible falsehood that could be used. Each could see he was being escorted by guards, each of whom was an invalid. As the journey progressed, the original party of 12 guards was supplemented by men who had embarked at Suez with infections, then subsequently been made healthy by Captain Alsop. Fit for duty once more, each of these lucky fellows realised he was now an 'escort' for the others. At least, that is how some of the cured men later described their, perhaps imagined, changed roles. Here was the story a worried man required, for each could say, if it came to it, that in Egypt he had been 'unexpectedly assigned to be a member of the guard on a ship that had carried invalids back to Australia'. Who would be any the wiser?

There was another much bigger face-saving falsehood that could be used — a real corker, one guaranteed to shut up over-curious enquirers. Borrowing the intention of genuine Gallipoli men on board, a man who had not been at Gallipoli could pretend that he *had* been there. 'Unfortunately, I was returned to Australia as an invalid because of what happened to me at Gallipoli.' Later in this account, we shall see how this bold lie played out, and how families believed it, and its long-term consequences.

What did all these troubled men expect to find on their arrival at Port Melbourne? Would they be publicly treated as fools and suffer more humiliations when they reached home? Mercifully, the army arranged a discreet arrival for the ship. On the wet, windy evening of Friday 24 September 1915, there were no curious onlookers as the *Wiltshire* slowly pulled alongside Railway Pier. Instead, on Saturday morning, the men on board were met only by a number of officials from the Commonwealth Quarantine Service, whose job it was to ensure that none could contaminate any innocent citizen after leaving the ship.

To guarantee that no one got away, an armed militia escort from Langwarrin supervised the movement of the men, with their heavy kitbags, from ship to wharf, and then onto a special railway train that was waiting with its hissing steam locomotive on the pier. The 275 were then escorted for the last stage of the trip, chuffing through the Melbourne suburban railway network, far off to the south, where their long journey from Egypt finally ended at the railway siding right next to the isolation camp. All had to go to Langwarrin, including the 70 men who, according to Captain Alsop, 'showed no signs of infection'.

Every man would now be medically examined at Langwarrin, and thus it would be the medical officers there who would decide which men would be released fit for duty, or be recommended for immediate discharge from the AIF because of medical unfitness, or remain in confinement for continuing treatment. For the men of the *nef de fous*, what might unfold for them at this place would determine their immediate futures. Would there be a happy ending, a release from the humiliation each had suffered since their infection had been discovered, far away and some time ago in Egypt?

CHAPTER FOUR

Robert Williams and Walter Conder

the isolation-detention barracks at Langwarrin

When the decision was made in January 1915 to send men with VD from Egypt to Australia, the army was faced with the urgent challenge of finding somewhere to put them. By early February, the first group of patients was heading home on the *Kyarra*, and more were following, so there was no time to lose. Because of the contagious nature of the diseases, and the public terror of them, the hospital would need to be akin to a detention barracks, able to hold men in complete isolation. Given the urgency, it would need to use existing facilities in an army camp.

If the isolation barracks were to be in a camp anywhere near civilians, agreement would need to be reached to allay their fears. The difficulty of achieving this was demonstrated when a proposal to establish it at the Liverpool camp near Sydney was refused by the NSW government because of local complaints. Even if permission had been given, it is unlikely that men with VD would have been tolerated for long at Liverpool. Throughout 1915, the citizens of Sydney were repeatedly made aware that there was much trouble at this camp, including drunken riots, which led to a royal commission to examine its deficiencies.

Another possibility was the big camp at Broadmeadows, near Melbourne. It had been opened in great haste in August 1914 to process

Professor J. Laurence Rentoul of Ormond College, Melbourne
University. In 1916, Rentoul became a chaplain-general in the AIF.
(NLA)

Victorian recruits to the AIF, and in early 1915 was still a maze of dusty
tents. There were other problems at Broadmeadows, as well, preventing
it from being considered as a place to put men with VD. Public concerns
were initially aroused by accusations made by a Melbourne Presbyterian,
Professor J. Laurence Rentoul, who announced that Broadmeadows was
a 'camp of evil'. He was referring to drinking, gambling, circulation of
pornography, and prostitution, which, according to Rentoul, went on quite
openly. Then, during autumn wet weather in 1915, the poor drainage and
leaking tents caused an outbreak of meningitis, and some recruits died.
As a result, a decision was made to establish the main Victorian recruit-
training camp at Seymour, 100 kilometres north of Melbourne, with
Broadmeadows supposed to be gradually scaled down in importance.

There was, however, another place near Melbourne that seemed
suitable. Three decades earlier, the Victorian colonial government had
reserved for military use a large area of unused land at Langwarrin on

A rudimentary field kitchen at a Victorian militia camp at
Langwarrin in the late 19th century. The bell tents in the
background were still being used in 1915 in the detention
enclosures for enemy aliens and VD-infected AIF soldiers. *(SLV)*

the Mornington Peninsula. A rudimentary camp was established with a
parade ground and tent lines, and roads named after military heroes like
Napoleon, Wellington, and Marlborough. Bushland was cleared to make
way for firing ranges, and pasture for military horses. A railway station
was built, and, in 1888, there was a failed attempt to establish a township
called Aldershot, after the British army camp in Hampshire.

Although regularly used by the Victorian colonial militia, the camp
was never properly developed. In 1899, when the Boer War began, it
received hundreds of volunteers for Victorian contingents, but they
were very disappointed with the leaking tents, poor sanitation and water
supply, and lack of proper kitchens and messes. After Federation in 1901,
the Australian government took control of the camp, and it continued to
be used by militia units and for the annual camps of army cadets from
Victorian schools.

After the outbreak of war in 1914, it was decided that people of German, Austrian, and Turkish descent would be interned as enemy aliens, and those in Victoria would be sent to Langwarrin. Hundreds of people were rounded up and interned in a newly built barbed-wire compound; they slept on the ground in old army tents, and water had to be brought by train and carted in. An officer of the Victorian militia, Major Archibald Lloyd, was in charge and commanded an armed militia guard. In April 1915, an escaper was shot and wounded when the militia fired at him; the same volley of shots killed another internee with a ricocheting round. By May, over 400 aliens lived at Langwarrin, and the numbers steadily increased.

In early 1915, because nowhere else could be found, it was decided that men with VD sent from Egypt would be put in a detention barracks at Langwarrin, next to the internee compound. A guarantee was given to the Victorian government that they would be completely isolated from the civilian population outside. It was assumed the barracks would be temporary and for not many men, so a small barbed-wire compound was built, tents were erected, and some alien internees were employed as cooks. The compound was also placed under the control of Major Lloyd and his militia guard. When the men brought on the *Kyarra*, *Moloia*, and *Ulysses* arrived, they, like the aliens next door, were required to sleep on the ground in old tents; even worse, because of the water shortage, there were no bathing facilities for them at all.

In March 1915, the first medical officer began making daily visits from Melbourne. He was Dr Whitfield Henty, a young general practitioner in Armadale who was a captain in the AAMC Reserve. After two months, he was sent to Egypt with the 3rd Australian General Hospital. His brief period at Langwarrin, brought to an end with an overseas posting, was typical of doctors who worked at the camp from then on. It was difficult to find doctors to work there at all, and the rapid turnover of those sent added to the chaotic conditions that soon developed.

After the Gallipoli landings in April 1915, the defence minister, Senator Pearce, approved sending all venereal cases from Egypt to

Langwarrin. After the first group of 261 arrived in May on the *Ceramic*, the camp struggled to house and feed its growing population of aliens and soldiers. What appeared to be a solution was a decision made by the defence department to concentrate most enemy aliens in Australia at a camp at Holsworthy, near Sydney. It took a long time to clear them from Langwarrin, and they had still not been moved out when, in July, the *Kyarra* delivered another 111 men from Egypt, followed by another 131 on the *Ballarat* the next month.

In mid-1915, there was a change of the commandant of the 3rd Military District, which covered Victoria. A suitable senior officer was needed to replace Colonel Robert Wallace, who had become ill. In July, Senator Pearce chose Colonel Robert Williams, initially in an acting capacity; later in 1915, he was confirmed in the role and promoted to brigadier general. His appointment as Victoria's military commandant would be of great significance for the thousands of AIF men eventually sent to Langwarrin.

As a young man, Colonel Williams started his working life as a teacher in Ballarat, then changed careers to become a journalist and the editor for *The Ballarat Courier*, and later became the town clerk of Ballarat West. He had joined the militia in Ballarat, and rose to become colonel-in-charge of the 2nd Victorian Infantry Brigade. In July 1915, he was aged 60 and had retired from military duties when he was suddenly recalled by Senator Pearce. Among the assignments of highest priority given to him was proper organisation of the overcrowded isolation barracks at Langwarrin.

His first challenge was finding doctors to work there. Major Andrew Grant, an elderly GP from Dandenong, had been making regular day visits, but had recently stopped. He had been accused of releasing an inmate before the man was cured; the resulting inquiry revealed that if a man infected with gonorrhoea drank copious quantities of water before taking a urine test, the result could be clear of pus threads. Later, and despite better methods for VD testing, other Langwarrin doctors got into trouble for releasing men who were only apparently cured.

In August 1915, Colonel Williams found two new doctors to replace Dr Grant. Dr Arthur Morris was a prominent Collins Street dermatologist in Melbourne, well known (along with his wife) on the social and charity committees of the city. He was not in the army, so, for him to become senior medical officer, Colonel Williams arranged a temporary commission as a captain. Morris was a venereal-disease expert, and appears to have been the first genuine specialist to work at Langwarrin.

He was assisted by Dr James McCusker, a young Scottish GP who had become involved with the AIF in Egypt earlier in 1915. McCusker was sent to Australia as a medical officer on the *Ballarat* to look after the notorious group of 'venereals' on board. After arriving in Melbourne, he joined the AAMC, believing he would be immediately sent overseas. He was made a captain, but was instead sent by Colonel Williams to work at Langwarrin.

In early September 1915, 414 more infected men arrived, delivered from Egypt by the *Port Lincoln*. AIF recruits with VD were also being sent to Langwarrin, and the overcrowding got worse. Colonel Williams visited the camp to see what could be done. He conferred with the staff, and talked with the inmates about their complaints, which were mainly about loss of pay. By now, most had been without it for months — and for many, this meant they could not get tobacco and alcohol. They knew there were supplies not far away at the pubs in Frankston, and they wanted their pay restored so they could go. Williams gave them a sympathetic hearing, but could not promise restoration of pay, or permit men to leave. After he returned to Victoria Barracks in St Kilda Road in South Melbourne, he told a reporter from the *Argus* newspaper about some of his experiences that day.

People in Melbourne were intrigued to read a story about Langwarrin. Two weeks later, the Reverend Henry Worrall, a famous and fiery Methodist morals campaigner, labelled the men in the camp who had returned on the *Port Lincoln* 'the nameless 400, of whom none of them were wounded or had ever pulled a trigger'. This, the inmates thought,

Brigadier General Robert Williams. *(AWM)*

was gravely insulting and wrong, so a protest meeting was held at the camp, led by the Gallipoli men. An anonymous letter that refuted Worrall's claim was sent to *The Argus*, pointing out that many of the soldiers in Langwarrin had been at Gallipoli.

In late September 1915, 275 more men from Egypt arrived at the camp. These were, of course, our 'boys ex-*Wiltshire*', as they became known at Langwarrin. They immediately discovered that it was worse than Abbassia, and some thought of trying to escape. Dr Morris and Dr McCusker examined each man and confirmed that a number did appear to have been cured by Captain Alsop during the voyage. Orders were made to send these lucky fellows to the Broadmeadows camp, with pay restored, for drafting to new battalions. Within a month or so, those released as fit for duty from Langwarrin found themselves back at Port

Melbourne, waiting to board troopships to take them back to Egypt.

Morris and McCusker also recommended that some of the *Wiltshire* men be discharged from the army because of their medical unfitness, but not because of VD. These included soldiers with old injuries and defects apparently unrelated to military service. Some of the Gallipoli men were recommended by the doctors to be discharged because of wounds and illnesses acquired in the Dardanelles, and also not because of VD.

A small number of men had their worst fears realised when Morris and McCusker recommended they be 'discharged–medically unfit–VD'. They had been found to have gonococcal arthritis, chronic gleet, persistent buboes, and other venereal conditions that might prove very difficult to cure. Men from Victoria in this category were transferred to hospitals in Melbourne or Geelong for a final decision. Those from elsewhere were sent from Langwarrin to be processed out of the army in the military district where they originally enlisted. Some sent home in this way chose not to go through with it — they escaped *en route*, and were posted as deserters.

But most of the men who arrived on the *Wiltshire* were not recommended by Morris and McCusker for release, or for discharge from the army. They were required to stay at Langwarrin and suffer ongoing VD treatments for many more weeks or even, for some, many more months. Between October 1915 and March 1916, most were released, in ones and twos, apparently cured and fit for duty, with orders to go to Broadmeadows or other camps in Australia to be sent overseas. Even so, about 40 of these fellows never made it to their destination; with pay once again in their pockets, they disappeared shortly after leaving the camp, and were also posted as deserters.

Wiltshire men who had to remain at Langwarrin would soon have to make space for hundreds more brought from Egypt on the *Ceramic* in October. There were now about 1,000 men with VD living in terrible conditions and unable to know how soon they would leave. Most had been without pay for a long time, and what especially galled them was the camp guard of militiamen, who had not volunteered for overseas service, and who stood between them and the world outside.

The frustration was bound to boil over, and it soon did. The first and largest breakout from Langwarrin happened on a clear spring night on 19 October 1915. During the day, Major Lloyd had refused a demand by some of the men to go to Frankston, but they decided to go anyway. Soon after dark, and in full view of some hapless sentries, a group of inmates approached the fence and threw greatcoats over the barbed wire. They scrambled over and disappeared into bushland. There was then a general rush at the wire by a much larger group — 'about 100', one of the sentries reported — and they, too, broke out and scattered into the bush.

When, some hours later, a group of about 50 arrived at Frankston railway station, they forced their way onto a Melbourne-bound train. The stationmaster telephoned ahead, and, by 11 o'clock, military and civil police officers had assembled at Caulfield station to set an ambush. Nineteen escapees were surrounded, there was a scuffle, and handcuffs were used to restrain three. By one o'clock in the morning, the prisoners were in cells at Victoria Barracks. The rest of the men who escaped had vanished into the night, and, the next day, newspapers were reporting that men from Langwarrin were on the loose.

There was a hastily arranged court-martial at Victoria Barracks for those captured at Caulfield. Each pleaded guilty to 'having broken out of camp in defiance of orders', and three also for resisting arrest. Major Lloyd and some Langwarrin sentries testified that, during the escape, they ordered the men not to leave. The prosecutor pointed out 'the necessity for keeping the men in isolation, inasmuch as their complaints might be communicated to others'. Sixteen escapees were given 90 days' imprisonment with hard labour; those who resisted arrest got 100. However, because all promised to return to the camp and remain there until cured, their sentences were suspended.

The following day, Major Lloyd was sacked by Colonel Williams and replaced as camp commandant. When announcing this to newspaper reporters, Williams also ordered the remaining escapees to give themselves up, and, threatening blackmail, said that 'their names and descriptions would be published and broadcast' if they did not. He then went to Langwarrin, had the remaining inmates paraded, and announced the decisions of the court martial. Williams then threatened future escapees with blackmail, and with arrest as deserters. A notice was placed by the army in newspapers, ordering those who had not returned to report without fail or face public shaming.

Some gave up voluntarily, and a few were brought back by police, but there were many still on the run, and their unknown whereabouts caused public concern. In the Victorian parliament, the minister for public health was asked

> what steps the Health Department was taking to protect the people of Victoria in regard to the prevalence of venereal diseases, and respecting the escape of soldiers from the isolation camp? It seemed that [Victoria] was being made the dumping ground for all the Australian soldiers that had been brought back from Egypt.[17]

Soon, another 40 escapees were rounded up and brought before a court-martial at Langwarrin. Some had taken part in the mass breakout, while others had walked out over the following days. Captain McCusker of the medical staff testified that the men on trial were all infected with VD when they broke out. The prisoners were each sentenced to 100 days' imprisonment, but their sentences were also suspended. Thus, within a week of the mass breakout, many escapees were back in camp with suspended prison sentences hanging over them, and all this news was published in newspapers.

In November 1915, the problems at Langwarrin were raised in the federal parliament when William Kelly, a NSW politician, urged the defence minister to stop bringing venereally infected AIF soldiers back to Australia. He said that better arrangements should be made in Egypt 'for their comfort'. Senator Pearce assured Kelly that he completely agreed, and also explained that Langwarrin would be closed and the inmates moved to new locations, including to other states. Soon after, Colonel Williams arranged for some NSW men to be sent to Milson Island, an isolation hospital on the Hawkesbury River, north of Sydney. Some South Australians were sent to the Torrens Island isolation hospital, near Port Adelaide, and a small group of Tasmanians was sent to Hobart.

Senator Pearce's comment in parliament started a rumour that the Langwarrin men would be transferred elsewhere in Victoria. Alarmed citizens of Bendigo heard that their city's prison was being considered as a destination. The matter was raised in the Bendigo Chamber of Commerce, where it was said that 'if it were true that the department intended to plant a number of men afflicted with this disease scourge in a large city like Bendigo, and so close to the playgrounds of two of the principal schools, it showed a great lack of consideration for Bendigo and the public health'.

Then, residents on the Mornington Peninsula launched a protest about the nearby presence of venereally infected men 'at the concentration camp at Langwarrin'. They were also alarmed because soldiers with venereal disease were using the drinking fountains and toilets at the railway station at Frankston. A railways official said that when the army moved diseased men by rail through the station, no one was notified this would happen, and that warnings should be given so that 'carriages might be set apart for them and subsequently disinfected'.

The breakouts, courts-martial, discussions in parliaments, and newspaper stories led to other consequences. The attention of Australia was drawn to the Langwarrin camp. The army began receiving letters from relatives of men known to have recently returned to Melbourne, enquiring as to the exact whereabouts of their man, and the nature of the wound or sickness he had acquired while abroad. To the horror of some of the men in Langwarrin who returned on the *Wiltshire*, parents and wives learned where they were, and began arriving unannounced at the camp.

All the troubles at Langwarrin helped make up the mind of Surgeon-General Fetherston that no more infected men should be sent to Australia from Egypt. He recommended that the 1st Australian Dermatological Hospital be formed to take over at Abbassia. Dr Arthur Morris agreed to go with the hospital when it left Australia in December 1915, and he worked with it in Cairo and later at Bulford. His position as senior medical officer at Langwarrin was filled by Captain McCusker, who stayed there until January 1916, when he departed for the overseas service he had been patiently awaiting.

In December 1915, the now Brigadier General Williams might have reasonably expected that his threats to blackmail and arrest Langwarrin escapees should have stopped the breakouts and ended the newspaper stories. But they continued anyway, and he had to announce that another 20 men had been captured after getting out of the camp. Williams arranged a court martial, but this time the sentences were not suspended: the prisoners were transferred to Pentridge Gaol, each to serve 100 days with hard labour 'such as his physical condition would allow'.

Among the men who broke out of Langwarrin between October 1915 and January 1916 were about 45 who had arrived on the *Wiltshire*. Most never returned; others were brought before the courts-martial. Within four months of their arrival from Egypt, almost 100 of the *Wiltshire* boys had escaped from Langwarrin or from the army. Some had been posted as deserters after their legitimate release from the camp; others, after they left illegally. Most were still on the run, and a small number who escaped were caught only to escape again.

It was a challenge for Brigadier General Williams to prevent men running away. It was also difficult for the camp to be closed or moved. At some point, it became obvious to him that treating men with VD as criminals while trying to force cures upon them was self-defeating. They were being punished enough by the diseases. Something had to be done to make the inmates want to voluntarily stay until they were cured, and then to willingly return to their military duties. Achieving that, however, would require a remarkable change of attitudes in the patients and in the army.

Brigadier General Williams visiting the Langwarrin
hospital in about 1917. *(NLA)*

General Williams' plan to convert Langwarrin from an isolation-detention barracks to a hospital slowly began to take shape from late 1915. He began by disbanding the militia guard and replacing it with the inmates themselves; he started restoring the pay of men who co-operated, and paid them for doing useful work; and he started searching for doctors who knew about the diseases and would stay for long periods. In particular, he needed an unusual type of army officer to take charge of the humane improvements envisioned by him.

It seems General Williams realised that a new commandant would not get the respect of inmates if he was another militia man. He would need to be an AIF officer — perhaps one who had fought overseas. In late 1915, there were not many such officers in Victoria who wanted to run a military backwater like Langwarrin. The man Williams initially found who appeared to fit the requirements was Major Ivie Blezard, then commanding a depot for returned invalids at the Melbourne Showgrounds.

Blezard had been in the 7th Infantry Battalion at Gallipoli, only to be shot in his chest and shoulder shortly after the landings. He had been evacuated to hospital in Egypt, then sent to Australia as an invalid. Having recovered sufficiently by November 1915 to resume work, he had been chosen by Williams to run the Melbourne Showgrounds depot, and then in January 1916 as Langwarrin's commandant.

Very soon, Blezard was in trouble. Although Williams had made concessions to encourage men to remain in the camp — including the restoration of pay — in January 1916, scores of inmates were still walking out. Some never returned, while others wandered off to local pubs and returned when they felt like it. Soon the general was firing rockets at poor Major Blezard, and again threatening blackmail:

> I wish you to make all the men who are in the Isolation Camp understand that if men get away immediately on pay being allocated to them, that the pay will be withdrawn. I want you also to make them understand that if men escape from Langwarrin and are captured, I will have them court-martialled and dealt with as deserters should be dealt with. If they are not re-captured, I will make public in the localities nearest their homes the fact that they are deserters from Langwarrin, and that a reward is offered for their apprehension. I cannot permit these leakages to go on further.[18]

To help Blezard at the hospital, Williams was searching for other suitable officers. His attention was drawn to another ex-7th Battalion man, a young fellow who had also been wounded at Gallipoli and who was now in Melbourne looking for a job that would keep him in the army. Without Williams knowing, this was the officer who would lead the conversion of Langwarrin to a roaring success as a venereal-disease hospital.

Major Ivie Blezard at the Broadmeadows camp in 1914. *(AWM)*

Walter Conder, also called 'Wally' or 'Bluey' Conder, had been born in Tasmania at Ringarooma, near Launceston, by coincidence not far from where Ettie Rout was born. He attended Launceston Grammar, where he became captain of the school and the senior cadets. A freckled redhead with the face of a pugilist, he was in fact a boxer, as well as a wrestler, a rower, and an outstanding Australian Rules footballer. After matriculating, he became a teacher at the school while studying part time at university and also serving as an officer in the militia at Launceston. Just before the outbreak of war, Conder moved to Victoria to teach humanities at Melbourne Grammar, and was subsequently picked to be a junior officer in the 7th Battalion of the newly formed AIF. He left Australia with the first contingent, and arrived in Egypt in December 1914.

Lieutenant Walter Conder (right) and another 7th Battalion officer, Captain Finlayson, in Cairo in late 1914. Conder's fondness for animals was evident during his years at Langwarrin from 1916 until 1921. *(Museums Victoria)*

Because of the AIF's troubles with drunkenness and venereal disease, General Birdwood had ordered General Bridges to steer the men into more wholesome pastimes. It had been decided that one of those would be boxing, and it was soon discovered that Lieutenant Wally Conder of the 7th Battalion was a boxing enthusiast with an entrepreneurial flair for organising tournaments. At the Mena camp, the battalion built a stadium, which Conder named the 'Stupendous Scene of Stoush', and he became the fight promoter and popular referee for many of the bouts staged there, until the departure of the troops for Gallipoli brought an end to the entertainment.

Walter Conder at the Langwarrin camp in August 1916 after he was
appointed to be the commandant. *(NLA)*

Conder landed at Gallipoli with the 7th Battalion on 25 April 1915,
but within hours was seriously wounded. He was hit by four Turkish
bullets in his legs, and then by three in his shoulder, paralysing an arm.
As he lay wounded, he was seriously concussed when a shell exploded
nearby. Lucky to be alive, he became one of the first evacuees from
Gallipoli, and within days was back in Egypt in hospital. In June 1915, a
medical board granted him six months' leave to recuperate in Australia,
so he left Egypt on the *Kyarra* alongside other wounded men being sent
home and 111 'venereals' being sent to Langwarrin. Back in Melbourne,
he began medical treatment, which became protracted. At this point, a
future in the army was doubtful, and he had to talk his way through more
medical-board hearings to maintain his hopes of being sent overseas again.

In January 1916, that hope faded when, at the age of 28, he was placed on the list of supernumerary officers — meaning his services were no longer required. That month, he was found by General Williams, who arranged for Conder to continue in the army as an honorary lieutenant, with a temporary appointment as the adjutant at Langwarrin. In August 1916, when Ivie Blezard was transferred to a training depot in Melbourne, General Williams entrusted Conder to take charge of the camp, promoting him to honorary major.

The close working relationship between Williams and Conder turned out to be very productive for Langwarrin, and very good for men who were sent there with VD. The hospital became so effective at curing and returning the men to duty completely healthy that it was not closed until 1921. Between 1915 and 1920, about 7,200 men passed through, with most admitted after Conder began to bring about the farsighted plans of General Williams.

In the development plan for the Langwarrin hospital, a great deal of effort was given to improving medical services. The military objectives were made very clear: increase the percentage of patients perfectly cured and returned to military duties, shorten the period of each treatment, and reduce the costs. To do this work, Williams recruited a new group of medical officers who were committed to staying. The doctors realised that, to achieve all the objectives, every aspect of a patient's health would need to be considered. Men admitted to Langwarrin with VD usually had other diseases as well. Many had badly decayed teeth, and some had oral VD infections. Finally, to reduce the possibility of a man becoming re-infected, his self-regard would need to improve and his attitude to sexual risk-taking would have to change.

Five doctors appointed by General Williams in late 1915 and in 1916 stayed for long periods, each leading an aspect of the medical plan. Captain Mathias Perl developed improved treatments for syphilis by experimenting with combinations and doses of the commonly used drugs. Major Charles Johnson led the development of bacteriological testing, and also experimented with methods for treating gonorrhoea

Major Walter Conder (right), at Langwarrin in 1917 with Major
Charles Johnson, the senior medical officer. *(NLA)*

using the salts and nitrates of silver. Captain William Potter, Captain
Alexander Cook, and Captain Henry Hunter Griffith were responsible
for other aspects.

To provide the facilities for medical work, the defence department
constructed a hospital near the original barbed-wire compound. A
number of modern barracks huts were erected for wards — enough to
accommodate 600 patients — and each had beds and a bathroom. Large
huts were built for an operating theatre, a treatment room for 'irrigating'
gonorrhoea patients, a dental surgery, and a dispensary. For the first time
since Langwarrin had opened as a military camp, modern kitchens and
messes were installed. Accommodation quarters for officers and medical
staff were built, and a post office was opened.

To provide abundant water, a bore was sunk and a new pumping
station built to deliver the water to an existing reservoir. With a supply

A rear view of the new hospital-ward huts constructed at
Langwarrin in 1916. The large rainwater tanks were part of general
improvements to the water supply made during that year. *(NLA)*

of water now available for irrigation, Conder arranged for the grounds
of the hospital to be landscaped. Patients made paths, planted lawns and
gardens, and cultivated hedges and shrubberies with plants and tools
supplied by donors. Under Conder's directions, about 2,500 trees were
planted, including pines, wattles, eucalypts, and English oaks.

An ornamental fountain was erected by patients near the main
entrance. A circular pond was dug and lined with cement; a pedestal
with a circular marble table was constructed in the middle; and a marble
statue, in classical Greek style, was installed on top. This was a proud,
semi-clothed maiden holding aloft an amphora. When an electric pump
was turned on, water flowed from the amphora and trickled down her
half-naked body to the pond below. For the men in the camp and visitors
entering, the symbolism of this lady of the fountain was obvious. She was
Venus, the cause of all the problems and the reason for Langwarrin, but
now safely captured to harmlessly delight all who saw her.

The ornamental fountain, built by patients, adjacent to the main entrance at the Langwarrin hospital. The statue is of a partly clothed maiden holding aloft an amphora. *(NLA)*

Conder asked for help from donors in Melbourne to make the hospital a comfortable place. He persuaded the Red Cross, the YMCA, the Victorian Racing Club, the Victorian Amateur Turf Club, sports clubs, businesses, and individual donors to provide funds and materials. He persuaded local community groups to overcome their suspicions and become involved. With all this assistance, a shower block with hot water, various well-equipped workshops, a Red Cross concert hall, a bandstand, a YMCA hut, and a canteen were gradually added. A military brass band was formed, using donated musical instruments. Men, women, and children from surrounding communities were made welcome to visit the patients and show interest in them.

By March 1916, the situation at Langwarrin had sufficiently improved for General Williams to invite the governor-general of Australia, Sir Ronald Munro Ferguson, to admire the results. Sir Ronald had made a visit in December 1915, and must not have been happy. Now, accompanied

The bandstand and Red Cross hut built at Langwarrin
in 1916 and 1917. *(AWM)*

by the chief of the general staff, Sir Ronald again inspected the camp, and addressed the patients before an audience of local citizens. This time, he complimented the men on the vast improvement, and congratulated the staff for their excellent work.

By Christmas 1916, Conder could demonstrate to General Williams, in monthly statistical charts he had made, that escapes and absences had practically stopped. Also at Christmas, the governor-general again visited Langwarrin, this time to open some of the new facilities. *The Argus* reported how he 'took the salute in a march past of the guard and the men of the camp, headed by the camp mascot (a diminutive pony gaily caparisoned and with tinkling bells) and the camp band'. Sir Ronald compared the deplorable conditions a year before with those now, and said that, in his opinion, Langwarrin was the best military camp in Victoria. He went on to visit Langwarrin often during the war, sometimes

The main entrance to the Langwarrin hospital in about 1917.
The sentry on duty was also a patient. *(AWM)*

accompanied by Lady Munro Ferguson in her role as president of the
Australian Red Cross.

How did a camp under threat of closure in 1915 still have thousands
of patients until 1920? Although the flow of infected men from Egypt had
stopped, there was still a need for a military venereal-disease hospital in
Australia. There were various reasons for the continuing demand: AIF
recruits became infected before going overseas; infected militia men
were admitted; and some of the soldiers invalided to Australia from
Europe with wounds or diseases were also infected with VD, as were
others repatriated during and after the war. But there was also a reason
to do with military requirements. At any one time, the number of AIF
soldiers in Europe languishing in hospital with VD was equivalent to
the full strength of an infantry battalion. The military and financial costs
this incurred meant that Langwarrin was needed to find better, faster,

Brigadier General Williams and local children planting trees at the
Langwarrin hospital in 1916. *(NLA)*

and cheaper cures. If that happened, a man who caught VD might find
himself back at the front much sooner than previously anticipated.

CHAPTER FIVE

Ernest Dunbar, John Dunbar, and John Beech

O, what a tangled web we weave,
when first we practise to deceive!

On New Year's Day 1915, at the Liverpool army camp near Sydney, a young man answered the patriotic call and volunteered for the Australian Imperial Force. On his attestation paper for enlistment, in answering the question 'What is your name?', he wrote 'John Dunbar'. But his name was really Ernest Dunbar, not John. He had been baptised as Ernest in 1890 at St Luke's Anglican Church at Scone in the Hunter Valley of New South Wales, where he grew up; and, as Ernest, was an outstanding pupil at St Luke's Anglican School. Yet he enlisted in the AIF using a different name.

Many thousands of AIF recruits did this, even though attesting with a false name was meant to be grounds for discharge from the army. They usually did it to hide something they thought might preclude them from enlistment. A man might have already tried to enlist using his correct identity, but been rejected. Another might have a criminal record or be on the run from the police, or from creditors. Plenty invented an identity that had an age within the permitted range for recruits. A volunteer might have had a German-sounding name, and thought that was unacceptable.

A pencil-on-paper sketch made by Ernest Dunbar in 1917, possibly
a self-portrait. He made two almost identical versions of this
drawing, but both are untitled. *(AWM)*

Other identity-changers wanted to conceal their enlistment from their
parents, or their employer. If a man was trying to enlist again after an
earlier period of service and was using a false identity, it usually meant
he had already been discharged medically unfit or for misconduct, or he
was a deserter. Omitting his original enlistment on the attestation form
would also be considered as proof of false attestation if he was caught.

Sometimes a new name involved a slight change of pronounciation,
or the spelling was different but sounded the same; sometimes the
names were completely new. Men also invented fictitious backgrounds,
occupations, and family details for their new identity, named a trusted
friend as their next of kin, and gave the friend's address as their own. At
places of enlistment, each attestation paper was meant to be verified by
an attesting officer. But it was difficult, often almost impossible, to verify

information provided by recruits — if there was ever an intention to do this conscientiously.

There is no obvious reason for Ernest Dunbar to have become 'John' when he enlisted. He didn't talk to his family about the change. There was a real John Dunbar who also lived in Scone — Ernest's cousin — and he was in Egypt as a corporal with the 1st Light Horse Regiment. Did Ernest deliberately copy his name, or was it just a very odd coincidence? There is nothing in his pre-war background to suggest that he was concealing any secrets at the time he enlisted. All we know is that, after the war, to his friends, he continued to use the name 'John' — perhaps he simply preferred it.

We know that Ernest's change of identity involved only a change of his first name, as all other details on his attestation paper were true. In his neat handwriting, he declared that he was 24 years of age, that he was born in Scone, and that his next of kin was his mother, Elizabeth Dunbar, who lived in Hill Street. She was married to Charles Dunbar, a stonemason whose Scottish ancestors had lived in Scone since the 1840s. Ernest was the second youngest of their seven children.

Ernest also wrote on the attestation paper that his 'trade or calling' was seaman. How had a fellow from an inland town like Scone become a seaman? As an adventurous teenager, he had started working on colliers at the port of Newcastle, down the Hunter Valley from Scone. Called 'sixty milers', these ships shuttled back and forth carrying coal from the mines at Newcastle to electricity-generating stations on the foreshores of Sydney Harbour. Seamen on colliers frequented hotels and boarding houses around the harbour, and Ernest often stayed at a boarding house in Pitt Street at Milsons Point.

At the Liverpool camp, he was examined by a doctor and measured to be five feet five inches tall, just under the minimum AIF requirement — not that it mattered. His complexion and hair were described as dark, and his eyes as brown. The doctor confirmed that 'John' Dunbar did not have a disease or physical defect that excluded him from being a soldier. He was then accepted into the AIF and drafted to the 3rd Reinforcements for the 13th Battalion. The main force of the battalion had just left Sydney, so

Soldiers all at Sea

Soldiers All at Sea, a pencil-on-paper cartoon made by Ernest
Dunbar in February 1915, *en route* to Egypt. A peril of long ocean
voyages for AIF men was seasickness. *(AWM)*

Ernest did basic training at Liverpool for a month.

In February 1915, he and other excited young men of the 3rd
Reinforcements boarded the troopship A49 *Seang Choon* and set out for
what they expected would be the greatest adventure of their lives. Ernest
intended to record this by sketching events as they unfolded; he was
an accomplished artist, and had packed in his kitbag a drawing book,
pencils, pens, and artist's ink. All of the sketches and cartoons he would
produce during the voyage and in Egypt would be made in the name of
'John' Dunbar.

In March 1915, the *Seang Choon* arrived, via the Suez Canal, at the
port of Ismailia in Egypt. Ernest and the reinforcements were taken by
train to Cairo, and, at the AIF camp at Mena, were united with their
battalion. They and the 13th Battalion then plunged into the hard work
of preparing for war. During the next month, they tramped, dug, and
shot their way all over the desert. In Ernest's spare time, he sketched

Colombo, a pencil-on-paper drawing made by Ernest Dunbar in
Ceylon in February 1915. *(AWM)*

street scenes and people in Cairo, although it appears he kept away from
the Wasa'a and out of trouble.

Barely a month after disembarking at Ismailia, he found himself at the
port of Alexandria on the Mediterranean coast, embarking on another
troopship, this one to take the 13th Battalion to Gallipoli, where it would
land with the ANZAC force. In the evening of 25 April 1915, the heavily
laden soldiers crowded onto landing boats, and were towed to shore
through the shot and shell descending from the hilltops. They were not the
first of the ANZAC men to arrive that day, and, on the beach, joined other
battalions that had been there since dawn, unable to move much further.

Slowly, the 13th Battalion advanced from the beachhead into the
scrub-covered hills, all the while under Turkish fire, before finally being
stopped in front of a hill known by the Australians as Pope's Ridge.
Within 24 hours, they had been transformed from soldiers-in-waiting,
and were now in the thick of an extraordinary, exhilarating, and terrifying

experience. There they were, in a strange land, being shot at and shelled by an invisible enemy in the hills above, while, all around them, mates were being wounded and killed.

A few weeks after landing, Ernest Dunbar was hit by a Turkish bullet in his left elbow. It had almost blown away the joint, and he was sent to the safety of a casualty clearing station on the beach. A few days later, he was evacuated to a British hospital ship standing offshore, and taken with hundreds of other wounded men to a military hospital on Malta. The AIF had a policy of notifying the next of kin of soldiers who were casualties, so an unintentionally misleading telegram was sent to Mrs Dunbar at Scone:

REGRET SON PRIVATE J. DUNBAR WOUNDED NOT REPORTED SERIOUSLY NO OTHER PARTICULARS AVAILABLE WILL IMMEDIATELY ADVISE ANYTHING FURTHER RECEIVED.

This news was greeted with consternation in Hill Street, because no soldier by the name 'J. Dunbar' had ever lived there — but a nephew, John Dunbar, lived a few streets away. Elizabeth sent a telegram to the secretary of defence:

Telegram very confusing please state whether J Dunbar or E Dunbar wounded.

Thus we learn how Ernest's family became aware that he might be serving in the AIF under another name. More confusion was created when the name 'J. Dunbar' appeared in a Gallipoli casualty list published in a local newspaper.

In July 1915, Ernest was sent from Malta back to Egypt on the A48 *Seang Bee*. In Alexandria, he was admitted, as 'John' Dunbar, to an army convalescent depot in an enormous Egyptian state palace called Ras el-Tin. While convalescing, he made what would turn out to be a fateful decision. Like Cairo, Alexandria had its own famous brothel quarter,

23. ALEXANDRIE — Sisters Street

A pre-war postcard of Rue des Soeurs in Alexandria, which at night
in 1915 was transformed into a red-light district of drinking halls
and promenading prostitutes.

in Rue des Soeurs. Australian troops called this place 'Sister Street',
and, although it was meant to be out of bounds for them, convalescing
Gallipoli men had a lot of back pay in their pockets. The Rue des
Soeurs was full of flaunting and inviting women from all around the
Mediterranean. A soldier who also caught VD in Egypt, Joe Maxwell,
later wrote about these irresistible ladies in a candid autobiography, *Hell's
Bells and Mademoiselles*. To Maxwell, they were 'hard bitten and raucous,
silky voiced and seductive, languorous as a purring cat, deceptive,
powdered, dissipated, decked out in blazonries like some lithe tiger
moving in the gloom'.

Evidently, Ernest Dunbar was unable to resist them. Within a
fortnight of his arrival at Ras el-Tin, he caught gonorrhoea and was
sent to Abbassia. Here he came under the care of Captain Harold Plant,
who commenced a course of sandalwood oil. This contained toxins to

The Ras el-Tin Palace in Alexandria, used by the AIF in 1915 as a convalescent depot for Gallipoli invalids. *(Barrett and Deane (1918))*

kill gonorrhoea bacteria in the urethra — but, if repeatedly syringed in high doses, the toxins could irritate the urethral lining, and might be absorbed into the bloodstream. Ernest's treatment made little progress, so he was selected by Colonel Brady Nash to be sent to Langwarrin. His being chosen to go back to Australia because of gonorrhoea would have consequences for Ernest that would last for the rest of his life. Without him knowing it at the time, his few moments of excitement in an Alexandria brothel had been a big mistake.

A few weeks later, he was sent from Abbassia to Port Suez, where he boarded the *Wiltshire*. In the afternoon of 31 August, the big troopship cast off, set course for the Red Sea, and made her fast voyage to Port Melbourne. On board the ship, Ernest came under the care of Captain Herbert Alsop, who continued the sandalwood-oil treatment, and who also discovered that Ernest's infection had become chronic, complicated by the urethral inflammation called gleet.

He was admitted to Langwarrin as Private 'John' Dunbar, formerly of the 13th Battalion. In his first days there, he was examined by Dr Morris or Dr McCusker, and concerns arose about his elbow wound as well as his stubborn gonorrhoea and gleet. He wasn't going to be one of the lucky ones released as fit for duty, but he wasn't recommended for discharge from the army, either. He was going to have to stay and continue his treatment; and, by now, he had been putting up with daily urethral irrigations with sandalwood oil for over two months.

It seems Ernest was not happy to have his pain and humiliation indefinitely extended like this, because — three weeks after arriving at Langwarrin, and the day after the mass breakout on 19 October — he went over the wire as well. He remained on the run until the following week, when he was captured and returned to Langwarrin and, as 'John' Dunbar, was arraigned before the second court-martial of Langwarrin escapees arranged by Colonel Williams. He was convicted and given 100 days' detention with hard labour, but the sentence was suspended.

Now with a suspended prison sentence hanging over him, Ernest was treated at Langwarrin for another six weeks. In the middle of December 1915, he was discharged from the hospital as fit for duty, having been finally made non-infectious after four months of sandalwood oil, and no army pay. He was then given orders to report to a training camp at Kiama, on the NSW south coast, where he was meant to join a reinforcement draft for the 13th Battalion, his old unit, and then return to Egypt.

At this point, with his VD episode behind him, and army pay once again in his hand, Ernest was evidently beset by uncertainty. It seems he might have reported for duty at the Kiama camp; but then, inexplicably, he disappeared. He was soon posted as being 'illegally absent', and in March 1916, with no further sign of him, Private 'John' Dunbar was declared to be a deserter from the AIF, and a warrant was issued for his arrest.

During the war, thousands of AIF men were declared to have deserted. The declaring of a man's desertion and the issuing of a warrant might

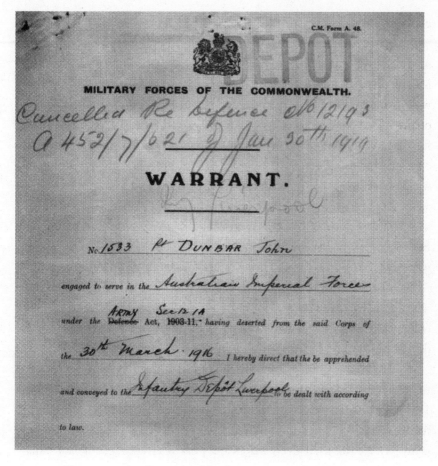

The warrant for the arrest of the deserter Private 'John' Dunbar,
issued in March 1916. *(NAA)*

lead to his arrest by civil or military police, and a court martial. If a man
deserted in Australia, his name could be published in the government
gazette and in newspapers, and a bounty could be paid to police officers
if they caught him. A harsh prison sentence could be given for such a
case, and the deserter be forced to forfeit his pay and entitlements to a
pension and medals, unless they were later restored. In Egypt, Europe,
and Australia, there were thousands of courts-martial for AIF deserters
who had given themselves up or were caught. There were also thousands

of deserters who were never caught, but who eventually had their entitlements revoked as well.

After 'John' Dunbar deserted, he made his way to Sydney and lived at Milsons Point, in a boarding house he had used before the war. Then he travelled to Scone, where, on arrival at the Dunbar family home, he became Ernest again. He told his mother that he had just come out of hospital in Melbourne, and explained away the mix-up over names in the casualty telegram and list. The arrival back from Gallipoli of the wounded Private Ernest Dunbar, and the cordial welcome given him by townspeople, were reported in a local newspaper.

At Scone, he discovered that his younger brother Randolph had enlisted in the AIF and had also joined the 13th Battalion. He had just embarked at Sydney to go to Egypt, possibly expecting to meet there with Ernest. Given this news, the confusion with names, and the secrets he was hiding, it was now essential for Ernest to get himself back into the AIF. To do this, he did something that must have seemed very clever at the time, but was another mistake he would later regret.

In April 1916, a young man, aged 25 years and ten months, with a dark complexion and brown eyes, standing five-and-a-half feet tall, presented himself at the army recruiting station at Newcastle. He neatly wrote on his attestation paper that his name was 'John Beech', and that he was a 'cook and labourer'. He wrote that his next of kin was Mrs Essie Harris (a friend of Ernest's), living in Pitt Street at Milsons Point in Sydney. To the question on the attestation form 'Do you now belong to, or have you ever served in, His Majesty's Army, the Marines, the Militia, the Militia Reserve, the Territorial Force, Royal Navy, or Colonial Forces?' he wrote 'No'. To the question 'Have you stated the whole, if any, of your previous service?' he wrote 'Yes'. He then signed the form as 'John Beech', and this was witnessed by the attesting officer. Shortly after, Private 'Beech' was drafted to begin training at Maitland with reinforcements for the 34th Infantry Battalion, a unit comprising men from the Hunter Valley.

There were already two soldiers named John Beech in the AIF, and Ernest probably knew at least one and possibly both. The first was a

Five to Six outside the Estaminet, a pencil-on-paper sketch made by
Ernest Dunbar in 1917. *(AWM)*

member of Ernest's 13th Battalion, who had been injured at Gallipoli some
days before Ernest was wounded. He was evacuated to Egypt, but, after his
recovery, continued with the 13th Battalion until the end of the war. The
other was Private John Thomas Beech, who had landed at Gallipoli with
the 2nd Battalion. The day before Ernest was hit by a bullet in his elbow,
John T. Beech was hit in his arm. He was invalided to Australia, where he
was discharged from the AIF as medically unfit. Did Ernest Dunbar take
his new false identity from one of these men, or from both?

In August 1916, Ernest left Sydney on the A68 *Anchises* to go to
England, and then to France and Belgium with the 34th Battalion.
The battalion waited a very long time to be committed to battle, but,
in June 1917, it moved into the front lines at Messines, where Ernest
banged away at the enemy with his .303-inch Lee-Enfield rifle. He drew
the scenes around him, especially the daily lives of battalion mates,
producing many fine sketches and cartoons, all of which were identified
as having been made by 'John Beech'. Ernest clearly liked the *estaminets*,

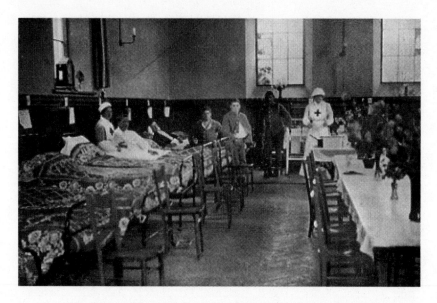

A ward at the Winchcombe Voluntary Aid Detachment hospital
near Cheltenham in Gloucestershire. Here, in 1917, Ernest Dunbar
recovered from his gassing at Passchendaele. *(Rebsie Fairholm)*

the ubiquitous bars so popular with diggers, and, in them, he made a
number of drawings. His four months of sandalwood-oil treatment in
1915 must have been fresh in his memory, however, because he never
again caught VD.

In October 1917, Ernest was wounded again, this time at Flanders. The
34th Battalion was fighting in autumn wet weather at the Passchendaele
Ridge, and the battlefield was a quagmire. The Germans fired everything
they had at the sodden Australians, and Ernest received a grazing bullet
wound to his mouth. He was patched up by field ambulancemen, and
two days later was back in action. But then German artillery began firing
mustard-gas shells. The weather was perfect for this nasty chemical
weapon: if gas came into contact with unprotected diggers, their eyes,
skin, and respiratory organs were damaged. Ernest was badly poisoned,
and was evacuated to England, to a hospital near Cheltenham in the
Cotswold Hills of Gloucestershire.

The Stuff to Give the Troops, an ink-and-watercolour sketch
on paper made by Ernest Dunbar at Christmas 1917, at the
Winchcombe VAD hospital. *(AWM)*

The change from the grim Passchendaele Ridge to the verdant
Cotswolds was a huge improvement for him. During a long
convalescence, he acquired a new sketchbook and artist's materials,
including watercolour paints, and produced some of his best wartime
pictures, once more identifying all as having been made by 'John Beech'.

In the hospital, it was obvious to doctors that his feet had been
deformed by the mud and water in the trenches, and they discovered
he also had neurasthenia. The hospital at Cheltenham was unable to fix
trench feet or shell shock, so, after three months, he was sent to another
hospital, at Dartford in Kent. While he was there, Germany launched
a massive springtime offensive in France to try to end the war with a
bold victory. The British and Australian armies had to take emergency
measures to stop this — every available soldier was needed, including
men in hospitals. Ernest soon found himself back in France with his
battalion, but it quickly became clear he was useless as a soldier because

The A43 *Barunga*. Before the war, she had been German-owned and called the *Sumatra*, but was seized in Sydney harbour in 1914. She was used as an Australian troopship until she was sunk. *(SLNSW)*

of his crippled feet. In June 1918, he was sent back to England.

At an AIF depot at Weymouth, it was decided that Private 'Beech' should be repatriated as an invalid. He was taken to Plymouth with 800 other Australian invalids, and they embarked on the troopship A43 *Barunga* to begin the long journey home. The following afternoon, as the ship crossed the Bay of Biscay, a torpedo fired at close range by a German submarine slammed into the front of the transport and exploded, creating a very large hole. Fortunately, the *Barunga* took a long time to sink, and, in a further stroke of luck, British navy destroyers were quickly on the scene to pick up survivors. Soon, all who had been on board were back at Plymouth.

A few weeks later, Ernest and other *Barunga* survivors were loaded onto the D19 *Carpentaria* to recommence their repatriation voyage. On board the ship, Ernest filled in papers needed by the repatriation department, and had to write his name as 'John Beech'. The *Carpentaria* reached Australia safely, and Ernest disembarked at Sydney in October 1918. Within days, he was on a train to Scone, heading for his second homecoming of the war. This was reported at length in *The Scone Advocate*, under the headline 'Private E. Dunbar'. Part of the story was as follows:

> Very few soldiers are blessed with the good fortune to return to the land of their nativity after having twice visited the fighting fronts, but in Private Ernest Dunbar we have an exception. One of the original Anzacs, Private Dunbar was invalided home from Gallipoli after being severely wounded, but having recuperated he re-enlisted and went to France nearly two years ago. He is now home again, suffering from shell shock and trench feet. But for his feet, Private Dunbar looks remarkably well, and converses most interestingly of his experiences abroad.

Back home from the war, Ernest now had to contend with the ramifications of his multiple identities. He appeared in the Australian army's records as two soldiers having no connections to each other. The most recent records, covering 1916–1918, were for Private John Beech of the 34th Battalion, who apparently lived at Milsons Point in Sydney. Older records, covering 1915–1916, were for Private John Dunbar of the 13th Battalion, who lived at Scone. There was an outstanding warrant for the arrest of that man, made in 1916 for his desertion in Australia, because John Dunbar had never been caught.

In Sydney, Ernest was admitted to an army hospital, where a doctor saw that his feet were so deformed that he had cut out the sides of his boots to fit the protruding parts. Although reconstructive surgery was contemplated, it was not done. At this time, he also started a process to obtain a repatriation pension for a disability caused by his war service. Then, in January 1919, exactly four years after his original enlistment as 'John' Dunbar, Ernest received a discharge certificate that said he was 'medically unfit — deformed feet'. The name on the certificate, however, was that of his invented identity 'John Beech'.

There was a problem for returned soldiers who had changed their identities but did not reveal this before they were discharged from the army. The Australian government provided generous repatriation pensions, and medical and hospital care to ex-soldiers who qualified; however, to prove their entitlement, a bureaucratic process had to be negotiated. Ernest Dunbar had qualified for the entitlements as 'John Beech', and so, to obtain them, the ruse might need to be kept up for the rest of his life. Alternatively, he could try to maintain his multiple identities, switching from one to another as circumstances developed.

A permanent solution was for Ernest to confess and have his correct identity restored; but, in 1919, there were risks in making that confession. The secret about his desertion as 'John' Dunbar would definitely be disclosed, and his venereal-disease secret might be unintentionally revealed to people who he felt must not know. In Australia during the war, informers often reported on deserters, and many were arrested. Ernest no doubt thought that this was a possibility if he confessed, and that inquiries might uncover all of his secrets, including the reason for his return to Australia in 1915 on the *Wiltshire*. Ernest could not know that the army was quietly abandoning its pursuit of deserters who had never been caught. He also couldn't know that, a year later, in 1920, a note would be added to the army records of 'John' Dunbar:

Deserted 29th March 1916. Warrant withdrawn, Defence 12193 of 30th January 1919

This was the result of a new regulation that applied to thousands of deserters who had never been caught. Then, another entry was added, this one recording that 'John' Dunbar had now been convicted of desertion without a trial:

Discharged in consequence of desertion being illegally absent from 15/12/15 to 21/7/20 (deserted from camp)

Pencil-on-paper cartoon made by Ernest Dunbar. His own
discharge in 1919 was not to occur in such exhuberant
circumstances. *(AWM)*

The actions to withdraw the warrant for 'John' Dunbar and discharge
him with ignominy occurred during a bureaucratic clean-up to finalise
the records of all deserters like him. With the villains identified, and
their entitlements forfeited, the army could move on to rewarding the
heroes. There would be a number of valuable items given by the army to
returned soldiers with good records of service.

One was a discharge certificate showing that a man had left the army
for an acceptable reason, because this entitled him to other benefits.
One was the little 'Returned from Active Service' lapel badge. This was
originally given to men who returned to Australia from service abroad,
unless they had been sent back for misconduct or venereal disease. In
1920, new rules included those sent back with VD, but excluded
those discharged by a court-martial, or found guilty of desertion. At
this time, many of the men who returned to Australia with VD on the
Wiltshire in 1915 were given the badge. Possession of it automatically

A 'Returned from Active Service' badge.

entitled the holder to join the Returned Sailors and Soldiers Imperial League of Australia, and receive an RSSILA lapel badge as well. The two little badges became much sought after by men not entitled to receive them, and they were sometimes stolen from their rightful recipients.

A discharge certificate also entitled a returned soldier to be awarded up to three imperial war-service medals, unless by being discharged for misconduct or desertion he had forfeited the entitlement. Originally, men discharged because of venereal disease also forfeited their medals; but, in 1922, that right was restored, and other *Wiltshire* men began to receive theirs. One of the medals was the 1914–15 Star, awarded to ex-soldiers who between August 1914 and December 1915 had served at Gallipoli or in the Middle East, including those who had served only in Egypt. Another was the British War Medal, awarded for service anywhere between August 1914 and November 1918. The Victory Medal was issued to all those awarded the 1914–15 Star, and to most men awarded the British War Medal.

A lapel badge issued by the RSSILA.

A good discharge certificate was also useful in life as a civilian. Together with badges and medals, it proved special status, and a man's good name, and could be used to obtain preferential treatment to obtain work, get loans, and buy property. It was proof of entitlement to the 'soldier-settler' schemes started in the 1920s, when tracts of farmland in Australia and plantations in New Guinea were given or sold cheaply to ex-soldiers. Later, during the Great Depression, a good discharge certificate held by an unemployed ex-soldier might help find him work, or receive charity from sympathetic citizens.

Ernest Dunbar had, by his desertion in 1916 as 'John' Dunbar, forfeited entitlements for that identity to receive a badge and the 1914–15 Star for serving in Egypt and at Gallipoli. However, because of the good discharge certificate given to his invented character 'John Beech', he received a badge and was awarded the other two medals. Ernest appears to have decided that his dealings with the army, and with the repatriation department for a disability pension, had to be as 'John Beech'. For other purposes and to friends, he called himself 'John', although, to his family, he was still Ernest Dunbar. Evidently, he felt he had to continue to keep separate his three identities, and to conceal the many secrets associated with each.

In early 1919, he began looking for ways to earn a living. This started in Sydney, where he found work for short periods in casual jobs. He also applied as 'John Beech' to the repatriation department for 'employment and sustenance', a temporary unemployment benefit that ex-soldiers called the 'susso'. Then, a few months later, he was living in the NSW coastal town of Kempsey and working as a 'hotel useful' at the Royal Hotel. That didn't last long either — he had to leave because the work was 'too severe on his feet'. Through all this, he patiently awaited news of the disability pension for 'John Beech' for which he thought he had applied in 1918.

In the early 1920s, Ernest moved to Melbourne, where he called himself 'John' Dunbar. He worked off and on in various mundane occupations, although by this time he could barely walk and was suffering from a number of diseases. So it was that Ernest sought refuge and healing at another place called Cheltenham, this one far from the Cotswolds in England. In 1924, when he was 33, he was admitted to the Melbourne Benevolent Asylum at Cheltenham, a charitable institution that cared for the poor and infirm who could not look after themselves. While he was there, someone realised that 'John' Dunbar's ailments were probably caused by war service, and an effort was begun to help him obtain a disability pension. It was then discovered that the pension application originally made in 1918 for 'John Beech' had lapsed. Because Ernest had moved so often, the repatriation department had lost contact with 'Mr Beech'.

In September 1924, it was decided that he should re-apply in the name he was presently using, which he had also used for his original enlistment in 1915 and that identified him as a deserter. This meant he would have to finally reveal the truth to the army, so Ernest was taken to Victoria Barracks to make a confession:

Sir, I write to inform you that I John Dunbar enlisted at Liverpool on the 1st of January 1915 as number 1433 in the 13th Btn and embarked from Sydney on 11/2/1915, returned to Australia 25/9/15 and went illegally absent on 30/3/1916. I then reenlisted on the 6th of April 1916 at Newcastle NSW as number 2035 John Beech in the 34th Btn and reembarked for active service on the 24/8/1916 and returned to Australia on 4/10/1918 and Discharged at Sydney on 2/1/19.

Quite quickly, the records for Private John Dunbar were united with those for Private John Beech, and the repatriation department's records were also amended. There was now proof to establish that this ailing ex-soldier had served in the AIF in two identities from 1915 until 1919, had been wounded at Gallipoli and gassed at Passchendaele, and in present circumstances might now qualify for the disability pension he sought. Unfortunately, within a few months, this became inconsequential.

In late 1924, it was discovered at Cheltenham that Ernest had both cancer and heart disease, and that his life was coming to an end. On 25 January 1925, he died at the asylum, and was buried, as John Dunbar and as a pauper, at the Cheltenham Cemetery. He had never married. His death occurred ten years after he first volunteered for the AIF, and just five years after his discharge in Sydney.

Ernest's premature death was one of tens of thousands of such deaths of returned AIF soldiers in the decades after the war. So many fit young men had cheerfully answered the nation's call to 'serve our Sovereign Lord the King in the Australian Imperial Forces', and had survived the war only to live the remainder of their shortened lives as invalids. The post-war dead are not included in the Roll of Honour at the Australian War Memorial, but they should also be remembered for having lost their lives as a consequence of their war service.

Ernest Dunbar left us a wonderful legacy: about 40 of his wartime sketches and paintings survived. In 1938, a sketchbook containing pieces produced by him in 1915 and 1916 was donated to the Australian War Memorial by a Mr W. Besanko of Melbourne. This contained sketches

Ernest Dunbar's confession letter, written in September 1924 as
'John' Dunbar, to reveal to the army his second wartime identity,
Private 'John Beech'. *(NAA)*

and cartoons that Ernest made on the way to Egypt and in Cairo in 1915,
as well as some made in France. In 1923, Ernest had given them to an
ex-soldier mate who he met when they were evacuated from Gallipoli to
Egypt. After the war, this man had boarded with Mr Besanko's parents in
Melbourne, and, after he died prematurely of tuberculosis, the Dunbar
sketchbook passed to Besanko.

Another collection of Ernest's sketches and paintings, produced in France and England between 1916 and 1918 and signed by 'John Beech', was given by him to Albert Clarke, a British soldier. The sketchbook remained in England until Clarke's death, when it passed to his son-in-law, Ernest Gardiner. Gardiner decided it should be returned to Australia, so he wrote to newspapers in Sydney. This led in 2006 to the collection passing to David Harrower, a Hunter Valley historian of the 34th Battalion, and curator of an exhibition of battalion artefacts in the Swansea RSL Club near Newcastle, where the 'Beech' collection was displayed until it was acquired by the Australian War Memorial.

After the war, thousands of communities across Australia remembered those who had fought and those who had died in the Great War. The citizens of Scone erected a number of war memorials, among which 'E Dunbar' is listed, along with seven brothers and cousins. Both of his collections of sketches held by the Australian War Memorial are recorded as having been produced by Private John Dunbar of the 13th Battalion. He is remembered in the histories of the 34th Battalion as Private John Beech.

Today, Ernest still lies in an unmarked grave at Cheltenham Cemetery in Melbourne, in the section where paupers were buried.

CHAPTER SIX

Maurice Buckley and Gerald Sexton

the great Sergeant Buckley, VC, DCM

Maurice Buckley's feet had barely touched the ground in Egypt when he became infected with VD. He arrived in July 1915 from Melbourne on the *Ceramic*, was soon sent to the Abbassia isolation hospital, and from there was selected by Colonel Brady Nash to go to Australia. Just over a month after he arrived in Cairo, Maurice was on his way back to Melbourne on the *Wiltshire*. This was a bad start for a soldier who would later become an Australian military hero.

Maurice had been working for a builder of horse coaches at Warrnambool, a coastal town in Victoria, when he volunteered in Melbourne for the AIF in December 1914. He was not immediately assigned to a unit, and had to wait his turn for almost four months. This was because Maurice was deeply involved in the world of horses; he was a horse-coach trimmer by trade, and a daredevil horseman by inclination, and wanted to be a trooper in the Australian Light Horse. Maurice clearly had an exuberant style of horsemanship: a horse-riding friend who knew him before the war later told a newspaper reporter that 'I had a lot of time for Maurice because he knew how to laugh and how to take a spill and still laugh'. However, none of the cavalry units could take him, until the 13th Light Horse Regiment was formed at Broadmeadows in March 1915. Even then, he was not selected to be part of the regiment's main force, which embarked for Egypt from Port Melbourne in May. Instead, he followed a month later on the *Ceramic* with the 1st Reinforcements, straight to an encounter with a prostitute in the Wasa'a — and chancroid. When the 13th Light Horse landed at Gallipoli in September 1915, Maurice was halfway back to Australia on the *Wiltshire*.

On his attestation paper, Maurice had written that his religion was 'RC', Roman Catholic; he had been brought up by his parents, Timothy and Agnes, in the Catholic faith, and educated at the Christian Brothers School at Abbotsford in inner Melbourne. His father had been born in County Cork in 1854, and had immigrated to Australia; he was a brickmaker by trade. His mother was Australian-born, and married Timothy in 1887 in Hawthorn under the magnificent stained-glass windows at the Church of Immaculate Conception. At the Buckley family home, 'Takee', in McArthur Street, Malvern, Maurice was part of a large Irish-Australian family of five boys and three girls. For Maurice, however, there would always be an inner tension between, on the one hand, his Catholic upbringing, and, on the other, recklessness and risk-taking.

When the *Wiltshire* arrived at Port Melbourne in late September 1915, he was taken with the others to Langwarrin, where, following a medical examination, he was detained for further treatment. He found himself incarcerated not too far from the Buckley home, yet unable to explain his sudden return to his family, who believed he was fighting at Gallipoli. Then, a few days after Maurice's arrival at Langwarrin, a family tragedy unfolded at Malvern. One of Maurice's younger brothers, Gerald, died at the age of 20, of cerebrospinal meningitis, at the Alfred Hospital. He had been an AIF recruit, a driver in the 12th Battery of the Australian artillery, and had been in training at a camp in Royal Parade. Gerald had been infected during an outbreak of meningitis, his death one of many from the disease in 1915 — all a result of infections spread in unsanitary AIF camps around Melbourne.

In January 1916, Brigadier General Robert Williams was exhorting his new commandant at Langwarrin, Major Ivie Blezard, to stop inmates leaving the camp on paydays and going to pubs in Frankston. Maurice Buckley walked out at this time, but he did not return. His disappearance was followed by the usual army procedures; and, in March, he was declared a deserter, and a warrant was issued for his arrest. But it seems that, once he was out of the camp, Maurice caught a train and headed straight for Malvern and an awkward meeting with his parents; it also seems that there was then a family conference in McArthur Street about how to deal with Maurice's fall from grace.

The solution for this big trouble — and Mrs Buckley played a large part in making the decision — was for Maurice to travel far away to another place in Australia, and re-enlist in the army under an assumed identity. The identity invented for him by Mrs Buckley was to combine two family names: that of the recently deceased Gerald with her own maiden surname of Sexton. Maurice Buckley would become 'Gerald Sexton', and, under this name, would go on to achieve enormous fame.

Maurice travelled to Sydney, and went to the AIF recruiting station at the Royal Agricultural Society Showground in Randwick. On his attestation paper, he wrote that he was 25 years old, that he was a horse groom, that he lived at Castlereagh Street in the city of Sydney, and that his next of kin was his mother, Agnes 'Sexton', who lived in Malvern, Victoria. He also declared that he had never before belonged to His Majesty's forces and that everything he wrote was true. In May 1916, he was accepted into the AIF as Private 'Gerald Sexton', a new volunteer, and a reinforcement for the 13th Infantry Battalion — the same unit from which Ernest Dunbar had so recently deserted. Maurice was then sent to the Liverpool camp to commence training with reinforcements for the battalion.

In July 1916 in Melbourne, Maurice's younger brother William decided to enlist, and, in September at Broadmeadows, he was accepted into the AIF as a reinforcement for the 58th Battalion. On 2 October 1916, Will left Port Melbourne on the troopship A71 *Nestor* for the voyage to England. A few days later, Maurice left Sydney on the *Ceramic*, the same troopship that had taken him to his brief stay in Egypt the previous year.

A post-war portrait of Sergeant Maurice Buckley, VC, DCM. *(AWM)*

On 16 November 1916, the *Nestor* arrived at Plymouth bringing Will; and a week later, the *Ceramic* arrived at Plymouth bringing Maurice. Like most reinforcements just arrived from Australia, they were sent to AIF training battalions in England before going to France — Will to one at Rollestone and Maurice to another at Codford. On 30 December 1916, Will left England from Folkestone with the reinforcements for the 58th Battalion; two weeks later, Maurice left England from Folkestone with the reinforcements for the 13th Battalion.

After Will arrived in France, and before joining his battalion, he disappeared for a while; for this, he was given a field punishment and had his pay forfeited. After Maurice arrived in France, he joined the 13th Battalion at Albert in the Somme Valley, but, as 1917 wore on, he apparently returned to his old, discreditable ways. He was absent without leave in June, and given the maximum field punishment for that offence, and was on the receiving end of ten days for the same in September. His brother Will also absented himself in June 1917, and again in October for a long time. He was caught, court-martialled, convicted of desertion, and given a long prison sentence, but this was suspended after Will served a short period.

In late 1917, however, it seems that a remarkable change came over Maurice: he appears to have discovered that he liked soldiering, and that he instinctively knew how to fight. As a result, in January 1918, he was promoted to lance corporal, a junior non-commissioned officer position of some responsibility. In April, he was promoted to temporary corporal during fighting to halt the German army's spring offensive; in June, he was promoted to corporal, and then to lance sergeant. In July, he was concussed by an exploding shell at Hamel; that same month, he was given another promotion, to temporary sergeant. It appears Maurice received all these promotions in 1918 because 13th Battalion officers had recognised his special military talents: he knew better than others how to handle the .303-inch Lewis gun, the light machine gun used by the British and Australian armies.

The gun had been introduced to the British army in 1914. If properly used, it was a great battlefield weapon, but to do so required skilful co-ordination by a team of four or five gunners. The first gunner fired the weapon from a prone, kneeling, or standing position; the second rapidly changed the pan-shaped ammunition magazines; and other men in the team carried a supply of filled magazines in heavy canvas bags, and protected the shooters with rifle fire. By 1918, the Lewis gun had become so important that every platoon in every Australian battalion had at least one Lewis-gun section. The task of these sections was to move to positions of advantage on the battlefield, bring their weapon to bear on the enemy, fire it to inflict maximum damage, and then move on, again and again.

For men in Lewis-gun sections, there was a problem that challenged their instinct for self-preservation. The section was meant to break from the safety of the trenches and move towards the enemy, firing, reloading, and clearing stoppages, usually in a no-man's-land swept by enemy gunfire. Doing this brought the gun into closer range of a target, considerably improved its accuracy, and provided many angles of attack. The Lewis gun was not supposed to be used at long range from a stationary position behind solid cover. Because of their dangerous work, a Lewis-gun section was a 'suicide club', in AIF slang, and the soldier who handled the weapon was a 'mug-gunner'. To encourage AIF Lewis gunners to act boldly, officers commended for bravery those who, in advance of an attack, cleared the way by suppressing enemy gunfire. Many medals for valour, including the Victoria Cross, were thus awarded to Lewis-gun men.

Maurice Buckley, Sergeant 'Gerald Sexton', was adept at organising and leading a Lewis-gun section, and was a fearless gunner as well. In August 1918, following a 13th Battalion action near Morcourt in the Somme Valley, he was recommended for the Distinguished Conduct Medal. The DCM was the second-highest award for bravery for NCOs and men in the ranks, and was often seen as a near miss for the Victoria Cross. The citation for the DCM awarded to Sergeant 'Gerald Sexton' was published in *The London Gazette* on 5 December 1918:

> For conspicuous gallantry and devotion to duty. On four separate occasions his company was suddenly confronted by enemy machine-gun fire. On each occasion this NCO in charge of a Lewis-Gun section brought his gun into action with great promptitude, quickly silencing the opposition. On one occasion, in some tall crops, he stood up in full view of the enemy, firing from the hip until he had put the enemy machine gun out of action. Throughout the day he displayed initiative combined with coolness.

So now this *Wiltshire* boy was demonstrating fearlessness in battle, and complete mastery of his weapon — qualities that enabled him to lead by example and deliver military success for the 13th Battalion. As it turned out, his actions that day at Morcourt were simply a dress rehearsal for what was to follow in the rolling hills near Le Verguier a month later.

Training of AIF Lewis-gun sections at Renescure in France. *(AWM)*

In September 1918, following a series of victories, Lieutenant General John Monash was driving the exhausted Australian divisions to make a break in the Hindenburg Line, Germany's last major line of defences. During this, on the outskirts of Le Verguier, near Saint-Quentin, Maurice carried out a most spectacular act of daring — for which it was later recommended that he be awarded a Victoria Cross. The long citation explaining his actions begins thus:

> During the whole period of the advance, which was very seriously opposed, Sergeant Sexton was to the fore dealing with enemy machine guns, rushing enemy posts, and performing great feats of bravery and endurance without faltering or for a moment taking cover.

The citation described how, through that day, Maurice, standing and firing from the hip, had used a Lewis gun to destroy enemy artillery and machine-gun positions and to force the surrender of many enemy

An AIF Lewis-gun section on a desolate battlefield in France. *(AWM)*

soldiers. In a burst of energy and fearless action, he had been all over the battlefield, had been constantly exposed to enemy fire, and had been instrumental in enabling the 13th Battalion's advance.

To be recommended for the highest award for bravery given to soldiers in the imperial forces was an amazing achievement; only 65 of these medals were awarded in an AIF of 330,000 men. According to the Victoria Cross regulations, the medal could only be awarded 'for most conspicuous bravery, or some daring or pre-eminent act of valour or self-sacrifice, or extreme devotion to duty in the presence of the enemy'. Maurice had certainly been extraordinarily brave — but had carried out his act of valour serving as Gerald Sexton, and it was this name that shortly afterwards appeared in newspaper accounts of his great day at Le Verguier.

On 14 December 1918, Maurice's award of a VC was officially announced in *The London Gazette*, with his name given as 'Sjt. Gerald Sexton', and soon this name began appearing in Australian newspapers.

Under the headline 'VICTORIA CROSS — AUSTRALIAN HEROES', the Melbourne *Argus* announced Maurice's award:

> The Victoria Cross has been awarded to Sergt. G. Sexton, 13th Batt. (Vic). He showed conspicuous initiative in capturing enemy posts and machine guns during an attack at Levelguil [sic]. At the head of his section he rushed a field-gun, which had been holding up part of the attack and killed the gunners, subsequently capturing 30 of the enemy from their dugouts. (Sergt. Sexton enlisted on May 6 1916 when 25 years of age. He was formerly a groom. His mother is Mrs. Agnes Sexton, of Taku [sic], Macarthur [sic] St., Malvern.)

In Malvern, the proud Buckley family was evidently faced with a dilemma, for their boy had suddenly become a public celebrity. How could they explain, to neighbours and parishioners, why he was using a false identity in the AIF? A decision was made for Maurice to reveal his correct identity to the army, and to explain that he had invented the false identity after deserting in Australia in 1916. In France, Maurice told his story to some officers of the 13th Battalion; and, from there, the news spread upwards, eventually reaching Corps headquarters, where it was realised that this was a matter that needed delicate handling.

After Sergeant 'Gerald Sexton' had been recommended for a Victoria Cross, a lengthy procedure to confirm the award had been followed. A senior officer was meant to have made an assessment, including checking the soldier's background, witness reports, and other particulars, before endorsing the recommendation and passing it on. The recommendation for Maurice's VC had been sent to the Victoria Cross Committee in London, which decided it had merit, and passed it on to the King for a final decision. How could Maurice Buckley's correct identity and background have remained hidden during an exhaustive VC process that had culminated with the King's approval?

It appeared that, under the AIF's regulations in 1918, Maurice might not be entitled to any medals, because he had been sent back to Australia with venereal disease in 1915; because he had deserted from the army at Langwarrin in January 1916; and because he had re-enlisted by using a false identity in Sydney a few months later. The regulations covering desertion alone provided that his actions should have at least caused his discharge from the army, and the forfeiture of any medals. However, there was a loophole: it might be possible for a medal to be kept by a recipient if extenuating circumstances could be found. An internal investigation was quickly begun to check Maurice's story and to find the necessary extenuating circumstances. One of the first people to be interviewed was Mrs Buckley in Melbourne, who, in December 1918, signed a statutory declaration stating that her true name was Agnes Buckley, not Sexton; that her son's true name was Maurice Buckley; and that he had 'absented himself' from the army and re-enlisted in a false name.

Evidently without explaining the reason for the inquiry, a request for background information about Maurice was sent to Major Walter Conder at the Langwarrin camp. In January 1919, his brief report was received at Victoria Barracks:

No. 633 Trooper BUCKLEY, Maurice, 13th Light Horse, overseas, ex 'Wiltshire' who was admitted this camp on 25/9/15, deserted 21/1/16. He re-enlisted as No. 6594 Private Gerald Sexton. 13th Battalion on 8th May 1916. It may be interesting to note that this man has been awarded the V.C. for Bravery in the field at Le Verguier, France 1918.

In January 1919, *The Argus* published a list of 64 VC awardees, including 'Sgt. G. Sexton', with the name 'MAURICE BUCKLEY' now appearing next to the name Sexton. Then, in early 1919, an urgent clerical effort was made by the army to unite the records of Gerald Sexton with those of Maurice Buckley, and to amend them. The name in which the DCM had been awarded was altered and re-gazetted in June 1919, without explanation; and, in August, the same was done for the VC. Meanwhile, in March 1919, at Hanzinelle in Belgium, Maurice, too, had been required to sign a statutory declaration that confirmed his and his mother's correct names, following which he was permitted to revert to his original identity.

Even while all this was happening, a decision had already been made that extenuating circumstances existed in Maurice's case: his earlier crimes were absolved by his later outstanding service. So, with the records made consistent and neat, and, most importantly, with no embarrassing truths appearing in the press, it was time for Maurice to receive his valuable medals. In 1856, when Queen Victoria and Prince Albert created the Victoria Cross, they had intended that investiture should be personally made by the Queen, and she had presided over the first ceremony in 1857. This established a tradition that a reigning monarch should make the presentation; but, during the First World War, many VCs were awarded, and it was not always possible to follow the tradition. Sometimes, investitures were made in the field by a very senior officer — a divisional commander, at the very least. However, for Maurice, there was a flattering surprise: both of his medals would be personally awarded by King George V. Accordingly, on 29 May 1919, an immaculate Sergeant Buckley attended Buckingham Palace in London, and, there, the King pinned to his chest first the Victoria Cross, then the DCM. So it was that a man who had returned to Australia in disgrace on the *Wiltshire* in 1915 had, four years later, reached the pinnacle of military success.

It appears that, after the ceremony at the palace, and while Maurice was on leave in London, boisterous celebrations went on for some time; and it also appears that his younger brother Will was there for them. We recall that, in 1917, Will had been convicted for desertion from the AIF, and had received a sentence of two years' imprisonment with hard labour, which was later suspended. In June 1918 in France, he was gassed, and remained in hospital recovering until August. After he returned to his battalion, Will disappeared again, only to be apprehended a month later. Brought before his second court-martial, he pleaded guilty to a charge of being AWL, and his earlier suspended prison sentence was re-instated. In December 1918, Will was admitted

Mosquito Farms, a pencil-on-paper sketch made by Ernest Dunbar
in 1917. AIF soldiers on leave in England liked to think they
attracted swarms of women. *(AWM)*

to a British military prison at Audruicq in France to resume his sentence. In January 1919, while working with a group of prisoners on a farm near Audruicq, he escaped, and then somehow made his way to London in time to celebrate his brother's awards.

Will and Maurice celebrated, excessively, it seems, and Maurice forgot to use Calomel and Nargol, or perhaps his supply had run out. In June 1919, he was admitted to the 1st Australian Dermatological Hospital at Bulford with gonorrhoea and syphilis. A course of treatment was commenced for him, using Wassermann tests and mercury injections for the syphilis, and urethral irrigations with silver for the gonorrhoea. Some days after Maurice entered Bulford, Will was caught in London by military police and taken to Wandsworth Prison. In early July, at his third court-martial, he was sentenced to nine months' imprisonment with hard labour, which was added to the remainder of his earlier, unfinished two-year sentence. He was then returned to Wandsworth to begin a term of imprisonment that was meant to last until 1921. Two days after Will began his sentence, Maurice walked out of Bulford, without permission, and made his way back to London. After six days, he was caught by military police, and, because he had again left an army venereal-disease hospital while still being treated, his misconduct was regarded as serious. At AIF headquarters in London, Maurice was reprimanded, penalised with forfeiture of pay, and told that a second period about to commence at Bulford would be regarded as 'disciplinary action'. He was taken back to the VD hospital, and his treatments resumed.

At the end of August 1919, Maurice was declared by a Bulford doctor to be 'non-infectious and fit to travel on a troopship', although it was noted that he now had chronic gleet. In early September, he joined the passenger steamer *Raranga* for his repatriation voyage, and arrived at Melbourne at the end of October. Unlike his quiet arrival from Egypt on the *Wiltshire* four years before, this time at Port Melbourne, his celebrity had preceded him, and he received a rousing welcome as a returning hero. Pupils of the Christian Brothers Abbotsford school were lined up at the South Melbourne army depot to greet their famous old boy, the great

Sergeant Buckley, who had become a household name over the length and breadth of Victoria. His return had been somewhat overshadowed by the wild reception given a few days earlier to Captain Albert Jacka, Australia's first VC recipient of the war; but, within days, Maurice was being entertained, together with Jacka, by the adoring citizens of Melbourne. For months to come, he was invited to speak at civic receptions and other public occasions in Melbourne and throughout Victoria.

There was to be no long and distinguished military career ahead for him, however; his service in the AIF ended shortly after his return, when, in December 1919, he was discharged from the army. A year later, when the army was sorting through the files of men who had deserted during the war, it was decided that Maurice would be awarded the three imperial service medals, including the 1914–15 Star for his brief sojourn in Egypt in 1915. A note was added in his army record explaining this decision: 'In view of having been awarded the DCM and VC for conspicuous gallantry in the field during his second period of service, it is recommended that all medals be issued.'

Maurice's brother Will also returned to Melbourne in late 1919. While serving his sentence in London, he had been transferred from Wandsworth Prison to the AIF's own detention barracks at Lewes, for a period of 'safe custody', before being placed on board the troopship A11 *Ascanius* for repatriation. On 23 September, the day the *Ascanius* departed from England, the remainder of his long sentence was remitted.

Maurice and Will resumed civilian life at home with their parents at 'Takee' in Malvern. With Maurice's amazing wartime experiences now in the past, it was time for decisions to be made about his future. Because of his fame, he attracted the attention of John Wren, a millionaire Melbourne businessman who, to some, had an unfavourable reputation, but who was a flamboyant hero of the Irish-Australian community. Wren liked to cultivate famous Catholic sporting and war heroes, and he was also close to the Irish archbishop of Melbourne, Dr Daniel Mannix. It was not long before Archbishop Mannix had it drawn to his attention that, among his flock, there were certain highly decorated ex-servicemen, who might

The leading group of the St Patrick's Day procession in Bourke
Street, Melbourne, on 17 March 1920. Some VC awardees are
leading on horseback, while others are seated in the limousine with
Archbishop Mannix. *(NLA)*

be prepared to serve the Church in useful ways. Archbishop Mannix
had been a controversial figure during the war because of his less than
wholehearted support for the war effort, and he had been a leader of
opposition to the prime minister's plans to introduce conscription. Now
with the war over, and Australia on the winning side, it was important that
Mannix, the Irish community, and the Catholic Church be seen in public
as loyal to Australia and the British Empire, and to have contributed to
the eventual victory.

Accordingly, John Wren arranged a special Catholic duty for Maurice.
In March 1920, he became a member of a delegation from the St Patrick's
Day Celebration Committee. They sought consent from the lord mayor
of Melbourne for a procession through the centre of the city on their feast
day. The Melbourne City Council had forbidden all processions in the
city 'excepting on great patriotic occasions', but this was aimed directly
at stopping St Patrick's Day parades, which were believed to promote

FOURTEEN VICTORIA CROSS HEROES
FORMING GUARD OF HONOR TO DR MANNIX
ST PATRICK'S DAY CELEBRATION, 1920.
COPYRIGHT.

Archbishop Mannix in an open car, surrounded by the VC awardees
who escorted him during the St Patrick's Day parade. *(SLV)*

sectarian discontent. Melbourne's establishment was firmly pro-British, and against mass displays of 'Irish Popery', when anti-British flags and banners might be carried. The council was swayed by the delegation, and it later became popular belief that Maurice had threatened to return his VC, forcing the council to permit the procession. It seems, however, that the lord mayor relented only after a last-minute undertaking was given by Dr Mannix that Union flags would be prominently displayed. Maurice then helped John Wren arrange for 14 Victoria Cross recipients, ten Roman Catholics, and four Protestants to provide a mounted escort for the open limousine of the archbishop. The VC men, splendidly dressed in uniform and decorations, and mounted on white chargers, led the procession in this way on St Patrick's Day, and the streets were crowded to see them.

The relationship with John Wren led to Maurice receiving assistance from him to start a contracting business. In January 1921, while managing road construction in south Gippsland in eastern Victoria, Maurice was seriously hurt in a horseriding fall. This was clearly the result of more daredevilry, although afterwards it was said to have been an accident. The circumstances of the accident were typical for a man who had been attracted to dangerous thrillseeking for much of his life.

Boolarra is a tiny town in the picturesque Strzelecki Ranges of south Gippsland, and Maurice had been living in a contractor's camp a few miles away. One Saturday afternoon, he rode into the town, it appears, to visit the pub. One thing led to another, and Maurice, the daredevil horseman, accepted a challenge to jump his horse over the railway gate adjacent to the new railway station. At the last moment, the horse baulked, Maurice was sent flying, and he crashed headfirst onto the road. According to the report of the coroner's inquiry, which appeared in *The Argus*,

he remounted immediately and rode away, without appearing to be hurt. The horse was a jumper, but was not put to the gates the right way. At half-past 7 o'clock that evening Buckley was found by Mounted-constable Ernest C. Edwards lying unconscious beside the Ganyah road, near Boolarra, where he had apparently collapsed, and fallen from his horse. He was taken to Boolarra, and later to Mont St Evin's Hospital. The Coroner said that it was the irony of fate that a man should, after having gone right through the war, be killed by a fall from his horse. He found that Buckley died from cerebral haemorrhage, caused by an accidental fall from his horse.

In fact, after being taken to Melbourne in an ambulance and admitted to Mont St Evin's hospital in Fitzroy, this almost indestructible man appeared to make a recovery, but then lapsed into a coma. He died from his injuries on 27 January, aged 29 and unmarried, and became the first of the returned Australian VC men to lose his life. A full military funeral was held for him in Melbourne, beginning with a requiem mass at St Patrick's Cathedral, and then a long procession down St Kilda Road to the Brighton general cemetery, where the pallbearers were eight Victorian VC recipients. *The Age* reported that

> the crowd in the vicinity of the cathedral comprised many thousands, and extended nearly to Collins Street. The cortege moved off with the VC men flanking the gun carriage, and Brigadier-General Brand immediately following on foot. Then came about 100 members of the 4th Brigade, marching four abreast, and the mourning coaches followed … The funeral passed down Collins Street, where the Town Hall flag was at half mast … Several hundred people were present at the graveside.

The remarkable life of another of the *Wiltshire* boys of 1915, Maurice Vincent Buckley, had ended. But what was going to be done to explain to posterity why this Australian hero had been awarded the VC and DCM in the name of Gerald Sexton? An innocent story would need to be invented, and an article in *The Age* published shortly after his death contained an early version:

> An element of romance was embraced in Sergeant Buckley's distinguished military service. Having, under a misapprehension, overstayed his final leave, and missed the boat upon which his battalion embarked, he hurried to Sydney, where under another name he re-enlisted in order to expedite his getting to the front. The second enlistment was in the name Gerald Sexton and under that name he won the V.C., his actual identity not being disclosed until a later period.

In 1936, the Perth *Western Mail* published a different version of Maurice's story, slightly closer to the truth:

> Having been originally allotted to the 13th. Light Horse, Maurice Buckley was invalided to Australia from Egypt and discharged in Victoria. He

decided to enlist again, and, to avoid awkward questions, went to New South Wales and, on this occasion, used his mother's maiden name.

Other accounts of Maurice's war service similarly glossed over what happened to him from his enlistment in 1914 to his desertion from Langwarrin. During the 1960s, in a series of articles about men who had been awarded a VC, an Australian army newspaper provided this misleading explanation:

He enlisted on December 18, 1914, under his correct name, and sailed with the 13th. Light Horse Regiment. No details of his service with the unit are available, but a significant event was his return to Australia and discharge on September 25 1915. After remaining a civilian for a period, he then went to Sydney and re-enlisted on May 16 1916, under his mother's maiden name of Sexton.

It was almost a century after Maurice's enlistment that truthful versions of his remarkable story began to appear. By 2009, *The Age* had forgotten its 1921 account, written to help conceal Maurice's secret past. A new, condensed, and not entirely correct story about him could now include this version of the long-avoided subjects:

The Australian troops were warned prostitutes who haunted the Allied barracks carried gonorrhea and syphilis. Buckley caught both. He was shipped home in September. In 1915, to be sent home to the army's 'pox camp' in Langwarrin, Gippsland, carried with it a serious stigma. For Buckley, his shame was compounded by the fact that he had not even seen the front. He found himself stranded at Langwarrin for five months, until in March 1916, he simply walked out of the camp.

The description accompanying Maurice's display in the Victoria Cross section at the Australian War Memorial also avoided explaining the gap in his service from 1915 until 1916, or the real reason for his change

Lieutenant William Dartnell, VC. The Victoria Cross and medal ribbons he is wearing were drawn onto the photograph after his posthumous award. *(AWM)*

of identity. Then, in February 2011, the memorial opened a new Hall of Valour for Australia's VC recipients. In the glass cabinet containing Maurice's story and medals, his return from Egypt to Australia with venereal disease is fully described.

Maurice Buckley is unique among Australia's First World War Victoria Cross recipients because of his combination of being treated in military hospitals for VD, his banishment from Egypt to Langwarrin, his desertion from the AIF, and his serving under a false identity when confirmed for a VC. However, other recipients did each of these things individually.

One other Australian soldier, William Thomas Dartnell, received a Victoria Cross for an act of bravery while serving under a false identity. He was 'Wilbur Taylor' Dartnell, who served as an officer in the British army in East Africa in 1915. After he was killed in a battlefield action while protecting wounded men, he received a posthumous VC. It is not clear why Dartnell chose to disguise his correct identity, or why

Private Jack Leak, VC, outside Buckingham Palace after his
investiture with the medal. His family, who all lived in England,
were able to attend the ceremony. *(AWM)*

he chose the names 'Wilbur Taylor'. It has been speculated that he
was concealing his whereabouts from his wife in Melbourne, and that
'Wilbur Taylor' Dartnell may have been a stage name when he was an
actor before the war.

One other Australian Victoria Cross recipient was declared a
deserter from the AIF. Private John 'Jack' Leak was awarded a VC
after single-handedly recapturing an entire trench system in July 1916
at Pozieres. The following year, he was found guilty by a field general
court-martial of 'when on Active Service deserting his Majesty's
service in that he absented himself from the line from 1 November
until 6 November 1917'. He was initially sentenced to penal servitude
for life, and the sentence was confirmed, but it was then commuted to
two years' imprisonment with hard labour. As so often happened to
AIF men convicted of crimes, Leak's sentence was suspended, and he

An over-painted photograph of Private Bob Beatham, with his
Victoria Cross painted onto his tunic. *(AWM)*

returned to his battalion in December 1917.

And there was one other soldier who was sent with venereal disease
from Egypt to Langwarrin in 1915 and was later awarded a VC. Private
Robert 'Bob' Beatham, who had been born in England, enlisted in
Geelong in January 1915, and was sent to Egypt as a reinforcement for the
8th Battalion, arriving in June. He was soon admitted to Abbassia with
VD, and in July 1915 was sent back to Australia by Colonel Brady Nash
on board the A70 *Ballarat*. After only six days at Langwarrin, in August
1915, he was discharged as fit for duty and sent to Broadmeadows, where
he rejoined the 8th Battalion. He was killed in action at Rosieres, near
Amiens, in extraordinarily heroic circumstances, and was awarded the
Victoria Cross posthumously in 1918.

Maurice Buckley and Bob Beatham were, of course, not the only
AIF Victoria Cross recipients to have been treated during the war for
a venereal disease. Given that at least 60,000 AIF men became infected,

it should be unsurprising that VC recipients were among them. Apart from Buckley and Beatham, at least seven other Australian VC men became infected during the war, and this occurred sometimes before and sometimes after investiture of their medal.[19] The VC men who caught venereal disease represent about 15 per cent of all Australian VC recipients; this is consistent with the percentage for all Australian soldiers. It also means, of course, that about 85 per cent of VC men, and Australian soldiers, did not become infected with VD during the war.

CHAPTER SEVEN

Richard Waltham and Harold Glading

the secrets of the dead

Richard 'Dick' Waltham was different from most other young men sent back to Australia on the *Wiltshire*. Most of those fellows were not well educated, and had started working at a young age on farms and in factories as labourers and apprentices. Their parents were not well-off, and had to work hard to provide for their children. Richard, by contrast, was from a well-to-do and prominent family of educated professional people. Nonetheless, soon after his arrival in Egypt in late July 1915, he, too, became infected with VD. He was admitted to Abbassia and, not long after, was selected by Colonel Brady Nash to be sent to Langwarrin.

Richard was born in 1894 at Heidelberg in Melbourne, the youngest child of Joshua and Constance Waltham. In 1867, as a young man of 21, Joshua had immigrated to Australia from Hull in England, and in Victoria became qualified as a licensed surveyor. In 1883, he married Constance Bromby, whose family was also from Hull. As a four-year-old child, Constance had arrived at Port Melbourne in 1858 with her parents and nine siblings; her father, John Bromby, had been invited to be the first headmaster of the Melbourne Church of England Grammar School for boys.

Dr Bromby was 49 when he brought his family to Australia, having had a distinguished career as a teacher and headmaster at prominent English private schools, and as a lecturer at St John's College at Cambridge University, where he earned a doctorate in divinity. He was also an ordained priest of the Anglican Church, as was his father, and had been a university preacher at Cambridge. In April 1858, he opened the doors of Melbourne Grammar School on St Kilda Road near South Yarra, and for the next 16 years established the culture and traditions of the school. As the clergyman-headmaster, Dr Bromby's duty was to impart high standards of Christian conduct, which he did with wit, passion, and humour — his captivating personality earned him popularity and respect.

After he retired from the school, Dr Bromby became the Anglican incumbent at St Paul's Cathedral in Melbourne. He was a leader of the Society for the Promotion of Morality, and an outspoken opponent of alcohol, prostitution, and venereal disease, but never by playing a firebrand preacher role. His elegant sermons about health, happiness, and virtue were prepared in a scholarly way, and he would use charm and wit in their delivery. An obituary in *The Argus* on his death in 1889 declared that the delightful Dr Bromby had been 'a rich thinker and fearless defender of the truth'.

So how could a grandson of his, Richard Waltham, become infected with venereal disease in Cairo in 1915, and be shipped back to Australia in disgrace?

When the war began in August 1914, Richard and his mother were living in Perth. The 1890s had been economically depressed times in Victoria, but a mining boom in Western Australia had provided employment on the goldfields for surveyors, so Joshua moved the family to Perth. They settled at Cottesloe, and Constance opened a music school on St George's Terrace in the city. She was a classically trained pianist: in the 1870s, she had been sent by Dr Bromby to Stuttgart to study at the Royal Conservatory of Wurttemberg, and, on returning to Melbourne, Constance had opened a school in Heidelberg to teach piano and singing. As a boy, Richard went to school at Lemyn College, a private primary school where his mother taught music. He was then enrolled at Guildford Grammar, where he completed his secondary education and experienced his first military adventures as an army cadet. In June 1914, just before the war, his father died. When Constance was widowed, she was 60, and all of her children were adults; Richard was 20, and farming with an older brother at Wanneroo, north of Perth.

Richard enlisted in the AIF in Perth in March 1915, and joined the 28th Battalion, then being raised by Lieutenant Colonel Herbert Collett at the Black Boy Hill camp. On 16 April, the battalion's first day, Richard was immediately promoted to corporal. This is exactly what would have been expected for a fine young fellow who was nearly six feet tall, intelligent, well educated, and from a good Perth family, and who had some military experience. With his background, he could expect to rise through the ranks, and perhaps to gain a commission as an officer.

At the end of June 1915, after training for two months, the 28th Battalion embarked from Fremantle on the *Ascanius*, bound for Gallipoli. A few weeks later, they arrived in Egypt. During a brief stay at an AIF camp near Cairo, the completely unexpected happened: when leave was granted for battalion members to visit the city, Corporal Waltham caught gonorrhoea. He was one of only a few men to become infected, and, as an NCO, his behaviour was regarded as disgraceful. Very quickly, he lost his rank, was struck from the battalion's strength, and was sent to Abbassia. Two months after leaving Australia, he was sent straight back by Colonel Brady Nash. On 10 September, when the 28th Battalion went ashore at Gallipoli, Richard was far away in the Indian Ocean on the *Wiltshire*.

Then, in the midst of this personal tragedy, during the voyage of the *Wiltshire*, two good things happened to him. The first was that he found a really decent new mate. The second was that his gonorrhoea was apparently cured.

Also on board the *Wiltshire* during the voyage from Egypt was a 26-year-old soldier from Sydney, Harold 'Harry' Glading, and he and

Richard Waltham in 1915 after he joined the
28th Battalion in Perth. *(AWM)*

Richard became mates. Harold was the son of John Glading, a Cornish immigrant, and Sarah Stapleton, who had been born on a migrant ship bound for Australia from England. John was a builder, and he married Sarah in Sydney in 1871; they went on to produce 11 children. When the war began, Sarah was a widow, and living with Harold and his teenaged brother Walter, or 'Wally', at their home, named 'Glen Eyre', in Bronte Road in Waverley.

Before the war, Harold had completed an apprenticeship as a printing machinist at *The Sydney Morning Herald*, and then worked at a printery in the city. He also trained as a member of the Australian Rifles, a militia unit in Balmain, along with his brother Wally. When the war began, Wally immediately enlisted and joined the 1st Battalion. He went to Egypt with the first AIF contingent, and, shortly after landing at Gallipoli, was wounded. In May 1915, his name and his brother Harold's appeared in a casualty report in *The Sydney Morning Herald*:

Sergeant Walter D Glading, who is reported wounded, was born in Balmain about 21 years ago. While in camp at Kensington he was appointed corporal. He left with the first battalion, and, soon after arrival in Egypt he was promoted to the rank of sergeant. When Sergeant Glading's casualty was announced his brother, Harold, aged 23 [sic], enlisted immediately, and is now at Liverpool.

In June 1915, just over a month after he enlisted, Harold departed from Sydney with the 19th Battalion on the *Ceramic*. When the battalion stopped briefly in Cairo, Harold — no doubt to his horror — became infected with syphilis. He was sent to Abbassia a week after Richard Waltham was sent, the 19th Battalion moved on to Gallipoli, and Harold was left behind in disgrace. When Colonel Brady Nash sent him back to Australia on the *Wiltshire*, he had been in Egypt for only a month. That was shameful enough, but Harold's shame was soon worsened when he learned what had happened to his brother Walter during that month.

At Gallipoli, Walter recovered from his wound and rejoined the 1st Battalion at about the time that Harold arrived in Cairo. On 6 August 1915, the battalion entered the fierce fighting at Lone Pine, and, almost immediately, Walter received a gunshot wound to his head. On 7 August, he was evacuated to a British hospital ship to be taken to Malta, but died of his wounds on the ship and was buried at sea. All this occurred while Harold was misbehaving in Cairo; it appears that, at Abbassia, he was given the news of his brother's fate. Evidently, he was haunted for the rest of his life by what happened to him and to Walter in August 1915.

Thus, when the two unfortunates Richard Waltham and Harold Glading were taken from Abbassia to Port Suez and thence the *Wiltshire*, they already had rather a lot in common. Their misbehaviour in Cairo had been uncharacteristic and inexplicable; despite all the warnings, each had still made a foolish choice. Because of their pre-war military experience and good character, each had been expected to make a big contribution in his battalion, but both had failed before firing a shot at the enemy. They could not join the fight at Gallipoli, which they were expected to do, and this was a heavy burden, especially for Harold. At Abbassia, they then had the misfortune to be selected to go back to Australia very soon after leaving.

However, Richard and Harold also had some good luck, which helped them avoid the troubles they had expected at home. First, they were not being sent back to their home military districts, but to Victoria, where they were unknown. Second, on board the *Wiltshire* as she steamed towards Australia, it appears they co-operated conscientiously with Dr Herbert Alsop, and willingly did everything he requested they do for a cure. When the *Wiltshire* arrived at Port Melbourne, Dr Alsop reported that 70 of his gonorrhoea patients were free of indications of disease, and Richard was among them. At Langwarrin, both men were medically inspected by Dr Morris and Dr McCusker, and they confirmed that Richard was cured, and that Harold seemed to be clear of syphilis. Within a few days, the two mates were out of the camp, with pay restored and orders to go to the Broadmeadows camp.

There, they were both drafted as reinforcements for the 8th Battalion, and were told they would shortly leave from Port Melbourne to join the battalion in Egypt. This was a remarkable reversal of fate for them: in Melbourne, without any fuss, and without their families knowing anything, their immediate pasts were expunged. They had avoided having to take the drastic actions that so many of their *Wiltshire* mates would soon take at Langwarrin to get back overseas. However, it does appear that Richard and Harold had already invented the excuses they would use if they needed to make their return to Australia seem innocent and logical. Richard's story would have been that, in Egypt, he had been assigned for guard duty on a ship returning to Australia with men wounded at Gallipoli. Harold's story would have been that he was one of the wounded men.

In late November 1915, Richard and Harold joined crowds of soldiers and well-wishers on the wharf at Port Melbourne, and then boarded the *Ceramic* for the journey back to Egypt, and, they thought, to Gallipoli. When the *Ceramic* reached Western Australia, she joined a convoy bound for Suez, and one of the troopships that Richard and Harold could see steaming with them was the *Wiltshire*, which had departed from Port Melbourne a few days before the *Ceramic*.

The 8th Battalion was a Victorian unit that had gone to Egypt a year earlier, and had landed at Gallipoli on the first day. It had suffered serious casualties during the following months; so, on board the *Ceramic*, Richard and Harold believed that they would soon take the places of men who had been lost at Gallipoli. They could not know that, very recently, Lord Kitchener and General Birdwood had made a short inspection visit to Gallipoli, which resulted in a recommendation, made to the war cabinet in London, to end the doomed Dardanelles campaign. A secret plan was then hatched to quietly withdraw the AIF, and this was put into action within a few weeks. When the *Ceramic* arrived at Port Suez, Richard and Harold discovered that the fighting at Gallipoli had ended, and the 8th Battalion was in Egypt again.

The departure of the A40 *Ceramic* from Port Melbourne on
23 November 1915. *(AWM)*

It remained there until March 1916 — recovering from the pounding
received in the Dardanelles, and training fresh recruits who had arrived
from Australia — after which it was one of the first battalions to go to
France. Richard had again been promoted to corporal, and he went
with the battalion to Marseille. Harold followed a few months later, and
was promoted to lance corporal. While they were separated, Richard was
found guilty of disorderly conduct and, for the second time in his military
career, was reduced to the ranks. Richard and Harold were both assigned
to B Company, and, when the 8th Battalion moved to front-line trenches
near the village of Pozieres in northern France, they went together.

Here, in July 1916, they had their baptism of fire. As soon as the
battalion arrived, it came under heavy attack from German artillery;
for weeks, exploding shells blew men to pieces and buried others in
collapsed trenches. One Friday night in August, the battalion was

ordered to attack across no-man's-land and capture enemy trenches. A thunderous British artillery barrage, intended to clear their way, opened fire, and the night sky was lit up by muzzle flashes and bursting shells. The Australian infantrymen gamely advanced, but the barrage had not weakened the German defenders, and the diggers were forced back by ferocious gunfire. The Australians tried again and again, but they were always beaten back. The attack ended in failure.

The 8th Battalion now had many wounded and dead scattered across the battlefield. When Richard and Harold and their B Company mates returned to the Australian trenches, they learned that two of their young officers, Lieutenant William Doolan and Second Lieutenant Reginald Dabb, were lying wounded somewhere in no-man's-land. Volunteers would have to go out, find them, and bring them back.

Battlefield rescues after failed attacks were hazardous undertakings. Although German gunners sometimes held their fire if they could see that rescues were underway, rescuers could easily be shot in the confusion of a night battlefield. One night, three weeks earlier at Pozieres, in another battalion, Sergeant Claud Castleton was single-handedly carrying wounded men to safety when he was shot dead; he was awarded a Victoria Cross for his selfless courage. The essence of the legendary mateship of Australian diggers was founded on a willingness to rescue their friends after failed attacks, whatever the cost.

So now, in the middle of the night of 18 August 1916, it became the duty of Richard Waltham and Harold Glading to go to the rescue of their young officers Doolan and Dabb, or any others they could find. Once again, they went forth from the B Company trenches. This time, Richard was struck in the head by flying metal — it is unclear if it was a bullet, a shell, or shrapnel — and killed.

Constance Waltham discovered none of the details of what had happened from the brief, sad casualty telegram she received. For this refined, sensitive woman, the loss of Richard was unbearable, and we know her thoughts returned again and again to him for the rest of her life. Her father had been a theologian at St John's College at Cambridge, and he would have understood the magnificence of what his grandson had done at Pozieres. It was through the revelations of St John that the spoken words of Jesus Christ had been recorded, to be later expressed in the poetic language of the King James Bible: 'Greater love hath no man than this, that a man lay down his life for his friends.'

At a time after the battle, Richard's body was recovered and identified from the little identity disc strung around his neck, and he was buried in a temporary cemetery for 8th Battalion dead near Pozieres. Later, it was discovered that Lieutenant Doolan had also been killed, and he was buried there, too. The cemetery eventually held 81 dead men, including 25 killed in the three failed night attacks of 18 August; by the end of the fighting at Pozieres, AIF cemeteries there held nearly 7,000.

Also after the battle, it was learned that Second Lieutenant Reginald Dabb was one of a number of 8th Battalion men who had been taken prisoner. For most of the night, he had lain on the far side of no-man's-land, his thigh fractured by machine-gun fire. He was recovered by German rescuers and evacuated to Germany, to a *reservelazarett* at Berg-Kaserne in Westphalia, a military hospital where his smashed leg was amputated. A few weeks later, he died of his wounds, and was buried in the Haus Spital Prisoners of War Cemetery in Munster.

Lance Corporal Harold Glading survived the night of 18 August 1916 at Pozieres. He was still with the 8th Battalion a year later when, during the Third Battle of Ypres, he received severe shrapnel wounds in his upper right arm. Harold was evacuated to a British military hospital at Birmingham in England, where he underwent a number of operations to remove pieces of shrapnel. Like so many wounded diggers who were evacuated to England, Harold used his reprieve from the war to contemplate his future. In the hospital at Birmingham, he decided it was time for a change. After he was discharged fighting fit, he requested a transfer to become an AIF machine gunner, and, in January 1918, he joined a training brigade. On the Salisbury Plain in Wiltshire, Harold learned to use the Vickers heavy machine gun, and, after he qualified, was sent back to France. At the vast Etaples depot of the British Expeditionary

Force, Harold joined the 25th Australian Machine Gun Company. He was then involved in the fighting at Villers-Bretonneux to hold back the German spring offensive, and continued to serve throughout 1918 as the Australians achieved one startling victory after another, until hostilities ceased in November.

In April 1919, when Harold was about to return to Australia, he was examined medically by AIF doctors, who found nothing wrong with him. Accordingly, following standard procedure before returning home, he signed a form stating he had no disabilities from his war service. He was then repatriated to Sydney on the Australian passenger steamer *Wyreema*, arriving home in June. There, he had a final medical examination, which again found that his health was good, although it was noted that he was slightly deaf in one ear. In July 1919, Harold was discharged from the AIF in Sydney. He had not applied for any repatriation benefits, except for temporary financial assistance until he found work.

In Sydney, Harold resumed life with his mother, Sarah, at 'Glen Eyre' in Waverley. He was now 31 years of age, but still single, and he remained unmarried for a very long time. He quickly found work at a printing company in the city, and also became a partner in a printing business in Randwick. He received a British War Medal and a Victory Medal in the mail, for his service in France from 1916 until 1918, and was also sent a 1914–15 Star for his month in Egypt in 1915. In 1924, an opportunity arose to move to a country town, and for the next 13 years he supervised the printery at *The Muswellbrook Chronicle*. The news of his joining the newspaper was published in it, with a reference to his war service:

> Mr H E Glading, for many years on the staff at Messrs. Turner and Henderson's printing works in Sydney, has joined the staff at the 'Chronicle' office, succeeding to the position of overseer. Mr Glading comes to Muswellbrook with splendid credentials as a first class printer. He is a returned soldier, having spent four years abroad with the AIF, serving in Gallipoli and France.

In Muswellbrook, Harold became very involved with clubs and organisations. He was a champion lawn bowler, a committee man of the local RSSILA and the School of Arts, and a member of a lodge. In 1937, in an unexpected change, he left Muswellbrook to become the licensee and proprietor of the Metropolitan Hotel at West Wyalong, in the central west of New South Wales. This did not last long, and he sold the hotel and licence and moved back to Sydney.

Some time after his return to Australia in 1919, Harold had communicated with Constance Waltham, the mother of his dead friend Richard Waltham. Constance was Richard's next of kin, and, in this role, she was a diligent guardian of his memory. At the time of his death, she was living in Melbourne, and she placed a notice in the 'Died on Service' section of *The Argus*, describing 'Corporal Richard Waltham' as the 'youngest son of Constance and the late J. F. Waltham, grandson of the late Dr Bromby.' More death notices for him were then placed by his sisters in Western Australian newspapers; each of the notices for Richard was just one among dozens for young men killed at Pozieres. For a few years, on the anniversary of his death, in-memoriam notices for him were also placed in newspapers in Melbourne and Perth.

As was the case with other next of kin of soldiers who were killed, the army provided Constance with very little information about Richard's life in the AIF, or the circumstances of his death. The only information she received were disconnected items in brief letters from the army. As a result, what she understood to have happened was in a number of ways quite different from the much more detailed version held by the army in Richard's service records, to which she had no access. In the version of events apparently in Constance's mind, Richard left Perth in 1915 as a corporal in the 28th Battalion, and was killed in France in 1916 as a corporal in the 8th Battalion. It seems she was proud that he held the rank, and her letters to the army always referred to him as a corporal. Constance had no way of knowing that he had been demoted in Cairo in August 1915 when he became infected with VD; or that, in France in 1916, Richard had again lost the rank because of misconduct.

In February 1917, Richard's death certificate was sent to her by the army. This came with a blunt letter, the contents of which must have come as a surprise:

> It is recorded this soldier reverted to the ranks on 8 August 1915. There
> is no report of any subsequent promotion, and the cable announcing his
> death and Army Form B 2090A (Field Service Report of Death) each
> refer to him as 'private'.

In 1918, Constance received in the mail the little identity disc that Richard had been wearing at Pozieres. In 1921, she received Richard's 1914–15 Star, but would not have known it was just for his brief visit to Cairo in 1915. In 1922, she was asked to provide some details about Richard for the register at the Pozieres British Cemetery in France; in another letter, she was given the location of his grave. In 1923, she was sent Richard's Victory Medal, British War Medal, and a Next of Kin Memorial Plaque, which was a medallion issued by the British government that came with a printed message of thanks from the King.

In 1919, Charles Bean was appointed Australia's war historian, and in the 1920s was kept busy writing *The Official History of Australia in the War of 1914–1918*. Before his appointment, Bean had suggested that, as well as making a war history, a national 'war memorial and museum' should be erected in Canberra, and this was approved. The memorial was to have a roll of honour listing the names of AIF soldiers killed in the war. To obtain more information about each of the dead, a short questionnaire was sent to next of kin, and, in 1922, Constance Waltham received one to complete for her son.

The questionnaire required a respondent to provide information that many could not have known, including the place where the soldier had been killed, and other military details. For example, Ernest Dunbar's father, Charles Dunbar in Scone, could not provide some details about his son Randolph, who had been killed at Fromelles in 1916. No one had ever told him the circumstances of his son's death. Next to the item

The main AIF cemetery at Pozieres, showing the large memorial
to 8th Battalion men killed in the months of July to September
1916. *(AWM)*

'Place where killed or wounded', Charles Dunbar wrote, 'In France
— all I know'. The only way that the next of kin could complete the
questionnaire thoroughly was to consult someone who had seen what
had happened, and evidently Constance Waltham found that witness in
Harold Glading.

We do not know exactly when Harold and Constance came into
contact, or how Harold provided details about her son's army career
and his death at Pozieres. It is clear that Harold was a loyal friend to
Richard, and that he protected Constance from upsetting truths about
him. He gave only information that she might like to know, and this was
recorded for posterity on the questionnaire she filled in. Next to the item
'Place where killed or wounded', she wrote with precision, 'Martinpuich
nr Pozieres'. In the section 'Any other biographical details likely to be of
interest to the Historian of the AIF, or of his regiment', Constance wrote
what she had been told by Harold Glading:

Left W.A. as Corporal on 9/6/15 in 28th Battalion. From Egypt returned as Corporal on board troopship with wounded soldiers to Victoria. At own request transferred to 8th Batt. Killed in night raid. Struck in forehead by shell while assisting to carry Lt. Dobb [sic] (wounded) to safety. Entered firing line 1 June 1916. Lt. Dobb died of wounds, while prisoner.

To the question that asked for the names and addresses of any other persons who might provide further information, Constance wrote:

Harold E. Glading, late of A.I.F.
'Gleneyre' [sic], Bronte St., Waverley, Sydney, NSW.

We know it is true that Richard was killed at Pozieres while attempting to recover wounded men after the failed night attacks of 18 August 1916. It is not possible, however, to verify a detail: was he attempting to carry Lieutenant William Doolan, or Second Lieutenant Reginald Dabb, or somebody else from the battlefield that night? The War Diaries of the 8th Battalion and 2nd Brigade provide no corroborating information, nor do the Red Cross files for the three men. In an 8th Battalion history published in 1997, no connection is made between Richard's death and the attempted rescue of Dabb, although descriptions of their fates appear in consecutive sentences.

In 1936, when the 20th anniversary of Richard's death was approaching, Constance sent a letter to the army and provided more of her version of his army career. We cannot know if she was aware that this was the story that Harold and Richard had invented to conceal why they returned on the *Wiltshire*.

... after being in Egypt for a time (1915), left Egypt as a corporal of a guard of 12 men on board a troop ship conveying wounded men from Gallipoli to Victoria. My son made an intimate friendship with one of the wounded men, H. E. Glading. He was granted permission in Melbourne to change his unit and left with H. E. Glading for Egypt in the 8th Battalion.

Constance believed that her son's war service had been exemplary and that he had been killed in heroic circumstances. She could be deservedly proud, and live her remaining years knowing he gave his life while attempting a battlefield rescue. In December 1943, she died at Subiaco in Perth. Constance was 92, and was survived by a large extended family, including ten grandchildren and seven great-grandchildren.

Harold Glading's decision to pretend he had been at Gallipoli appears to have been made soon after he was admitted to Abbassia in August 1915. What happened in Cairo must have seemed so shameful that it would need to be concealed for the rest of his life. His catching syphilis was terrible enough by itself, but it had also stopped him from going to Gallipoli, meaning he hadn't even been fighting for his side when his brother Walter was mortally wounded at Lone Pine.

Almost 20 years had passed after Harold's return from the war when he finally married. He was 49, and his bride was 34; they married in 1938 at Campsie Congregational Church in Sydney. He had first met Alice Felecia L'Homme in Sydney in 1926, when she was just 22, and it appears their relationship resumed in the 1930s after Alice, still single, was transferred to Marcus Clark's department store in Newcastle, not far from Muswellbrook. Alice had been born in 1904, at Milton, on the south coast of New South Wales, near Ulladulla, where her father, Alphonse L'Homme, was a watchmaker. An immigrant from France, he had married a local, Mary Knapp, in Milton in 1899.

Soon after Harold and Alice became married, they started a new life at Belmont, a holiday resort on Lake Macquarie, north of Sydney, where they opened a small mixed business. But not long after she started living with Harold, Alice became aware that he was frequently ill. His deafness was noticeable, and his right arm, which had been wounded by shrapnel at Ypres often caused him pain. By 1940, Harold's nosebleeds, vomiting, and headaches so alarmed her that she insisted he have a full medical check. To her surprise, this revealed he had serious heart diseases, the kidney disease chronic nephritis, and diabetes. The doctor decided that Harold's poor condition at such a young age must have been related to his war service. He recommended that Harold apply for repatriation benefits to cover the costs of medical care. Again to Alice's surprise, Harold refused to do this — because, he said, of his 'pride'.

They struggled on at Belmont with the mixed business, their marriage produced no children, and Harold's health became progressively worse. By the 1950s, he was virtually an invalid, so, in 1956, they sold up and moved to Ulladulla, to live at a house called 'Stray Leaves' in St Vincent Street. In August 1958, at the age of 69, Harold died at Milton-Ulladulla hospital as a result of coronary and artery diseases, and diabetes. He had lived his last years bedridden, and Alice had spent almost all their married years devoted to his care.

In 1963, she made a claim to the Repatriation Commission for a war widow's pension, believing the diseases that killed Harold were caused by his war service. However, to satisfy the commission's stringent requirements, Alice needed to produce irrefutable evidence. She was amazed to discover that, despite her providing what she thought was clear proof, her application was rejected. She was told that, in all the years since Harold's discharge from the army, he had never applied for the benefits due to someone who was suffering war-related illness, and that the diseases he had died of were caused by old age. For the next six years, Alice exhausted every avenue of appeal to have the decision reversed. During this process, and without Alice knowing, the Repatriation Commission requested the records for Harold covering his treatment in 1915 for an unstated disease. For reasons unknown, they were never provided; perhaps they were lost. The records contained notes made by Captain Plant at Abbassia and by Captain Alsop on the *Wiltshire* describing the toxic treatment given to Harold, and the fact that it was for syphilis.

Nine years after Harold's death, an event occurred that caused one of his secrets to be revealed to Alice — and she could not believe it. On

25 April 1965, Australia commemorated the 50th anniversary of the Gallipoli landing, and many large ceremonies were held. In 1967, the prime minister, Harold Holt, announced that a special commemorative medallion would be issued to ex-soldiers who were at Gallipoli, or to the families of those who had died. Alice wrote from Ulladulla to the army department, requesting a medallion on behalf of her late husband. In her letter, she provided, as proof of his Gallipoli status, a brief summary of what Harold had told her:

Corporal Harold Ernest Glading.
No. 1372 19th Battalion
No. 3975 25th Machine Gun Coy.
Enlisted 14/4/1915 Embarked 25/6/1915
Served at Gallipoli & France

From this, we learn that Harold had told Alice he was at Gallipoli, and that he had been a member of the 19th Battalion. She could not know he was in the battalion for just a few months; had he not gone to Abbassia, it would have taken him to Gallipoli. Inexplicably, not included in Alice's summary was any mention of his membership of the 8th Battalion, which Harold joined in Melbourne after leaving Langwarrin; he was with it for two years, and at Pozieres and Ypres. Why had he not mentioned this to Alice?

She received a reply informing her that, according to the records, her late husband had not been at Gallipoli, and that, consequently, her request for the medallion was denied. Alice was incredulous. She wrote again, challenging the decision, and started a back-and-forth correspondence with the army department. She offered a 'historical extract', which purportedly proved that Harold had been at Gallipoli, and said that she possessed Harold's 'Gallipoli medal' — but what she described was his 1914–15 Star.

Her letters created a quandary for the army: this was a sensitive matter, and a truthful explanation could be upsetting to an elderly widow. Eventually, a colonel prepared a detailed internal report showing why it was impossible for former Lance Corporal Glading to have served at Gallipoli. This rebutted the 'proof' that Alice supplied, and included minute calculations of the exact timings of Harold's arrival in Cairo, his infection, and his departure from Egypt. The truth was contained in one sentence:

> It would be too much to expect a soldier whose unit went to Gallipoli to explain that he did not go because he was hospitalised with VD.

The report concluded that, 'In view of the official evidence, we cannot but again reject the widow's application.' Despite this, we know that Alice still firmly believed it was all a mistake, and that everything Harold had told her was true. We do not know if she ever learned anything more by the time she died at Ulladulla.

Richard Waltham and Harold Glading were not the only men who were sent from Egypt to Australia in 1915 on the *Wiltshire* and later used excuses to conceal the real reason for the trip. There were plenty of other fellows who later pretended they had been guards on the ship, or had been at Gallipoli when they were not. Some also pretended that their 1914–15 Star was a 'Gallipoli medal'. There were other relatives of *Wiltshire* men who also applied for a Gallipoli medallion on behalf of their man, and who were surprised to discover his secret.

CHAPTER EIGHT

Albert Crozier and Michael Willis

just a silly streak — he was young at the time

Albert Crozier was born in Sydney, the youngest child of Alice and Robert Crozier, who was a horse-cab proprietor. The family lived close to the city at Forest Lodge, where Bert was raised with his brothers, Will and Reg, and sisters, Myra and Elsie. The family was not well off, but Alice and Robert Crozier were caring parents who ensured that their children were properly educated to read, write, and do arithmetic at a commendably high standard. Each of the boys started working quite young — Will in the printing trade, and Reg and Bert in the leather-footwear industry. When the war began in 1914, Bert had risen in the shoe factory to be a 'bootclicker', an expert at cutting as many sets of boot and shoe uppers as possible from a sheet of leather, one of the most skilled and highly paid jobs in the industry.

When he first volunteered for the AIF at the Liverpool camp in December 1914, Bert was 21, and the first of the Crozier sons to try to enlist. He was a wiry fellow but short, and this caused a problem. The minimum height for joining the AIF at the time was five feet six inches, but Bert measured five feet four-and-a-half. In April 1915, he tried again, and, although nothing had changed, he was accepted. In his clear, strong handwriting, he wrote on the attestation paper that his next of kin was his mother, Alice, and that he had never previously served in the King's army. He was a typical new recruit. He took the oath and was drafted to join the 5th Reinforcements for the 1st Battalion, which was in Egypt, on the verge of leaving for Gallipoli. Two months later, Bert departed from Sydney on the *Ceramic*.

After arriving in Egypt late in July, Bert soon became swept up in the excitement and drinking that accompanied going into Cairo on leave. He became infected with syphilis, and, before long, was out of the 1st Battalion and into Abbassia. Here he became acquainted — for the first time, but not the last — with Wassermann tests, injections of Arsenobenzol, and the daubing of mercury on his syphilitic lesions. When this treatment had little effect, he became another of the unlucky men chosen by Colonel Brady Nash to be sent back to Australia on the *Wiltshire*. It is apparent in hindsight that Bert's troubles in Cairo in 1915 were caused by a very casual attitude to life; as we shall see, there would be many more boozy nights and bad decisions.

By the time of his being sent home, Bert's brothers were also in the AIF. Reg enlisted about a week after Bert had, and placed in a reinforcement draft for the 1st Australian General Hospital in Cairo. Will enlisted a few months later, and was meant to be going to Gallipoli to join the 3rd Battalion. In October 1915, Reg departed from Sydney, followed a month later by Will. By the time his older brothers left Australia, Bert was already back, and in Langwarrin, and itching to get out.

After five weeks, he was discharged as fit for duty, with orders to go to Broadmeadows to join a new unit. However, somewhere between the isolation hospital to the south of Melbourne and the Broadmeadows camp to the north, he disappeared. Many men who left Langwarrin for Broadmeadows did not complete the trip: with pay restored, they seem to have become irretrievably distracted by the pleasures of Melbourne town in between. Very soon, Bert was posted as a deserter, and a warrant was issued.

About four months later, a short, wiry, blue-eyed young man presented himself at an AIF recruiting place in Melbourne and volunteered for enlistment. He said he was Michael Willis, aged 22 and working as a carter. From whom did Bert borrow this new identity? We know there were two men in the AIF called Michael Willis, but neither could ever have been in Bert's proximity, and it is unlikely that he borrowed his new names from them.

In June 1915, the minimum height for AIF recruits was lowered to five feet two inches. At his enlistment as 'Michael Willis' in March 1916, Bert was found to be five feet three inches tall — even shorter than he had been a year earlier at Liverpool — so he could now be accepted without any fuss. In his same strong handwriting, he filled out a second attestation form, and once again declared he had never previously served in the King's military forces and that everything he wrote was true. His attestation was duly sworn, witnessed, and certified by the recruiters, and he was accepted into the AIF for the 38th Battalion.

When Bert had originally attested, he had written that his mother, Alice, was his next of kin. For his attestation as 'Michael Willis', he nominated his sister Myra Pinson. We do not know if Myra knew at the time that he had done this, although she certainly knew later. We also do not know how Bert explained his re-appearance in Australia, or his need to re-enlist in the AIF using false names. Myra remained Bert's next of kin for the rest of the war — although, as we shall see, his mother also became involved in dealing with the army on his behalf.

Following his successful re-enlistment, Bert was sent to Broad-meadows, where he belatedly completed the journey from Langwarrin that had begun four months before. From Broadmeadows, he was meant to go to Bendigo to join the 38th Battalion, which had just been formed there. However, an outbreak of meningitis in the Bendigo camp caused the unit to transfer to Melbourne, where it was reconstructed using fresh recruits, like 'Michael Willis'. The battalion's main body departed from Port Melbourne in June 1916, but Bert was in the 2nd Reinforcements, and did not leave until August, on the *Orontes*.

When the reinforcements arrived in England, they were sent, as usual, to a training camp; afterwards, they went to the Salisbury Plain and joined the 38th Battalion. In November 1916, when all preparations

Albert Crozier in mid-1916 at the Broadmeadows camp. At the
time, Bert was serving as 'Michael Willis', but he gave his correct
name to the photographer. *(AWM)*

had been completed, the battalion left from Southampton for the port of Le Havre, in France. Soon they were living in billets at Strezeele near Armentieres, which was immediately behind the Western Front. Here they could hear the dull booming of artillery, and at night could see the glow from explosions illuminating the sky.

Bert's casual attitude got him into much trouble. Even before arriving in England, he was punished at sea for 'breaking ship', which meant that, when the *Orontes* was in a foreign port, he had gone ashore without permission. Now in France, 'Michael Willis' received more punishments for absence without leave, including a very severe one by a court-martial.

In France, Bert was exposed to the heavy-drinking culture of the AIF, and he evidently became very attracted to alcohol. Although army regulations existed to control drinking and drunkenness, they were inconsistently enforced by officers and NCOs, many of whom were drinkers themselves. The Western Front was awash with all kinds of booze, and *estaminets* and temporary bars followed the troops around. If men wanted to, just before battles, they could bolster their courage from big jars of British navy SRD rum.[20] When they were away from the fighting, or on leave in London or Paris, binge-drinking sessions were a popular form of entertainment. A whole new AIF jocular language of drinking was invented to describe alcohol, drunkenness, and drinking situations.[21] Later, diggers who survived brought this language, and their drinking and other addictions, home to Australia.

Smoking tobacco was also enormously popular with Australian soldiers, and English cigarettes — Woodbines, Senior Service, and Players — were supplied in their millions to the imperial forces. The epidemic of wartime smoking occurred long before the health risks were known: smoking was so normal, it was possible for brands to be given the seal of approval of King George V, and for Australian branches of the British Medical Association to start tobacco funds 'for the comfort which our Australian boys at the front may derive from a smoke'.[22]

In June 1917, at Messines in Belgium, Bert received a severe gunshot wound when a bullet passed through the axillary fold where his arm joined the shoulder. This wound had several consequences for him. First, he was sent to England for long medical treatment at a hospital at Birmingham. His sister Myra Pinson, in Australia, the next of kin of 'Michael Willis', was duly informed by the army that this had happened. Second, while recuperating in England, Bert apparently forgot all about his nasty episode with syphilis in Egypt two years before. Evidently, he was also not bothering to use Blue Light kits: he was admitted to Bulford with syphilis and gonorrhoea. He told a doctor he had been infected by an 'amateur' prostitute in Edinburgh a month before, which meant that the infections were very advanced. He had to go through another long course of Wassermann tests and injections of Arsenobenzol and mercury for the syphilis, and urethral irrigations of silver for the gonorrhoea.

A third consequence of Bert's wound was that, in June 1917, a week or so after the attack at Messines, a letter was sent to Myra by the 38th Battalion's Church of England chaplain, the Reverend Captain Henry Hayden. The letter began, 'You will have received the sad news of your brother's death long before this note reaches you', and went on to describe how 'Private Michael Willis died like so many of his comrades a brave and gallant gentleman ... a noble death for God, King and Country.' Myra had been in constant contact with Bert, and so, although greatly perturbed when this letter reached her, she doubted her brother was dead. She wrote to army headquarters in Melbourne to question Chaplain Hayden's letter, thereby provoking immediate corrective action. A 'please explain' memo was sent to AIF headquarters in London, and internal correspondence about this alarming error continued for months until early 1918, when the mistake was corrected. Eventually, an apology was sent to Myra; in it, the chaplain was blamed. In fact, it was not the chaplain's fault at all, but that of the officer who had told him that 'Michael Willis' was dead rather than wounded.

All the attention drawn to 'Michael Willis' by Bert being wounded, and the killed-in-action mix-up as well, so worried the Croziers in Sydney that they decided to inform the authorities who he really was.

Without revealing his period of service in 1915, Bert's mother, Alice Crozier, wrote a letter to the army to say that her son

> Albert Edward Crozier enlisted under the name Michael Willis and left Australia with the 38th Battalion ... and was wounded last year ... at Messines ... and I would be very grateful if you would see he is placed on the records in his proper name it is at his request also there was no serious reason for him to do this for he was never in trouble in his life not before a police court and up to the time of enlisting never was away from home for one night. Just a silly streak he was young at the time.

The army replied by informing her that when 'Michael Willis' had enlisted, he had declared that his parents were dead. Alice was asked to make a statutory declaration averring that she was Albert's mother. This was done, witnessed by a police magistrate, and sent with an accompanying note asking that Bert 'not be penalised (my three only sons are doing their duty for their country abroad)'. Then began a long, slow process within the army bureaucracy to verify Mrs Crozier's claim. Until that happened, Albert would need to keep serving as 'Michael'.

While this was occurring in Australia, Bert was sent from England to rejoin his battalion in France in early 1918. Soon, he was in trouble again, punished for 'leaving the ranks when ordered not to do so'. During the German spring offensive, the 38th Battalion fought a series of battles in the Somme Valley, and Bert was involved. Then, a few months later, he was wounded for a second time. The battalion was moving under enemy fire into trench lines at Vaire Wood when Bert was hit by a bullet in his right fore-arm. He was taken to an Australian hospital at Rouen, and, during his long stay there, the 38th Battalion advanced to the Hindenburg Line, far to the east.

When Bert rejoined the battalion, final preparations were underway for what was hoped would be the capture of a section of the Hindenburg Line along the Saint-Quentin Canal. The attack was launched at dawn at the end of September 1918, with the diggers advancing into an outlying

An entrance to a Saint-Quentin Canal tunnel, part of the
Hindenburg Line of defences captured on 29 September 1918.
(AWM)

maze of desperately defended German trenches. Bert was hit by a bullet
again, this time deep in his right thigh. The wound was bad — the worst
of the three he received — and he was taken straight to a field hospital,
and then back to England to a hospital in Manchester. He had been shot
during the last days of the 38th Battalion's final attack of the war. By
October 1918, the Hindenburg defences had been breached, and the
German army had begun its final retreat. The following month, the war
ended.

Bert took opportunities during his convalescence in Manchester to 'do
a bunk', and, on one occasion, was absent from the hospital for five days.
Then, after he was sent to the AIF's clearing hospital at Hurdcott, he was
punished again, this time for 'neglecting' to obey orders and 'neglecting'
to identify himself. Bert was also sent to AIF headquarters in London
to sign a declaration that enabled his correct identity to be restored. In
December 1918, now Albert Crozier once more, he was invalided home

to Sydney because of the wound in his thigh.

Since 1916, the army had been investigating men who had returned to Australia in 1915 on the *Wiltshire* but had deserted after being sent from Langwarrin to Broadmeadows. One of these was Private Albert Crozier, whose whereabouts was unknown. The army was unaware of the connection between that soldier and Private 'Michael Willis' in France, and Mrs Crozier had not helped them make it. In early 1919, army headquarters in Melbourne finally connected the two, and their records were united and corrected. For reasons unknown, nothing was done about Bert's desertion in 1915. In Sydney in April 1919, he was given a good discharge certificate: 'medically unfit, disability — gunshot wound right leg'. This was written for his correct identity, and, later, he received the three imperial service medals, including the 1914–15 Star.

Bert's older brothers, Will and Reg, had also fought in France, and were also repatriated in early 1919. In July 1916, Will had been captured at Fromelles, and he had spent the rest of the war as a POW in Germany. Reg had been twice wounded by shrapnel, and had been in hospital in England when the war ended. So, with all Crozier brothers safely in Sydney by Easter 1919, we can be sure there were hearty Crozier-family celebrations, and the women of the family, including Reg's wife, Pearl, must have been relieved and proud to have their men back. The ugly scars of Bert's three bullet wounds and Reg's shrapnel wounds must have provoked interest and awe.

The family might have noticed, however, that Bert was now a heavy drinker, that drinking was an important part of his daily routine, and that there seemed to be no end to it. Perhaps they hoped that, after getting over the war and settling down, Bert's drinking might stop. He could resume his good place in the footwear industry, find a nice young woman to marry, acquire a new home, or even a war-service farm, and start a family. Maybe he had a yearning, like so many other returned men of his age, for the respectable life of a family man. With enormous encouragement from their communities, and with uplifting inducements from the government, thousands upon thousands of ex-AIF men put the

Pay night in an Estaminet

During 1917, Ernest Dunbar made a number of drawings of Western Front drinking scenes. This one is *Pay Night in an Estaminet*, made with ink, pencil, and wash on paper. *(AWM)*

war behind them and followed that path.

There were also thousands of other returned men for whom post-war life would not be so fulfilling. They were the fellows whose war experiences were so unnerving that they could never enjoy normal life again. They had survived the horrors, but now carried permanent reminders in their physical disfigurements and mental torments. Bert Crozier would never make the healthy adjustments needed to succeed as a civilian, nor find release from his addiction to alcohol. What seems to be evident is that Bert used alcohol to abate his pain, or perhaps pretended to himself that he was doing so. This might have been because of the ballistic traumas he still suffered from the gunshot wounds, or because of the long-term effects of the toxic treatments he had for VD, but none of that is clear.

Slowly but surely, he made the long descent to being unemployable and homeless, and stealing to get clothes to wear and money to live on. Within a decade of his discharge from the army, Bert was an outcast, living rough at the fringes of society, and sometimes in prison. He would never marry, and would never know the particular satisfaction that having a family could give. In the 1920s and 1930s, he drifted restlessly between the cities of Sydney and Melbourne, and the towns of Goulburn, Yass, Canberra, and Queanbeyan. He became a habitual petty criminal, and was frequently arrested and brought before magistrates in many cities and towns. To maintain a semblance of respectability in the police courts, he usually described himself as a 'bootclicker', but it had been years since Bert had clicked any leather uppers for shoes and boots.

Through the years of the Great Depression, he was arrested for stealing, drunkenness, abusive language, 'loitering with intent to commit a felony', and breaking and entering, and was often in prison. His police record was so depressing that he decided it was time for another identity change. Back in Sydney in 1936, he became 'George Gordon', and was then repeatedly arrested under that identity as well. As 'George Gordon', Bert was given three months' imprisonment with hard labour for stealing from a department store. After his release, he stole a handbag from Woolworths and received six months, and then another six months for stealing pairs of socks. Bert was a regular at Parramatta Gaol, and also at the Concord Repatriation Hospital — not that it did him much good.

The magistrates who knew him, and had to make decisions about him, were sometimes surprised by his thinking ability. On one memorable occasion, he helped the Queanbeyan police court clarify a point of law, by pleading not guilty to a charge of drinking intoxicating liquor. At an earlier criminal hearing at the court, Bert had promised to refrain from liquor. Soon after, he had been found by police drinking methylated spirits at the showground in Yass. The 'metho' Bert was drinking was probably obtained from a hardware shop, and normally sold as a fuel. Because of its toxicity, it was not meant for human consumption, but was frequently drunk as a cheap alternative by people who could not afford to buy liquor, and by those who were banned from buying or drinking it.

In April 1939, Bert was brought before the Queanbeyan court to explain himself. He argued that he had not broken his promise, because methylated spirits was not intoxicating liquor. The two justices of the peace hearing the case consulted with the police prosecutor, and then made a surprising decision. They were unsure if methylated spirits was classed as intoxicating liquor under the *Liquor Act*, because it could be bought at shops that did not require a liquor licence for its sale. The bench found the charge disproved, and Bert was discharged. This victory for metho drinkers was broadcast to the world the following day by the newspapers in Sydney. But the following month, the incorrigible Bert was before the Queanbeyan court yet again, this time for drunkenness and using insulting words, and on three charges of stealing.

While he was locked up at Queanbeyan police station, a drifter mate called Michael Grady stopped by to see Bert — and stole a cheque from the police-station counter. Both Grady and Bert were taken to court, where Grady was charged with stealing the cheque, and both with having stolen a towel and a shirt from the Tourist Hotel. The police magistrate sentenced Grady to nine months' imprisonment, and Bert to six months'. In sentencing Bert, the magistrate addressed him to say he was 'evidently a man of intelligence, who could shape his life in the right direction if he so desired'.

In March 1940, this returned soldier was found on the main street in Newcastle, asking for money from passers-by. Bert was arrested, and a stipendiary magistrate sentenced him to 14 days of imprisonment with hard labour for 'begging for alms'.

In 1939, Australia had entered the Second World War. Two years later, Bert decided to enlist in the Second AIF. From 1940, the age limit for AIF recruits had been raised to 40, but Bert was 47, so he would need to 'make an adjustment'. In March 1941, at Paddington in Sydney, he presented himself to join up. For this new attestation, he provided the name of his widowed sister Elsie Leibick as his next of kin, and gave her address in Bondi as his own. Following his medical examination, when the bullet-wound scars in his shoulder, fore-arm, and calf were noted, he was classified as fit for military duties 'Class 1 (Special)'. The 'special' annotation meant that Bert's military service in the First World War was sympathetically recognised, and also that his age had been lowered to 45, the cut-off for 'specials'. In reality, he was being recruited as a labourer, a kitchen orderly or some other low-skilled occupation needed at the time by the army.

In April 1941, Bert was drafted for service in the Northern Territory, and, while waiting in Sydney for this adventure to begin, he continued his relentless drinking. Two days after enlisting, he went absent without leave, and was fined; then he did it twice again, and was also punished for drunkenness. In May 1941, Bert was once more found drunk, and, at this point, the army decided he was an alcoholic. His enlistment only came to an end, however, when it was discovered that Bert had concealed his criminal past. It was for this reason that he was discharged. His third period of service in the Australian army had lasted just over two months.

Following his failed enlistment, Bert continued his restless wandering, drinking, and petty crime. In 1947, he was caught taking ten bottles of wine from a hotel; in a police court, he told the stipendiary magistrate that it was his 54th birthday, and that the wine was for 'a bit of jollification'.

In the winter of 1953, he was back in Goulburn, where he stole a pair of pyjamas from a shop and was caught by police. In court again, he told the magistrate that he was drunk at the time; he was convicted of theft and fined £10. The following summer, when Bert was 60, he was in Goulburn again, and this time was arrested and charged with vagrancy. He pleaded guilty; a long list of his previous convictions was read, and he was sentenced to two months with hard labour.

By 1954, nearly all of Bert's relatives were dead. His mother, Alice, had died in Sydney in 1939, and his brother Reg had died there in 1943. In 1950, Reg's widow, Pearl, had died, and, that same year, Bert's sister Elsie had died. In 1951, his unmarried brother Will passed away, and, in 1954, his brother-in-law Les Pinson also died. Now, the only ones left were Bert, the rootless alcoholic, and his respectable widowed sister Myra Pinson, who lived on the North Shore, and who had helped and protected him so much during his AIF years. Bert had outlasted almost all of his siblings, despite his hard life.

In August 1954, he was 61 and living in inner Sydney, and it was there that events conspired against him to bring his remarkable life to its sorry conclusion. At the time, he had been living for six weeks in a tenement house at 16 Albion Street in Surry Hills, a place where alcoholics and drifters found cheap rooms, not far from the trams and traffic in Elizabeth Street. In 1954, this suburb was a neglected slum of old warehouses, hotels, and dilapidated houses. There were many pubs in the area, including the old London Hotel on the corner of Albion and Elizabeth Streets, and no doubt Bert was known at many of them. By this time, his body had suffered about 40 years of heavy drinking, and it is very likely he had started losing his mind.

On the cool, clear night of Monday 16 August, just before nine o'clock, Bert, very drunk, was unsteadily making his way along the footpath outside the London Hotel. He was not far from his new home, but moving away from it — a small figure shuffling along in a shabby, brown army greatcoat. Further to the north, on Elizabeth Street, a Holden taxi driven by Roy Negus was slowly approaching. At the very moment that Negus passed the Albion Street corner, Bert suddenly veered onto the roadway, into the path of the cab. Later, Negus told police, 'I don't know where he came from. I did not see him till I had almost struck him.' Negus slammed on the brakes and skidded to a halt, but too late. Bert was hit by the centre of the cab's grille, and his head was slammed into the bonnet.

He was thrown by the impact onto the roadway, unconscious and terribly injured. The police arrived, an ambulance was called, and Bert was taken to Sydney Hospital, not far away, where resuscitation was attempted. It was noted by emergency staff that he smelt strongly of alcohol. Bert died at six o'clock the following morning. His unidentified body was taken to the city morgue, where it was inspected by a forensic examiner, who recorded that the cause of death was multiple serious fractures and lacerations.

That morning, there was a problem identifying Bert. The police made inquiries in Albion Street, and their investigations led them to the shabby boarding house at number 16, where they spoke to the manager, Edwin Holland. That afternoon, Holland identified the body as Albert Edward

A police photograph of the taxi driven by Roy Negus on the night of
16 August 1954. The buckling of the bonnet was made by the
impact with Bert Crozier. *(State Records Authority of NSW)*

Crozier, lately one of his tenants. Separately, the police had also taken the
fingerprints of the dead man and, from Bert's criminal records, were able
to make a corroborating identification. A few days later, his remains were
taken to the Rookwood Crematorium and, after the simplest of funeral
services, cremated. By coincidence, the traffic collision that mortally
wounded Bert in 1954 had happened just a few miles from where he had
been raised 60 years before, in the Crozier home at Forest Lodge.

It was still not known why Bert had stepped into the path of the taxi,
although it was thought that alcohol might have played a big part. After
his death at the hospital, blood and urine samples were taken from his
body and sent to the chemical laboratory of the department of health, and
analysis showed that Bert had a very high concentration of alcohol. The
following month, after two hearings at the Coroner's Court, the coroner
decided there was no evidence whatsoever of criminal negligence by the

cab driver. The coroner found that Bert had been very drunk when he collided with the taxi, and that he had died from injuries accidentally received.

Of the many military and civil court proceedings involving Bert during the 40 or so years before 1954, the coroner's hearing was the only one where he was not present to explain his actions. The evidence against him was that Bert Crozier was a drunk and a drifter, with a criminal record, and that he had, in effect, caused his own death. There was no one in court to explain how Bert had been seriously damaged by wounds and diseases in a terrible war, or that what he had done on Elizabeth Street was the end-stage of a long tragedy.

CHAPTER NINE

Graham Butler and John Cumpston

Australia receives a shock

During the First World War, there was considerable public discussion in Australia about the extent of venereal disease in the AIF. This had begun after Charles Bean's article appeared in newspapers in January 1915, and continued with reports about infected men arriving at Port Melbourne from Egypt. Speculation was again aroused by news of the breakouts at Langwarrin, and the isolation camp became well known. Public discussion, however, was ill-informed: the defence minister and the army rarely provided relevant information, and none about the extent of the problem. On the rare occasions that announcements had to be made, an impression was given that venereal disease in the AIF was insignificant and under control.

Much of the wartime public discussion was led by morals crusaders — usually clergymen and people dedicated to the prohibition of alcohol, including its prohibition in the AIF. That AIF soldiers often drank to excess was well known, and the purported link between drunkenness and venereal diseases in soldiers was highlighted by prohibitionists. Without any official statistics, however, discussions about the AIF's venereal-disease problem had to be based on invented estimates. The estimates were often exaggerated, sometimes wildly so, and seemingly designed to provoke outrage.

The Reverend Robert Hammond, during the 1930s, at one of the
orphanages he established in Sydney. *(SLNSW)*

There were at least three kinds of Australians who were likely to be
outraged when these 'statistics' were announced. The first comprised
those who followed the morals crusaders, and who firmly believed that
in the AIF there was a hidden 'Red Plague', their term for VD. The second
kind was Australians who believed that the AIF was glorious and could
do no wrong; they upheld a heroic image of the Australian soldier, and
would react with indignation if the legend was challenged. The third
kind, allied with the second, was members of the Returned Soldiers and
Sailors Imperial League of Australia, who usually reacted strongly to
anything they construed as a slur on themselves.

The Reverend Robert Hammond of the Anglican Church was a well-
known and respected Australian churchman who, in 1916, became
president of the Australasian Temperance Society. In 1918, he claimed
that 10,000 AIF men infected with venereal disease had been sent back

The Australian morals crusader Gifford Gordon, in Washington,
DC, during the 1920s campaign to prohibit the sale of liquor in the
US. *(LoC)*

to Australia from abroad — a figure that was repeated by other morals
campaigners. The Reverend Hammond was wrong, and his claim was
questioned. Nevertheless, it could not be corrected, because, at the time,
no one, apart from the army, knew how many infected men had actually
been sent back. Where did Hammond's figure come from? He might

have heard about the 10,000 men treated for VD in Egypt in 1915 and 1916, and perhaps had assumed they were all returned to Australia.

Among the clergymen repeating Hammond's claim was the Reverend George Brodie, a leader of the Temperance Committee of the Presbyterian Assembly of Victoria. In 1918, Brodie claimed in a submission to the Victorian government that '10,000 men had to be sent back to Australia before reaching the firing lines because of venereal disease'. Another advocate for temperance, Mr A. J. Dalgleish of the Victorian Alliance, visited country towns in Victoria in 1917 making stirring speeches to prove that consumption of alcohol was hindering Australia's war effort. He regularly claimed that 4,000 infected men were being sent to Langwarrin every year, and 'that drink is mainly responsible for that'.

At about this time, another temperance crusader in Melbourne, Mr Gifford Gordon, a Church of Christ pastor, launched a social movement he called 'Strength of Empire'. This demanded the prohibition by Australian governments of the sale and consumption of alcohol during the war; and for governments to deal firmly with 'the question of social purity and the prevalence and cure of venereal disease'. Gordon travelled around Australia giving lectures and establishing new Strength of Empire branches. Towards the end of 1918, he began making the claim, widely reported, that '100,000' AIF men had been infected with venereal disease. In March 1919, he arrived in Western Australia, where he faced a hostile reception from returned soldiers. During a Strength of Empire meeting at York, a town east of Perth, the following exchange occurred:

Questioner: Did you state in Perth that one-third of the Australian soldiers suffered from venereal disease?

Gifford Gordon: I made a statement, but I do not know whether the figures are correct.

Questioner: Are you prepared to apologise and withdraw unreservedly your false and wicked accusation made against the men who defended your liberty?

Gordon was made to withdraw his claim on the spot, and later published an apology. Shortly after, the general secretary of Strength of Empire, Thomas Wilson, discovered the figure of 100,000 quoted in an article in the 22 March 1919 edition of *The Medical Journal of Australia*. This contained comments that had been made in Paris in 1918 by Lieutenant Colonel Graham Butler of the AAMC. At the conference on venereal disease held by the Allies, Butler revealed that, during a period of six months in 1917 to 1918, about 100,000 men had reported for prophylactic treatment for VD at AIF depots in the United Kingdom (and also that, in the same period, 75,000 Blue Light kits had been issued, and 50,000 condoms had been purchased by soldiers). To Butler and his AAMC colleagues, prophylactic treatment was the early precautionary use of Calomel ointment and Nargol jelly at a Blue Light depot soon after a soldier might have been exposed to infection. Thomas Wilson did not know that; he assumed it meant the treatment of actual infections. When he used the information to vindicate what Gordon had said, he came under crude attack from returned soldiers for his 'blockheaded' comments. Yet, despite these protests, the revelation that 100,000 prophylactic treatments, whatever they were, had occurred in the AIF in just six months had the effect of stimulating public speculation, and this was reported in newspapers.

In 1923, Lieutenant Colonel Butler agreed to accept the position of official historian of Australian army medical services during the war, and to collaborate with Charles Bean on the war-history project. Butler had been a medical officer with the AIF at Gallipoli and in France, and in 1918 had been sent to AIF headquarters in London to assemble the medical records of the war. This included gathering information and collating statistics about venereal disease, some of which he presented at the Paris conference. He later expanded this work in Canberra, and his elegantly written account of venereal disease in the AIF was published in *Volume III — Special Problems and Services* of the medical history.

Butler told the full story, from 1914 until 1919, and explained the evolution from punishing soldiers who caught VD to the comprehensive

The two official Australian First World War historians,
Graham Butler and Charles Bean, photographed at the Australian
War Memorial in the 1940s. *(AWM)*

scheme for issuing prophylactic kits and using early, abortive, and
hospital treatments. The statistics he included indicated that at least
60,000 men, or 14–15 per cent of an army of nearly 417,000, were treated
for VD infections up to 1919.[23] In another volume, Butler published
figures showing that venereal disease was prominent among all causes

for temporary withdrawal of soldiers from the front line. *Volume III* was published in 1943, 25 years after the First World War had ended and when a new world war was underway. Had all this detail been released soon after the First World War, it would surely have caused an outraged reaction by morals crusaders, by upholders of the legend of the heroic digger, and by the RSSILA.

As it happened, some of Butler's venereal-disease statistics were released soon after the war, but not by him or by the army. They were in a bulletin issued in August 1919 by the Australian Quarantine Service. From late 1918, large numbers of Australian troops being repatriated from Europe began arriving at Australian ports. At the time, a large and lethal pandemic of Spanish influenza was abroad in Europe, so there was concern in Australia that returning troops might bring the virus home. The quarantine service was asked to examine the influenza risk and propose ways to prevent its arrival. In the course of the research, it was discovered that returning AIF men might also have other infectious diseases, including VD.

Dr John Cumpston was director of quarantine during the war, and was also a lieutenant colonel in the AAMC and an advisor to the director of medical services. There were a number of regulations he administered that prohibited 'any person suffering from any loathsome or dangerous communicable disease' from entering Australia. Under the *Quarantine Act*, the master of any ship entering an Australian port was required to give written notice of any case of gonorrhoea, syphilis, or chancre on his vessel. Since 1915, quarantine officers had been inspecting troopships arriving in Australia from Egypt and England, and hundreds of crewmen with VD had been detained in quarantine; soldiers with VD sent to Langwarrin were also regarded as being in quarantine there.

In 1919, Dr Cumpston decided to identify all infectious diseases that repatriating AIF soldiers might bring. In the course of this, it was discovered, in information provided by the defence department, that a large number of AIF soldiers had been infected with a venereal disease while abroad. This was so important that Cumpston decided a separate bulletin should be prepared to describe what had happened. Accordingly, in August 1919, the quarantine service published Bulletin Number 17, *Venereal Disease in Australia.*

Included in this was considerable information about the incidence of VD in the AIF during the recent war, including rates of infection for soldiers in Australia and for men who had served overseas. The information was taken from reports and statistics gathered by the Department of Defence since 1914, mostly those compiled by Lieutenant Colonel Butler, and also from material compiled at the isolation hospital at Langwarrin. Since 1916, the staff there had been conducting informal social surveys to try to discover why so many young soldiers became infected, and to discover links, if any, between alcohol consumption and getting VD.

A statistical summary in the bulletin, based only on data collected up to September 1918, showed the size of the problem:

The numbers of men who have suffered from venereal disease after enlistment and during service between August, 1914, and September, 1918, have been —

In Australia	13,038
Abroad	40,950
	53,988

The total of 40,950 does not include the number of venereal disease cases in Egypt after March, 1916. It would be a quite moderate estimate to add 1,000 for these, making the total number of venereal patients 55,000.

The venereal figure of 55,000 represents persons irrespective of the fact that one person may have had more than one attack.

News that 55,000 Australian soldiers had been infected with venereal disease was very soon published in newspapers throughout Australia, and there was uproar. Some articles carelessly stated that 55,000 infected soldiers had returned from abroad and were being discharged from the AIF. Stories appeared under banner headlines such as 'LIBELLING THE RETURNED SOLDIERS', 'SOLDIERS DEFAMED', and 'THE RED PLAGUE AND RETURNING SOLDIERS'. The president of the NSW Returned Soldiers and Sailors League said Dr Cumpston had made 'ridiculous and exaggerated claims'. The NSW minister for health, David Storey, told the *The Sydney Morning Herald* that his state had 'adequate machinery' to prevent the spread of infections from returning soldiers; but he also said:

> Moreover, as one who has always taken the deepest interest in the members of the AIF and their gallant struggle with the German, I take the responsibility of questioning the accuracy of the information which Dr Cumpston has based the statement attributed to him. It appeals to me as slandering our brave men to state that practically one in every six has been contaminated by this dreadful disease.

The newspaper reports and public furore had an unintended consequence for some returned soldiers: suspicion arose in the minds of parents, wives, and fiancées, and prospective in-laws as well, that their man might be concealing something. We know from the records of the *Wiltshire* men that, following the Cumpston bulletin, private letters of enquiry from such relatives were sent to the army. In reply, they were usually informed that 'it is not permissible to furnish any information in regard to a soldier's medical history, all records being treated as confidential documents'. In September 1919, however, a prospective mother-in-law was told the truth about her daughter's fiancée, with a warning that 'this information is not to be divulged to anyone other than members of your own family'. Men who did have a secret wondered if the army could be trusted to keep it, and some sought assurance that it was safe. The replies they received usually advised them that 'due discretion will be exercised in replying to any enquiries about you made by private individuals'.

Then Sir James Barrett entered the debate. He had returned to Melbourne after his four years of service in Egypt, and had recently published, with Percy Deane, his history of the AAMC in Egypt and his long article about wartime VD in *The British Medical Journal*. His unpopular advocacy of prophylaxis in 1915 having been later vindicated with its wholesale adoption by the AIF, he was now regarded as an infallible expert. The Victorian state council of the Returned Soldiers and Sailors League had met in Melbourne to consider a suitable response to Dr Cumpston's bulletin, because the league considered 'that the soldier generally was being misrepresented'. It was decided that Sir James should be asked for his advice in order to 'place the position fairly before the public'. His carefully worded report was released by the league in September 1919.

Sir James wrote that an 'exaggerated view had arisen in the public mind respecting the prevalence of venereal disease among soldiers by reason of statements published by Dr Cumpston'. He wrote that, as a percentage of the 417,000 soldiers mobilised for service in Australia and overseas, 55,000 infected men represented about 13 per cent, and that 'to those who have not examined the venereal disease problem closely, the figure may appear excessive'. He then explained, delicately, that a number of factors needed to be considered:

> During the war a soldier is removed from home influence; he is exposed to temptations hitherto unknown to him. On the other hand, never before in his life has his health been cared for with the same degree of thoroughness. The army is aware of the extent of the infections, and is able to express it in fairly precise terms. In addition, a commander in chief employs every moral agency possible by which the spirits of his men can be maintained, and their good sense encouraged and developed. Every good general appreciates the value in his army of men who are not only valiant, but contented.

Sir James claimed that, because of the extreme care taken by the army, the incidence of VD in the AIF was lower than in the civilian

Sir James Barrett in Sydney in 1930. He is wearing his First World War 'Returned from Active Service' lapel badge. *(Fairfax; NLA)*

population, and he quoted many alarming statistics from Britain, Germany, and the United States to demonstrate this. He concluded with an observation:

> So far as Australia is concerned, there is no doubt whatever, in my mind, that the infection in civil life far exceeds that in the Australian Imperial Force. What has happened, however, is that the public has received a shock. They have hitherto played the part of the ostrich, and refused to believe these estimates, and now they are face to face with statistics compiled with military precision, and from which there is no escape.

In the 1920s, Sir James became an outspoken campaigner for open public discussion about the high incidence of venereal disease in Australia. He again and again returned to the theme of what he called the 'ostrich' or 'hush hush' mentality, which he believed prevented the spreading of venereal infections from being stopped. He became a leader of the Australian Association for Fighting Venereal Disease, helped develop its public-education campaign, and travelled extensively to give lectures and show films and a slide show about human biology, the diseases, and healthy family life. He became an early advocate, against much opposition, for the provision of sex education for adolescent boys and girls, frequently quoting statistics showing that young men and women were most likely to become infected. Always ahead of his time, decades before it occurred, he repeatedly urged the introduction of lessons in human physiology and reproductive biology to high-school curricula.

It was not as if Sir James devoted his post-war years to campaigning about venereal diseases only; his interests were many and varied. He became a president or chairman of a remarkable number of organisations, including the British Medical Association in Australia, the Town and Country Planning Association, the Japan Society, the Royal Empire Society, and the Royal Life Saving Society. He was a conservationist, and advocated protection of Australia's native flora and fauna through his work of developing national parks. In Melbourne, he was heavily involved with classical music, bands, and a number of symphony orchestras. He was also a founder of the Bush Nursing Association, which provided community health-care in rural areas where there were no doctors. Sir James is perhaps best remembered, however, for his long association with the University of Melbourne, which had begun in 1901. Following the death of Sir John Monash in 1931, Barrett succeeded him as vice-chancellor, and, from 1935 until 1939, he was the university's chancellor.

Sir James died in April 1945, aged 83. His funeral was attended by large crowds, and the cortege wound its way from his home in Toorak through the streets of Melbourne and through the university to the Melbourne General Cemetery in Carlton, where he was buried. In obituaries, he was lavishly praised for his extraordinary contributions to medicine and medical education, to the university, and to public life. He was also remembered for 'saving the lives of thousands of soldiers' through his advocacy of preventive measures against venereal disease in the AIF.

And what of the man who had been charged with selecting the men to be sent back, Barrett's AAMC colleague in 1915 in Cairo, Dr John Brady Nash? After his return to Australia in January 1916, Brady Nash resumed his duties as a member of the NSW Legislative Council, and as a director of the Royal Prince Alfred Hospital. In June 1925, after some months of illness, he died, aged 68. He was buried in Sandgate Cemetery, near Newcastle, where for much of his life he had practised medicine as a GP and surgeon. A long obituary in *The Sydney Morning Herald* recalled his life and distinguished public service, including his voluntary membership of the army medical corps in peacetime, and his service as a lieutenant colonel in 1914 and 1915 during the war.

CHAPTER TEN

Major Conder and the End of Langwarrin

*a triumph of science and sympathy
over righteousness*

In September 1916, the last of the men brought to Langwarrin from Egypt a year before on the *Wiltshire* was released as fit for duty and sent to Broadmeadows to be drafted to a new battalion. Most of the men who had arrived with this poor soul had only been in Langwarrin for some weeks or months, but he outstayed all of them. By this time, many of the *Wiltshire* boys were again serving overseas, or were on the way. Richard Waltham and a number of others had been killed at Fromelles or at Pozieres, and others had been wounded. Harold Glading was in France with the 8th Battalion; and Ernest Dunbar, Maurice Buckley, and Bert Crozier, each using an assumed identity, were heading to the fighting.

Also by September 1916, Major Walter Conder had just recently been put in charge and was overseeing Langwarrin's conversion from a penal camp to a hospital. Numerous improvements had already been made, and more were to come. Brigadier General Williams was still commandant of the 3rd Military District, and still giving Conder all the backing he needed to make the changes. They worked closely together to make what Colonel Butler later described as a hospital in which patients in surroundings both mentally and physically attractive could recover from one of nature's cruelest punishments, and where science and sympathy could triumph over righteousness. The effort was to mend and help every man sent there, to send him away a wiser human being, a decent citizen and a better trained soldier than when he entered the camp.

When General Williams retired in 1919, he received considerable praise for the success of Langwarrin. He, however, gave most credit for that to Walter Conder. Later, Williams wrote that he had merely 'supplied the canvas, easel, pigments, palette and brushes' — it was Major Conder who had 'painted the picture'. Williams wrote admiringly of Conder's humane care for 'the poor devils held in bondage' at Langwarrin, and of his giving 'light and leading and achieving a personal triumph over the powers of darkness so great and beneficial I can never sufficiently appraise it'.

Conder's personality and unusual talents were suited for the job. He was respected by the soldiers in Langwarrin because he had been wounded at Gallipoli; he also impressed them with his exercise routine of galloping a horse around the military reserve, and of boxing and wrestling with men who were game. He had a nice diplomatic style, which enabled good relations with most people he met, and smooth co-operation with townspeople close to the camp. Conder became well known in the district — even a kind of celebrity — and his activities were often reported in local newspapers. What he was perhaps most known for was his enthusiasm for securing donations for the hospital, and his talents there as an entertainment impresario.

Conder charmed numerous organisations and individuals into making valuable donations, and he attended many fundraising events on behalf of the patients. He obtained pets, books, newspapers, workshop tools, horticultural tools, seeds, plants, shrubs, trees, garden ornaments, sports equipment, theatrical costumes and scenery, art materials, musical instruments, Christmas gifts and decorations, food and beverages for special events, medical equipment, and entire buildings. All of these things were provided to the hospital by donors in Melbourne, while men, women, and children from nearby towns became visitors and voluntary helpers.

Conder's talent for arranging entertainment for the patients became legendary — so much so that, after he left the hospital, he received offers of positions in the entertainment industry. In 1916, he encouraged the formation of a hospital brass band using instruments obtained from donors, and, later, he had a bandstand erected. The members of the band initially came from the militia guard, but they were largely replaced by musical patients. The Langwarrin Military Band became so good that it was in demand all over the Mornington Peninsula to play at patriotic concerts, carnivals, fetes, bazaars, and commemoration ceremonies such as those held on Anzac Days. At the hospital, the band played for the governor-general, senior military officers, and other visitors, as well as when there were military parades.

Conder arranged for regular concerts to be performed in the hospital's Red Cross hall, usually on Sundays, and these became famous and were well attended by visitors. The band played as an orchestra, and patients performed as singers, solo musicians, comedians, mimes, and ventriloquists. The role of 'talking' horse in the ventriloquist acts was taken by Langwarrin's mascot, a pony that the men named Carbine after the bay stallion that won the 1890 Melbourne Cup.

Conder also arranged for entertainers from Melbourne to give free performances. One Sunday in 1918, the entire Tivoli Revue Company of 50 performers and technicians arrived to stage the popular revues *Time Please* and *Honi Soit*. This was organised by Conder with the head of Tivoli, Percy Crawford, and the troupe included its American producer, Lester Brown; two famous comedians, Barry Lupino and Billy Rego; the glamorous pantomime actresses Ethel Bennett and Beatrice Holloway (who came with her mother); and Noel Geddes, a theatrical star. The arrival of these celebrities was greeted by throngs of local men, women, and children.

The ornamental wooden archway at the entrance to the military VD
hospital at Langwarrin. *(NLA)*

Not all citizens of Melbourne approved of Conder staging his light-hearted concerts at Langwarrin, especially on Sundays, and there were sometimes objections. After a concert in 1918, Conder was sternly criticised by a local dignitary because children had performed a pantomime, and on the day of rest. Conder defended himself in a letter to the *Moorabbin News*; he opened by stating that he had been 'misreported' if anyone thought he had used the term 'wowser' to describe critics of the concerts. He then wrote:

> I regret there should be any trouble concerning Sunday concerts. Personally, I do not favour Sunday concerts, but I am in favour of anything, on Sundays or weekdays, that is for the benefit of soldiers. We of this camp have been bitterly attacked by a section of the community whose minds are so rotten and contemptible that they see no good in anything. I would say to those people that this camp has sent over 6,200 men to fight for them week-day and Sunday, and that 700 of these men have paid the supreme sacrifice.

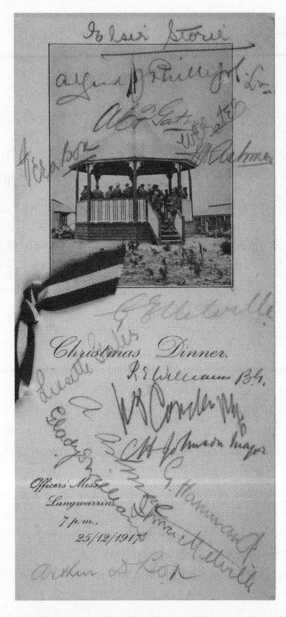

A page from the menu of an Officers' Mess Christmas dinner held
at Langwarrin in 1917. The autographs of Brigadier General and
Mrs Williams, Major Conder, Major Johnson, and other officers
and guests are visible. (*Museums Victoria*)

The Langwarrin military band, fallen in and ready for a parade at
the Langwarrin hospital. *(NLA)*

Conder had troubles with other citizens as well. The hospital became
so interesting that it began attracting unwanted visitors. Extraordinarily,
in 1917, a woman visitor became sexually entwined with a patient,
only to be discovered in the act. She was escorted off the premises, and
Conder had to launch an inquiry to determine how this remarkable
breach of the rules had occurred. Evidently, he became so concerned
about visits by women who might be having affairs with patients that he
posted a corporal at Frankston train station to intercept them and turn
them back. One day, the corporal refused to allow two young women
to proceed from the station to the hospital. Days later, Conder received
an angry letter from a solicitor informing him that the women were his
respectable daughters, and Conder was berated for the inference and
discourtesy.

A glamorous Tivoli Revue star posing in 1918 with a local
schoolboy, Carbine the Langwarrin hospital mascot, and some
NCOs. *(NLA)*

In November 1918, the armistice came and the war ended. Soon,
rumours began circulating that the Langwarrin hospital would be closed
and the patients released before they were cured. The principal medical
officer of the 3rd Military District, Lieutenant Colonel Sturdee, said
'there was not a particle of truth' in the rumour, and that 'the only men
being liberated from the hospital were those who required no further
treatment'.

The end of the war led to discussions in the Department of Defence
about the future of the hospital, and of the entire Langwarrin military
reserve. The director of medical services for the AIF estimated that the
hospital would be needed until 1920 for soldiers returning from Europe
who were found to be infected with VD. Instead, preparations began to

close the camp in 1919, because the patients and staff, including Major Conder, were eager to get out of the army and resume civilian life.

In May 1919, a farewell function for Conder was held by the citizens of Frankston. This was a gala affair with many attending, and included an 'excellent musical program', and speeches of tribute by the mayor and prominent citizens, including one made 'on behalf of the boys and girls of the district'. Conder was presented with an illuminated scroll, decorated with photographs and 'handsomely framed'. The scroll said in part that:

> We are deeply conscious that under your wise, salutary rule the military camp was transformed from a potential menace to a centre of beneficient activity and an ornamental asset of the district, while regenerating and passing onto the battle front many thousands of brave soldiers.

The farewell function, however, was premature. The defence department soon realised that the prediction of the director of medical services had been correct, and that the Langwarrin hospital, and the services of Major Conder, would still be needed. In 1920, while still at Langwarrin, he was made a Member of the Order of the British Empire for his wartime services. When the hospital finally closed in 1921, another 'gala night' farewell function was held for him — this one arranged by the Progress Association of Langwarrin.

From 1920, Conder's main duty was overseeing disposal of the hospital's assets by tender and at auction sales at the site. Almost all of the buildings were sold for removal, some to government organisations and others to private bidders. The Red Cross hall, where Conder's Sunday concerts had taken place since 1916, was returned to the donor for removal. Six of the hospital-ward huts were acquired by the State Electricity Commission of Victoria, dismantled, and re-erected at Morwell, near the brown-coal mines of the Latrobe Valley, to be used as workers' accommodation. In December 1920, *The Argus* reported that the huts were discussed in the Victorian Legislative Assembly:

During the discussion on the Electricity Supply Loan Bill, Mr Prendergast complained that the commissioners had recently caused to be erected at Morwell, for the use of employees, six huts which previously had been inhabited by venereal patients at Langwarrin camp. The Morwell men objected strongly to living in such homes, and asked for an assurance that no more huts would be transferred from Langwarrin.

A book should be written about the interesting life of Walter Conder; in this one, there is room only for a brief account of his activities after Langwarrin closed. He left the army, but retained a connection by being placed on the Reserve of Officers at his original AIF rank of lieutenant; he continued to be well known in Melbourne, however, as 'Major Conder'. In 1922, he accepted an appointment as governor of Pentridge Gaol in Melbourne, and as inspector of prisons for Victoria. This did not work out: his humane ideas about prisoner welfare were resisted by prison authorities, and Conder resigned after 18 months.

He was then hired as a manager with the theatre company J. C. Williamson and Co. In 1923, wireless broadcasting was just becoming established in Australia, and Conder's job was to develop a new Williamson enterprise, the radio station 3LO in Melbourne. He became instrumental in establishing the popularity of radio broadcasts, and 3LO became a successful commercial broadcaster. In 1930, the station was acquired by the Australian Broadcasting Company, which later became the Australian Broadcasting Commission (now the Australian Broadcasting Corporation).

Major Conder was not appointed to be the first general manager of the ABC; but, in 1933, after a period working as chief organiser of the Melbourne centenary celebrations, he became the second. Coming from commercial radio, he decided that ABC programs should be entertaining and have the widest possible appeal to the general public. Conder arranged for broadcasts of light entertainment, of news events as they happened, and of sports, including boxing and wrestling. During his work with the centenary committee, he had suggested that an air race from London to Melbourne should be part of the celebrations. This famous event took place in 1934, and Conder arranged for the ABC to broadcast the arrival of race aircraft at Flemington racecourse. That year, a new ABC chairman, William Cleary, was appointed. He had completely different tastes, and intended that broadcasts should mainly be of classical music, intellectual talks, and educational programs. The differences between Conder and Cleary could not be resolved; in 1935, Cleary had his way, and Conder left the ABC.

He then entered a long period, probably the nadir of his life, of moving between unemployment and short periods of work. In 1936, he formed a company to run the Ivan Brothers' 'Top of the World' international circus; but, after a number of shows in Sydney, the circus failed. Between 1937 and 1940, Conder lived in Sydney, and the name 'Major Conder, former manager of the ABC' was often in the newspapers — especially for his prosecution by the taxation department, a lawsuit for breach of contract, and bankruptcy and sequestration orders issued against him. He was declared bankrupt in 1940, arrested for contempt of court after he failed to appear, and briefly imprisoned in Pentridge.

The Second World War had begun in 1939, and, in June 1940, Conder joined the army in Melbourne, and was supposed to become commandant of the VD isolation hospital at Puckapunyal. He was rescued from this fate by Lieutenant General Thomas Blamey, whom Conder had known in Melbourne and who was now commander of the Second AIF. An application was made to the Bankruptcy Court for Conder to be permitted to go to the Middle East as General Blamey's amenities officer, and this was successful. Re-instated as a major, his job was to be the showman again, and to organise morale-boosting entertainment for soldiers of the new AIF in Egypt and Palestine. Conder arranged events there until 1942, including a huge surf carnival on a beach in Palestine using surf-lifesaving equipment he had shipped from Australia.

He returned to Australia, left the army, and in 1944 began working for the Americans — managing first a hostel for soldiers in Queensland, and then the American Red Cross Club in Sydney. In 1945, Conder married

Walter Conder (right) in the 1920s, when he was manager of radio station 3LO in Melbourne. *(NLA)*

Cora Wood, a hospital matron, and they sailed to England, where Conder joined the Australian Department of Information to give lectures about Australia to prospective British emigrants. From 1947, he managed the historic Swan Hotel at Bedford, north of London. And then, in 1952, he and Cora emigrated to New Zealand, where he managed breweries, a hotel, and the Tattersall's Lottery. His remarkable life came to an end when he died at his home in Nelson in 1974.

Brigadier General Robert Williams had been Conder's collaborator in all the enlightened improvements at Langwarrin. In 1917, Williams was mentioned in dispatches, and also appointed a Commander in the Order of St Michael and St George. His wife died in 1918, and, the following year, he retired from military duties and resigned as the town clerk of West Ballarat. He then returned to the world of newspaper journalism, which he had left 20 years earlier, and, from his home in Ballarat, became a leader writer for the Melbourne *Herald*. This led to a seat on the board of the Herald and Weekly Times, a position that Williams occupied until 1935, when he was 80. In the 1930s, Williams also wrote for the newspaper where he had begun as a journalist, *The Ballarat Courier*. In 1943, at the age of 88, he died in Melbourne.

One area of excellence for which the Langwarrin hospital received favourable notice during the war was its venereal-disease research. This was driven by the army's need to reduce the immense costs of treating tens of thousands of men for VD in England and France, and to reduce the time they were withdrawn from front-line service. The scientific work at Langwarrin was performed by doctors recruited by General Williams in 1915 and 1916, especially Dr Mathias Perl and Dr Charles Johnson. They succeeded in shortening the periods of treatment for each type of disease, and halving the average cost of treatment.

The Langwarrin experiments caused much interest in the medical profession. They were often reported and discussed in *The Medical Journal of Australia*, and were the subject of conferences of doctors held at Langwarrin by medical associations. Other pioneering work at Langwarrin included studies of the dental-health and oral-infection aspects of venereal disease, and the use of what are now called occupational therapies, with activities for patients such as horticulture and gardening, and music and theatrical productions. Walter Conder liked animals, and encouraged their collection and care by the patients. Informal use of what is now called animal-assisted therapy occurred, using Carbine, the beautiful pony, and other tame animals, including deer, kangaroos, swans, guinea pigs, cats, and dogs.

The medical experiments begun at Langwarrin stopped when the hospital closed. Had they continued, they might have examined the long-term health consequences of gonorrhoea, syphilis, and chancroid infections for soldiers and their families after the war. This might have also included studies of the long-term effects of the toxic drugs used to treat these diseases. It took a long time for scientists to fully understand the serious health consequences of poisoning humans with even very low doses of mercury, arsenic, and silver. In Australia, years later, each of those heavy metals, and most drugs derived from them, were banned for human consumption. The irritation of human skin tissue by sandalwood oil was understood, but the long-term effects of its absorption appear to still be unknown.

Some of the Langwarrin doctors continued as venereal-disease specialists after the war. Dr Arthur Morris, a dermatologist who was senior medical officer at the isolation camp in the chaotic months of the spring of 1915, went to Egypt with the 1st Australian Dermatological Hospital, and moved with it to the UK. In 1917, he returned to Melbourne and resumed his dermatological practice in Collins Street. He was prominent, with Sir James Barrett, in post-war discussions about wartime venereal disease, and he publicly urged ex-soldiers who had been infected with syphilis to have regular Wassermann tests, and for their wives to be tested as well. At the age of 52, Morris died of pneumonia in Melbourne in 1931.

Dr Mathias Perl joined the medical staff at Langwarrin in November 1915 and worked there for two years, specialising in syphilis research. He left the army in 1917, and returned to his Melbourne practices in Windsor and in Collins Street in the city. Perl died in Melbourne in 1936.

Dr Charles Johnson was recruited to Langwarrin in 1916, and was senior medical officer in 1917 when members of the Victorian parliament visited and were impressed by what they saw. This led to his joining the Victorian health department and, in 1918, establishing Melbourne's first public venereal-disease clinic for men, and then, in 1919, the first one for women. Dr Johnson worked as their medical superintendent for the rest of his professional life, and, as well, contributed to the public discussions and government inquiries of the 1920s and 1930s that dealt with venereal diseases. Johnson died in Melbourne in 1940.

Within 20 years of the closure of Langwarrin, the Australian army faced a new venereal-disease challenge. After the Second World War started, Australian troops were sent once again to Egypt and the Middle East, and, in 1940 and 1941, VD incidence rates among them became very high. There were still centres of vice and venereal disease in Cairo, and Alexandria's brothel quarter was still in Rue des Soeurs, where a new generation of Australian soldiers became infected. As in 1915, men with VD were stigmatised, and detained in isolation barracks, and, until 1941, they also lost their army pay. Curing syphilis was still undertaken with arsenic-based drugs, and also a metal called bismuth. However, by now, a new class of drugs, the sulphonamides, had become available for treating gonorrhoea. Then, after 1943, the antibiotic known as penicillin became widely available, and it revolutionised the treatment of both diseases by providing fast, perfect cures, with less risk to patients than the heavy metals used before. Penicillin was utilised by the AAMC in all theatres of war to rapidly treat many bacterial diseases, including VD, and VD-infected soldiers could be returned fit to their units within days, not after weeks or months as before.

During the Second World War, there was far less venereal disease in the Australian army than between 1914 and 1919. But after the Second World War ended in 1945, the army remained obsessed with keeping VD rates as low as possible, and this occurred in peacetime and in war. For example, Australian soldiers who served in Malaya after 1950, and later in Vietnam, were regularly medically inspected, and army units were expected to return VD statistical reports to headquarters. This occurred as if VD was still a serious threat to military efficiency, which it was not. It was, however, and especially during the war in Vietnam, a political concern. Unfounded rumours abounded about purportedly 'virulent oriental strains' of VD in Vietnam that were resistant to antibiotics. Many American soldiers and sailors from Vietnam arrived in Australia for rest-and-recreation visits, and the Australian government worried that they might bring VD with them.[24] In a politically sensitive war, the Australian army could not have its own soldiers returning home carrying such diseases, or give an appearance that it was not taking them seriously. Even in the late 1970s, after Vietnam, army reservists were still being paraded for 'short arm' inspections at Puckapunyal, although it was unlikely that symptoms of VD would ever be found.

Soldiers at Langwarrin with some of the many animals accumulated
by Major Conder for the enjoyment of patients. *(NLA)*

The penicillin that, after 1943, cured Australian soldiers infected with
gonorrhoea and syphilis, was developed by a team of medical scientists
led by an Australian — the pharmacologist Howard Florey, who in
1945 was awarded a Nobel Prize for his remarkable achievement. Had
penicillin been available before the First World War, the suffering of men
and women infected with VD could have been stopped, and the moral
stigma might have greatly diminished. If penicillin had been available
in Egypt in 1915, voyages to Australia like that of the *Wiltshire* — and
the pain, shame, and secrets of her 275 passengers — may have never
occurred.

What happened to the *Wiltshire* after that voyage? She continued
to be leased as a troopship for Australia until 1917, and until 1919 was
chartered voyage by voyage. When her war service ended, she resumed
making the run between Britain and the Antipodes. Then, in May 1922,

WILTSHIRE - WRECKED
GREAT BARRIER ISLD. N.Z. 11422

The *Wiltshire* breaking up and sinking in rough seas in 1922 at
Great Barrier Island, New Zealand. *(SLNSW)*

she was wrecked at night in wild weather in Rosalie Bay at Great Barrier
Island in New Zealand, in the final stage of a passage from London to
Dunedin. No lives were lost when she hit rocks and sank in relatively
shallow water, but rescuing her passengers proved to be difficult and
dangerous. Years later, she became one of the most popular and accessible
underwater wreck dives in New Zealand, and still is today.

What happened to the Langwarrin hospital after it closed in 1921? By
1923, everything was gone from the site — except for the over-2,000 trees
planted under Walter Conder's directions during the war, the stormwater
drains, a crumbling reservoir, and a number of open trenches where pipes
had been removed. The water pump and electricity cables had been sold,
and the telephone poles and wires taken away. The road metal, and the
white-painted stones that had neatly lined the hospital's roads, had been
sold. Over 7,000 men had passed under the big wooden archway that
formed the camp entrance, but it, too, was taken away and re-erected
over a war-memorial avenue in Frankston. The camp's railway station on

Arbours of the mature trees at the wartime hospital site in the
Langwarrin Flora and Fauna Reserve.

the spur track from Frankston had been stripped of its buildings. It was
almost as if the hospital had never existed; judging by the speed at which
it was dismantled, that may have been the intention.

After 1923, the expected decision by the defence department about
the future of the Langwarrin military reserve took a very long time to
be made. In the 1920s, part of it was leased to the Langwarrin Progress
Association and used as a recreation reserve. The open land that had
originally been used for artillery ranges, and pasture for military horses,
was leased to farmers for grazing cattle and sheep. Much became
overgrown with native scrub and stringybark trees, but Conder's pines,
wattles, eucalypts, and English oaks continued to flourish at the old
hospital site.

Nowadays, this is all that remains of the fountain of Venus.

During the Second World War, the Langwarrin range was occasionally used by the army. In 1943, methods for air-dropping military supplies were tested there, in daytime and at night, as were ways of packing the containers so that their contents were undamaged on impact. This was to develop a way of supplying fragile stores to troops in New Guinea and to coast-watchers on Pacific islands. The war ended in 1945, and the Langwarrin reserve returned to its scrubby silence, and Conder's trees continued to grow.

In the 1960s and 1970s, the reserve was occasionally used by school cadets and the army reserve for part-time military training. Finally, in the late 1970s, the Department of Defence made its decision: the entire Langwarrin reserve was to be handed to the Victorian government, earmarked as a conservation area. In 1980, it was named the Langwarrin Flora and Fauna Reserve.

Today, visitors entering the Langwarrin reserve from McClelland Drive find themselves immediately adjacent to the site of the First World War hospital. Its presence is obvious in the arbours of mature trees, some originally planted by Conder's men between 1916 and 1918. In among the trees, in the rubble and earth, many small traces of the hospital's existence can still be found: parts of the foundations of buildings, fragments of bottles and jars, pieces of porcelain, bricks, and metal objects. Quite close to the car park, in their own little arbour, are the circular remains of the ornamental fountain that was built by the patients. Venus is gone; but, for almost a century, her pedestal has resisted the ravages of nature and man, and defiantly remains in place — a memorial to all those soldiers, including our *Wiltshire* boys, and the doctors, dispensers, orderlies, and men of the guard who were there with her during the war.

Misconduct, Bravery, VD, and VCs

Sergeant Maurice Buckley and Private Bob Beatham appear to be the only Australian Victoria Cross recipients of the First World War who were sent home in 1915 with venereal disease from the Abbassia detention barracks in Cairo to Langwarrin. This occurred long before each was recommended for a VC. Beatham was posthumously awarded his after he was killed in August 1918 at Rosieres, during a solo attack on trenches full of German soldiers. In close combat, he was repeatedly shot, but his actions resulted in the destruction or capture of many enemy positions. The following month, Buckley had his big day at Le Verguier.

In Egypt in 1915, catching venereal disease was punished by the army in a variety of ways, and soldiers with VD were regarded as pariahs on board ships taking them home. Men who were drunks and rule-breakers were also sent back for early discharge from the army. In the minds of commanders such as Kitchener and Birdwood, such undisciplined men were unlikely to ever be efficient soldiers, and very unlikely to be valorous in battle. It was perhaps unimaginable in 1915 that such men could later become very brave soldiers on battlefields in France and in Belgium.

During the war, army regulations were announced that made it difficult for AIF soldiers who had committed particular acts of misconduct to receive awards and medals. When the 'Returned from Active Service' badge was announced in 1916, men who had been returned to Australia with VD, as well as those with criminal records, were excluded from receiving it. In theory, this meant that Buckley, Beatham, and over 1,300 men sent home with VD from Egypt in 1915 could never be awarded the badge. All men who deserted from the army, including men of the *Wiltshire* such as Buckley, Ernest Dunbar, Bert Crozier, and others who had committed certain crimes, also forfeited their entitlements to service medals, bravery awards, and other benefits — in theory, at least.

In Europe, however, a strange and remarkable discovery was made: it was possible for AIF soldiers with records of drunkenness, crime, misconduct, absence without leave, and VD to also be outstanding soldiers. In France and Belgium, battalion officers sometimes found themselves writing after-battle recommendations for incorrigible misbehavers to be awarded medals for bravery. These were for men who, according to strict compliance with regulations, might have already lost their entitlement to receive an award. In a great many cases, medal entitlements had to be restored; as we know, reasons were found to restore Maurice Buckley's after he was recommended in 1918 for a VC. Following the war, the entitlement rules were progressively relaxed, and thousands of men who were previously denied badges and medals could then receive them.

Of those returned in disgrace to Australia on the *Wiltshire* in August 1915, some were later awarded medals for outstanding bravery in France and in Belgium. Apart from Maurice Buckley, two other *Wiltshire* men, Rupert Barrie and Walter Moore, received the Distinguished Conduct Medal, both also receiving theirs in 1918. Gordon Linsley was later commissioned in the field as a lieutenant, and, in 1918, posthumously awarded a Military Cross. At least six *Wiltshire* men were later awarded Military Medals: Thomas Popple in 1916; William Stein, William Brown, and John Burke in 1917; and Eric Swallow and William Thomas in 1918. In 1917, Frederick Banwell was personally commended for gallantry by General Birdwood; the general might not have known at the time that, in his own words, Banwell had been 'rotten from women' in 1915.

Many *Wiltshire* men were later killed in action, or died of their wounds. The first to lose his life after leaving Langwarrin was Thomas Galloway, killed at Fromelles in July 1916. As well as Richard Waltham, three others died in the fighting around Pozieres in August and September 1916: Thaddens Leach, George Leunig, and Arthur Reed, who was captured, and, in Germany, died of his wounds. William Lock was wounded by a grenade in November 1916, and died the same day; and Frank Kluck was killed the following month.

The fighting around Bullecourt and Bapaume in April and May 1917 claimed the lives of Bertram Thomas, William Hull, Francis Power, Thomas Ryan, Richard Warn, William Stein, Frederick Collins, Harry Minnie, and William Baker. William Platt was killed in a shell explosion at Warneton in Belgium in July 1917, together with his brother George; they were in the same dugout when this occurred. John Harman and Daniel Fitzgerald were killed at Polygon Wood in September and October 1917.

In 1918, Sydney Jenkins was killed at Warneton, Alfred Hill at Villers-Bretonneux, and Gordon Linsley died of shrapnel wounds received at Dernancourt. John Burke was killed in August 1918, as was 19-year-old Leo O'Toole, who had originally enlisted aged just 16. Kenneth Annear was killed near Peronne in September.

The individual stories of all those mentioned above, and of others who were sent back on the *Wiltshire*, are often interesting, and in many cases remarkable, as well as sad. There are tales of escapes from Langwarrin, of army deserters, and of identities being changed so the men could re-enlist. There are stories of wives and families discovering the truth of their man's return from Egypt, and of their attempts to get him out of Langwarrin, or divorce him. After *Wiltshire* men left Langwarrin and got back in the army, there are stories aplenty of bravery in battles, and of terrible shrapnel wounds and deaths from diseases. Most of the men never became infected again with VD, but some did.

Apart from Maurice Buckley and Bob Beatham, at least seven other Australian Victoria Cross awardees had been treated in army venereal-disease hospitals. The percentage of VC awardees treated is about the same as for the entire Australian army, which means that about 85 per cent did not catch VD. For some who did, it occurred before they were recommended for the award; for others, it occurred after.

That some VC men also became infected with VD is unsurprising in an army containing at least 60,000 who were treated. It may have also been because VC awardees tended to be, like Buckley and Beatham, seemingly reckless with their personal welfare. To qualify for a VC, a soldier usually had to perform, at great personal risk, an individual battlefield act that enabled a much bigger victory to then occur. Many VCs were awarded, some posthumously, for single-handedly destroying or capturing enemy strong points that were stopping attacks by Australian battalions. Selfless acts of heroism like this might in some circumstances be regarded as reckless, or foolish, especially had they failed. It was also often said by AIF officers that only selfish, reckless fools inflicted VD on themselves.

The First World War military exploits of Lieutenant Joseph 'Joe' Maxwell, VC, MC and Bar, DCM are very well known. He received all those high medals for bravery within just 12 months, and became the second-most-decorated soldier in the AIF after Captain Harry Murray, VC, CMG, DSO and Bar, DCM, Croix de Guerre. The achievements of Murray and Maxwell were extraordinary, and have never been repeated. Joe's post-war fame was boosted when, in 1932, he published his war stories in *Hell's Bells and Mademoiselles*, which became a bestseller.

Joe was a boilermaker from Sydney, and just 19 when he volunteered for the AIF in 1915. He was steadily promoted through the ranks, and eventually received, after a few false starts, an officer's commission in 1917. His Victoria Cross was the last and highest award he received, and it came after an attack by the 18th Battalion on the Hindenburg Line near Estrees, in October 1918. After his company commander was wounded, Joe took charge, and, under intense fire, reached the enemy trenches. Joe pushed forward alone and captured two machine guns, killing the crews. Later, with two of his men and an enemy hostage, he encouraged about 20 Germans in an outpost to surrender. In the course of this stunt, Joe was briefly taken prisoner, but he drew a pistol, killed two of his captors, and escaped with his men as they were shot at from behind. He then returned to the same German outpost, and this time it was captured.

Earlier in the war, Joe had been at Gallipoli with the 18th Battalion, but was evacuated because of sickness in December 1915. In Egypt, he ended up recuperating at the convalescent depot at the Ras el-Tin Palace in Alexandria. This is where Ernest Dunbar had recovered from his Gallipoli wound in July 1915. Now, in early 1916, it was Joe Maxwell's turn to catch VD in the infamous Rue de Soeurs; soon, he, too, was in the Abbassia hospital in Cairo, where he remained for over a month. Joe wrote fondly of Rue de Soeurs in *Hell's Bells and Mademoiselles*, and also of girlfriends in France — which was perhaps why reviewers called the book 'candid' and 'vulgar'.

Joe was a boisterous, cheeky young fellow; just before he began his series of medal-winning exploits in France, he was involved in a brawl with police in London when they tried to break up a rowdy nightclub party. He escaped out a window down into the street. At the time, he was about to join an officer training course, but this was stopped by the army because of the brawl. His spectacular wartime experiences became the highlight of his life; he wrote about it in his book when recalling his thoughts after the war ended:

How wildly elated I was when the news had flashed through that Germany had accepted the terms of the Armistice. Yet, was I really glad? The Armistice sounded the death-knell of a carefree, colourful, and reckless existence. No more the thrill of having survived another 'stunt'. The thrills of promotion and honour gained. How could I again settle down to the humdrum of civilian existence?

Joe settled down in Australia to become, of all things humdrum, a gardener. Before this occurred, he was one of the VC heroes honoured in the 1920 St Patrick's Day parade in Melbourne organised by Maurice Buckley for John Wren and Archbishop Mannix. After the start of the Second World War, he unsuccessfully tried several times to enlist in the army; on one occasion, in a false name. In 1967, following many years of ill health, Joe died after collapsing in a street in his home suburb of Matraville in Sydney.

Private Bernard Gordon enlisted in Townsville in September 1915, and joined the 41st Battalion. He left Australia in May 1916, and, during the voyage to the UK, was convicted for being AWL, and detained. Before the battalion moved to France, he spent almost seven weeks in Bulford being cured of VD. In France during 1917, he was found guilty three times for being AWL, and also once each for 'conduct to the prejudice of good order and military discipline', 'leaving the ranks without permission', and 'urinating on the parade ground'. In October 1917, he was wounded by shrapnel and hospitalised, and, while on leave in London, was convicted for drunkenness.

Then, some time in 1918, Bernard started behaving himself, and in June was rewarded with promotion to lance corporal. In July at Hamel, he single-handedly destroyed a German machine-gun post, and later stalked and killed an enemy sniper. For this, Bernard was awarded a Military Medal. Three weeks later, near Bray, he again single-handedly attacked an enemy machine-gun post, killing the gunner and capturing the post, which turned out to contain an officer and ten men. Still alone, he then cleared more trenches and captured another 50 prisoners and six machine guns. For these acts of conspicuous bravery, he was recommended for a Victoria Cross. Shortly after this, Bernard was again wounded by shrapnel, and was evacuated to England before being repatriated to Queensland in January 1919. For most of his post-war life, he worked as a dairy farmer near Beaudesert; he died at Torquay, Queensland, in 1963.

Private John 'Jack' Hamilton was a butcher in Sydney when he enlisted in 1914. Jack was awarded a VC following the bloody fight at Lone Pine on Gallipoli in August 1915. When this happened, he was in the 3rd Battalion, and was only 19. His unit was heavily attacked with grenades, as, for six hours, he lay in an exposed position to fire at enemy grenade-throwers. This act of daring encouraged his mates, and the enemy was driven away with heavy losses.

Shortly after this, he became ill with dysentery, and was evacuated from Gallipoli to hospital in London. While he was there, his award of a VC was confirmed and gazetted; but, even though he was now a military celebrity, he soon began to misbehave. In January 1916, he was absent from camp, and was also convicted of using insubordinate language to an officer. Jack also caught VD, and until April was in and out of British army hospitals at Portland in Dorset and at Bulford being cured. In March, he was convicted again for absence without leave. At this point, it appears that an older and wiser head had a frank chat with young Private Hamilton about his misconduct. As a VC-holder, his behaviour was meant to be exemplary; instead, he was acting the fool. Whatever was said, the salutory effect was almost instant, and the rest of his AIF service was trouble-free.

In May 1916, he was sent to Egypt to help train reinforcements arriving from Australia, and was promoted to corporal. After rejoining the 3rd Battalion and moving to France, Jack fought at Pozieres, Mouquet Farm, and Flers during 1916, and was promoted to sergeant in 1917. Back in England in 1918, he joined a course at an officer-cadet battalion, but the war ended before he could be commissioned. After the armistice, he became a second lieutenant, then a lieutenant, and rejoined the 3rd Battalion in France. Jack was repatriated to Sydney in August 1919, and, the following year in Melbourne, he was also one of the VC men in the St Patrick's Day parade. In Sydney, he became a wharfie, a shipping clerk, a storeman, and a packer, and was active in the waterside workers' union. During the Second World War, he was an army officer in Australia and New Guinea. He died in the Concord Repatriation Hospital in 1961.

Corporal Thomas 'Bede' Kenny was also just 19 when he joined the AIF in Sydney in August 1915. He was raised in Bondi in an impeccably Catholic family, and went to the Christian Brothers' College in Waverley. Bede was a young man of outstanding character, and when he enlisted had just begun training as a chemist. In early 1916, he arrived in Egypt with reinforcements for the 2nd Battalion, and he served with it for the rest of the war. He became popular and respected in this unit, and an exemplary soldier. After the battalion moved to France, Bede fought at Pozieres in a 'bombing' platoon, hurling grenades into enemy trenches.

The following year in April at Hermies, Bede's platoon was stopped by heavy fire from a German strong point. He ran alone into the enemy, bombing and firing, and captured the gun crews and their weapons. For this, he was recommended for a VC; yet what he had done was entirely characteristic and, in the battalion, half-expected. It was said that, at the time of the announcement, he was reading a newspaper, and exclaimed to a mate, 'Look at this! Someone with my name has won a VC!' Bede was immediately promoted to lance corporal; but, shortly after, he was diagnosed with trench feet and evacuated to England.

He ended up in a hospital in Dublin, a perfect place for an Irish-Australian to be. During his stay there, no doubt to his horror, Bede caught VD. He was sent back to England and admitted to Bulford, where he remained for a month. In July 1917, he was released from the hospital to return to duty, but instead disappeared. Where did Lance Corporal Kenny go, and what was he doing? Nearly three weeks later, he re-appeared, at AIF Headquarters in London, and thus saved the army the trouble of having to find and arrest him.

As a young man of known good character recently recommended for a VC, Bede's misconduct was inexplicable. He was paraded before Colonel Reginald Browne, a wise old soldier who as a civilian had been a journalist with *The Brisbane Courier*. Bede had to explain himself to the colonel, and, as well, admit, no doubt very shamefully, that he still had VD. His honesty and good sense in turning himself in must have impressed Colonel Browne, because Bede was punished with just an admonishment for the AWL offence, given forfeiture of pay, and was sent back to Bulford for another two weeks.

He was then ordered to join a challenging course at the British army school of physical training at Aldershot, where soldiers were sometimes sent for a comeuppance. While he was there, in October 1917, the award of his VC was confirmed. After many months of strenuous physical training, boxing, wrestling, and bayonet fighting, and despite his bad feet, Bede passed the course. In May 1918, after a year away from the 2nd Battalion, he rejoined it in France. The following month, however, he was wounded during fighting in the Merris–Vieux-Berquin area, and, despite playing this down, was sent back to England. Just before being invalided home, he was promoted to corporal. He arrived in Sydney in October 1918, and was discharged in December. Just as he had been before his AIF service began, he once again became an impeccable and staunch member of Sydney's Catholic community, and remained one until his death in 1953.

Private Edward 'Jack' Ryan was from Tumut, in the Snowy Mountains of New South Wales, and was 25 when he enlisted in late 1915 and became a reinforcement for the 55th Battalion. His Victoria Cross came late in the war, for displaying conspicuous bravery during an assault on the Hindenburg Line near Bellicourt in September 1918. During this ferocious fight, Jack and some mates captured an enemy trench, but were soon evicted by fierce enemy gunfire. They then discovered that their retreat was blocked by enemy grenadiers, so Jack organised a charge using grenades and bayonets. The Australians killed some of the Germans, and then Jack alone attacked the rest with grenades, driving the enemy away. His actions enabled the German trench to be retaken by the battalion; but, during his solo effort, he was shot in a shoulder, causing him to be evacuated to a hospital, where he remained until after the armistice.

In May 1919, he was invested with his VC by King George V at Buckingham Palace, a week before Maurice Buckley attended his ceremony there. Jack's celebrations in London must have been just as impressive as those held for Maurice, because he, too, ended up being admitted to Bulford as a result. This was the second time Jack had to endure a VD cure; in 1917, he had been treated for infections at an AIF hospital in France.

During his army service, he had never been in any serious trouble; but, shortly after his release from Bulford in 1919, Jack went before a district court-martial to face four charges of misconduct, including insubordination. He pleaded guilty, but was penalised only forfeiture of a day's pay and released. In September 1919, he left England to return to Australia, and in 1920 was discharged in Sydney. He was also one of the VC men who appeared at the St Patrick's Day parade in Melbourne that year. However, Jack's days of glory soon came to an end: he became one of the many returned soldiers who had difficulty adjusting to life as a civilian. He never married, was unemployed for most of the post-war decades, and, during the Great Depression, became an itinerant swagman. Jack died of pneumonia in 1941 in a hospital in Melbourne.

In May 1915, Clifford 'Cliff' Sadlier was working as a salesman in Perth when he enlisted, and, aged 22, went to Egypt to be a nursing orderly at the 1st Australian General Hospital in Cairo. In early 1916, he joined a troopship to nurse Gallipoli invalids returning to Australia. Later that year in Perth, he transferred to the infantry, and left Fremantle on the A8 *Argyllshire* with reinforcements for the 51st Battalion. During this voyage, Cliff spent almost three weeks in the ship's isolation ward with VD, but had been cured by the time the *Argyllshire* reached England. In May 1917, he joined the battalion in France and was soon promoted — first to corporal, then second lieutenant. The following year, as the German army's great spring offensive got underway, he became a lieutenant.

He was recommended for a Victoria Cross after the second battle at Villers-Bretonneux, which had been occupied by Germans during their offensive. Throughout the night of 24 April 1918, many attacks were launched by Australian battalions to dislodge the enemy. The 51st Battalion began its assault into vicious artillery and machine-gun fire, and the platoon led by Clifford was stopped in its tracks. He organised a grenade and Lewis-gun attack on a German machine-gun nest, and a wild fight ensued. Cliff was shot in the thigh, but the nest was destroyed. In spite of his wound, he led his depleted platoon to destroy another machine-gun nest, and then, on his own, captured another with his revolver. During this final solo attack, he was shot in an arm and forced out of the fight. Within days, he was evacuated to a hospital in England, and a few months later was repatriated on account of his wounds.

He arrived in Adelaide in October 1918, and was brought by train to Perth with another Western Australian VC recipient, Lance Corporal John Carroll. At the Perth railway station, they were greeted with a cheering crowd, and speeches by dignitaries. A few months later, Cliff received his discharge from the AIF, and went into business in Perth as a manufacturer's agent; later, he was a clerk with the repatriation department. Although married twice after the war, he had no descendents when he died in Busselton in 1964.

Although born in New Zealand, Lawrence Weathers' parents were Australian, and, when he was a boy, the family moved to South Australia. When the war began, he was 25, married, with two boys, and working as an undertaker in Adelaide. He enlisted in the AIF in February 1916 after his brother Frank was killed at Gallipoli in June 1915. Very soon after Lawrence enlisted, he was admitted to the venereal-disease compound at the Torrens Island quarantine hospital in Adelaide, where he stayed for over a month. He embarked from Adelaide with the 43rd Battalion in June, bound for England, and in November 1916 went to France. There, in January 1917, he was again admitted to hospital with VD. Lawrence was shot in the leg at Messines in June 1917, and as a result was away from the battalion for six months. He was promoted to lance corporal in March 1918; in May, he was gassed at Bois L'Abbe, putting him out of action for a month.

Early in the morning of 2 September, Weathers took part in an assault launched by the 43rd Battalion against a heavily defended German trench complex near Peronne. Machine-gun fire from an enemy strong point stopped the advance. Single-handedly, Weathers attacked the enemy position and killed its leader. After stocking up with many grenades, he climbed onto the German parapet and, completely exposed to enemy fire, began hurling them into the trenches below. By the time Lawrence had finished, he had captured three machine guns and 180 prisoners. Very soon after, he was promoted to temporary corporal. Then, a fortnight later, he took part in a battalion assault on the Hindenburg Line between Rosnoy and Bony. Here, he was seriously wounded when an enemy shell exploded nearby, and he died at a regimental aid post run by the 41st Battalion, not knowing he had been recommended for a Victoria Cross for his heroic deeds two weeks before. Lawrence was buried in a temporary AIF cemetery between the villages of Hargicourt and Lempire, and, after the war, his remains were transferred to the Unicorn war cemetery at Vendhuile. The award of his Victoria Cross was gazetted in London in December 1918.

Apart from his being awarded a posthumous VC, an outstanding feature of Lawrence's army service — if we can overlook his episodes with VD — was a perfect record of conduct. This was extremely rare in an AIF populated by so many rule-breakers; historians who have examined hundreds and hundreds of individual service records have been hard-pressed to discover any where a man never once committed an offence, however trivial.

Preventing, Curing, and Testing for Venereal Diseases in the Australian Army, 1914–1919[25]

During the First World War, most Australian soldiers who became infected with VD caught gonorrhoea; the others suffered from syphilis and chancroid. Although soldiers were usually infected with one venereal disease, it was common for men to have gonorrhoea and syphilis simultaneously, and occasionally to have chancroid as well. Catching VD once, and enduring a cure, was enough for most men; others became infected often, some with different diseases on different occasions.

Until the rapid developments in medical science in the late 19th century, no definite way had ever been found to prevent the diseases being transmitted, except practising abstinence from premarital and extramarital sex. As well, although doctors had searched for centuries to find reliable and safe VD cures, none was ever discovered; men and women who caught gonorrhoea, syphilis, and chancroid might suffer them, as outcasts of society, for the rest of their lives.

During the decades before the war, breakthroughs in medical science had enabled each of the venereal-disease bacteria to be identified and classified, and progress had been made in developing prophylactics, tests, and cures. However, none of these were guaranteed effective when wartime promiscuity erupted in 1914, and reliable ones were still not available by 1919 when VD faded away as a problem for the Australian army.

During that time, gonorrhoea was the most common sexually transmitted disease, not only in the Australian army but in all human societies. It was caused by the bacteria *Neisseria gonorrhoeae*. Humans were its only host, and it was very contagious. Gonorrhoea was spread through semen or vaginal fluids during sexual contact with a partner who was infected; for a man, *Neisseria gonorrhoeae* lodged in his urethra, which became blocked by thick pus that continually leaked. If the disease was not treated effectively, or at all, it could cause long-term effects for a soldier, some of them serious. After returning home, he could easily infect his sexual partners in Australia, including his wife, and his children might be infected at birth and become blind. Gonorrhoea was colloquially called 'the clap' — perhaps from *clapier*, an old French term for brothel.

A common side effect of gonorrhoea was gleet, a non-infectious urethral inflammation accompanied by discharge of pus. Gleet could be exacerbated during gonorrhoea cures when syringe and douche nozzles were repeatedly inserted deep in the urethra to flood the bacteria with toxins. It was an obstinate complaint, which could persist for months, even years; soldiers apparently cured of gonorrhoea could long after still have gleet. Another side effect of gonorrhoea was gonococcal arthritis in the skeletal joints of infected soldiers. They might be discharged from the army medically unfit because of arthritis without anyone realising they had the gonococcal form. Another side effect was prostatitis, an infection and enlargement of the prostate gland. Yet another side effect related to gonorrhoea was orchitis, an infection in the soldier's testicles.

When the war began, syphilis was known as the most dangerous sexually transmitted disease, caused by the spirochete bacteria *Treponema pallidum* subspecies *pallidum*. It was transmitted by contact with the syphilitic sores of an infected person during sexual activity; the contact point for a man was usually the skin of his genitals. Syphilis appeared in stages, and insidiously disappeared after each early stage, although the invisible bacteria remained. The primary stage was appearance of painless sores variously called buboes, ulcers, or lesions on the skin area of contact. If no cure began at this point, the sores disappeared, and a second stage commenced with skin rashes on hands or feet, sometimes elsewhere; after a while, they disappeared, too. Although there were no longer any visible symptoms, the bacteria had entered a long stage of latency, and, during this time, a carrier might feel normal and well. The disease, however, was gradually transforming to a tertiary stage, and causing serious long-term damage to the spine, heart, brain, and other vital organs, and this could be fatal. A common long-term consequence of undetected syphilis was brain degeneration, which led to what was called General Paralysis of the Insane.

As with those afflicted by gonorrhoea, a soldier with undetected or incorrectly treated syphilis could infect others, and this infection could be passed on to unborn children. The children of syphilitics — those who survived the pregnancy and birth — could be hideously deformed, and might have to live in special sanatoriums. Syphilis was the second most common venereal disease caught by Australian soldiers; like sufferers throughout the ages, they called it 'the pox'.

Chancroid was also called soft chancre and hard chancre. Before the war, it was identified as a sexually transmitted bacterial infection caused by the streptobacillus *Haemophilus ducreyi*, spread from one person to another solely through sexual contact. For a man, painful sores called chancres appeared on the skin of his genitals, and he could infect others while the chancres remained. Chancroid occasionally caused long-term effects, such as permanent scarring where a chancre was destroyed. It was the least common venereal infection among Australian soldiers in the First World War.

Protecting against venereal diseases

In Australia in 1914, the conventional method for protecting against venereal infections was for men and women to abstain from premarital or extramarital sexual relations. If sexual intercourse was confined solely within faithful marriage, it was impossible for infections to spread. Marriage contracts were supposed to protect society from the spread of VD, so sex outside marriage was taboo, immoral, and proscribed by religious convention and civil laws. It was believed by many that God had created venereal diseases to punish the sin of sexual promiscuity. Devices or methods that might be used as barriers against venereal infections were also immoral, and also prohibited by churches and laws.

For Australian soldiers in Egypt and Europe who disregarded those taboos and prohibitions, there was no completely effective protection against venereal infections. For example, thick vulcanised rubber condoms, then called sheaths, were available. They were meant to be contraceptive devices for the then new and morally controversial practice of birth control. Sheaths might be discreetly prescribed by doctors only for reducing the possibility of conception during sexual intercourse between husband and wife. For the moral majority, this was bad enough in itself; but using sheaths as prophylactics to prevent the spread of VD was outrageous. By the end of the 19th century, governments in many parts of the world, including in Australia, had banned sheaths as 'obscene, lewd, or lascivious materials', and the advertising of them was banned as an obscenity.

Irrespective of what they were used for, rubber sheaths were thick and uncomfortable for men to wear, and, because they broke often, were unreliable for preventing pregnancies or infections. Although, during the wartime VD emergency in Europe between 1916 and 1919, the AIF made sheaths available to soldiers who wished to buy them, other more reliable prophylactics were recommended by army doctors, and these were provided free of charge. The recommended prophylactics were particular ointments, creams, or jellies, to be smeared over the sexual organs of both partners immediately before and after sex.

If a soldier exactly followed the instructions, he was to thoroughly clean his genitalia, as was his partner hers, and then both would form a temporary barrier against infection using a thick film of the disinfectants

Calomel ointment and Argryol or Nargol jelly. The Calomel contained mercury, which was meant to kill syphilis and chancroid bacteria, and the jellies contained colloidal silver to kill gonorrhoea bacteria. Immediately after intercourse, the cleaning and disinfecting was meant to be repeated. If a soldier forgot to do all or any part of the procedure, he was meant to immediately go to an army medical clinic, where disinfection could be performed under supervision. Army doctors called the post-coital disinfecting at a Blue Light clinic 'preventive early treatment', and soldiers were reminded over and again that doing this early greatly decreased the chance of infection.

During the war, the safe-sex campaigner Ettie Rout suggested similar methods for soldiers to use:

> If you become infected with V.D., the fault is really your own. Either do not risk infection at all, or, risking infection, take proper precautions. These are quite simple. If you take the following precautions *without delay* you are very very unlikely to contract disease:-
>
> 1. Use vaseline or some other grease (such as calomel ointment) *beforehand*, to prevent direct contact with the source of infection. (Note: Any personal discomfort or unpleasantness grease causes is counteracted by the woman's having douched beforehand, as should always be done for the sake of cleanliness. A mere film of grease is sufficient to fill up pores of the skin, cover over abrasions, and prevent penetration of microbes, and it greatly facilitates subsequent cleansing.)
> 2. Urinate *immediately* after *each* connection to wash away all infective material, and to prevent the invasion of the urethra by the microbes of V.D.
> 3. Wash thoroughly with soap and water, because ordinary soap is destructive to germs — of syphilis and of gonorrhoea — and bathe parts with weak solution of pot. permang.
>
> You had far better carry a blue-light outfit with you as a 'town dressing', in the same way as you would carry a 'field dressing'. If you

cannot get an outfit, carry a tiny bottle of pot. permang. lotion and a scrap of cotton wool. If you swab yourself *carefully* with this, you will not become diseased. Remember always *it is delay that is dangerous*. If there has been delay, use a syringe sufficiently large for the contents to flood the urethra and slightly distend it, so that every nook and cranny is cleansed.

Whatever you do, make certain of *going home clean*. Be sure of your health and doubly sure before you embark. While you are in the army and on this side of the world you can be cured easily and privately. If you go home infected, there will be embarrassment and expense to yourself and *great danger* to the women and children you love.[26]

It is evident, however, that many Australian soldiers did not, or perhaps could not, follow such elaborate procedures. Others were notoriously indifferent to the risks they took. In displays of bravado, risk-takers might boast of their disdain for common-sense precautions, and openly flaunt their venereal-disease symptoms as a kind of hilarious joke. There was also talk of soldiers deliberately becoming infected to avoid front-line service, although that is hard to verify. The careless attitude of many young men was a source of amazement, disappointment, and irritation for their officers, and for the army doctors who had to treat them for VD.

The army also maintained that there was a relationship between drinking alcohol excessively and becoming infected with VD. In the AIF campaign to prevent the diseases, frequent reminders about the consequences of drunkenness were given to men going on leave. A man affected by drink might drop his 'moral guard' and easily be tempted to have sex with prostitutes, to his later regret. Drunkenness of soldiers was often blamed by temperance organisations in Australia for their venereal infections, and having been drunk when an infection occurred was a common explanation given by soldiers, and an excuse. Being drunk also meant that a man was less likely to take prophylactic measures, or to quickly report for early treatment at an AIF clinic.

Testing for gonorrhoea and syphilis

After observable symptoms were gone, few of the tests for syphilis and gonorrhoea were simple to prepare or easy to administer, and they required almost perfect conditions during sampling and testing to produce reliable results. Because of this unreliability, testing might be done many times during a cure to produce a consistent trend in results. Such comprehensive testing was not always possible, and soldiers might be discharged from hospital as cured or non-infectious after minimal testing, or none at all. Sometimes, they still carried live bacteria in their bodies — and there are numerous examples of men who were discharged from Langwarrin and Bulford being re-admitted shortly after with the same infection.

Testing for gonorrhoea

For doctors working in army venereal-disease hospitals, the certain diagnosis for gonorrhoea was generally much easier to make than for syphilis. An obvious visible symptom of gonorrhoea in a soldier was a white, yellow, or green discharge of pus from his urethra.

A simple and commonly used test for gonorrhoea during a cure was to observe for pus threads in a sample of urine given by a soldier. As the cure progressed, urine samples were expected to gradually clear. Soldiers quickly learnt that, if they drank large quantities of water before a urine test, they might be able to produce a clear sample. Soldiers might also offer as their own a sample of urine provided by a mate whose sample was clear. There were, however, scientific methods to test for gonorrhoea, and their results could not be so easily cheated.

At Langwarrin and Bulford, two science-based tests were used to detect how much *Neisseria gonorrhoeae* was still present during a cure. One test was called the Pappenheim's method, after the German haematologist Artur Pappenheim. This involved preparing a microscope slide containing a stained film of pus taken from a soldier. If *Neisseria gonorrhoeae* was present, it appeared bright pink under the microscope.

Another staining method, named after American scientist William Leszynsky, turned the bacteria black.

Testing for syphilis

The visible signs of primary-stage syphilis were buboes on the skin where contact had been made with those of the donor. After the disease progressed, and observable symptoms disappeared, a reliable test was needed to detect the invisible bacteria. During the First World War, this was the antibody test for syphilis developed in Germany in 1906 by three bacteriologists: von Wassermann, Citron, and Neisser.

The Wasserman test, as it was called, was performed on a sample of blood drawn from a soldier's arm into a hypodermic syringe, and the degree of reaction by syphilis antibodies showed the infection's intensity. Conducting the test required great skill by a laboratory technician, but it usually revealed the presence of *Treponema pallidum pallidum*. Sometimes, a test might produce false-negative reactions, or false-positive reactions to other diseases. The Wassermann test was meant to be repeated often during a syphilis cure, in order to measure progress, and tens of thousands were performed between 1914 and 1919 in Australian military hospitals where venereal diseases were treated.

Cures for gonorrhoea, syphilis, and chancroid
Quack remedies, home treatments, and patent medicines

Before the late 19th century, and because of the trouble that venereal diseases caused, apothecaries and quack doctors often invented what they claimed were remedies. Despite advances in medical science, some were still being openly sold when the First World War started. Most quack remedies, home treatments, and patent medicines for VD were advertised as fast, effective, painless ways of restoring health, which was never entirely truthful and was sometimes frankly fraudulent. Because of the shame that accompanied the disease, and the need for buyers to keep their infection to themselves, sellers offered confidentiality and guarantees that a cure could be self-administered at home in privacy.

These remedies might give temporary symptomatic relief, but they had no properties that could provide a permanent cure. Many quack preparations contained mercury, although silver, arsenic, and other heavy metals were also used. Sometimes they were made from vegetables and herbs. Some had a high alcohol content, or were fortified with morphine, opium, or cocaine. Remedies containing alcohol and narcotics were popular with those who consumed them, and profitable for the makers.

When, after all this, no cure was forthcoming, a soldier usually ended up revealing his disease to an army doctor. At this point, his secret was in the hands of army policy and his own ingenuity, as we have seen.

The unreliability of cures

During the war, there was no single best medical cure for gonorrhoea, syphilis, and chancroid. In army VD hospitals, specific cures were, from time to time, recommended for each disease, but doctors were encouraged to experiment in a search to find better, faster, and cheaper methods. When experimenting appeared to produce encouraging results at any of the Australian VD hospitals, the news was communicated to the others. Throughout the war, there was an imperative to find cures that would shorten the time a soldier was withdrawn from the fighting because of VD.

Although great advances were made in developing science-based cures before the war, and although the new methods were more effective and safe than their predecessors, no 'cure' was ever completely reliable. Each required preparation and administration in almost perfect clinical conditions, and patients needed to co-operate fully during painful procedures that had to be performed over a long period of time. Men with advanced or multiple infections could be difficult to cure perfectly; in fact, some were discharged from the army as incurable.

None of the drugs came from the manufacturer ready for use, but had to be made up in a hospital pharmacy by a dispensing chemist. Dispensers needed to be highly skilled: many ingredients were sensitive or unstable, and lethal if not properly diluted. Exactly correct doses needed to be administered to patients at the correct intervals in a rigorous schedule. Patients needed to endure repeated hypodermic injections, urethral syringings and douchings, and the application of caustic substances onto their genitals. Men could easily interrupt this by resisting or interfering, while some might intentionally sabotage a cure to delay a return to active duty.

Most of the drugs to cure gonorrhoea and syphilis, and their associated testing materials, had been developed and patented in Germany and Austria before the war began. After 1914, the original Hoechst and Bayer products gradually became unobtainable outside Germany, so manufacturing chemists in Britain, France, and the United States began making copies and variations for doctors in the Allied armies.

The use of mercury, arsenic, and silver

During the First World War, common cures for gonorrhoea, syphilis, and chancroid were drugs and medicines derived from the heavy metals mercury, arsenic, and silver. These were well-known for their antibacterial action — mercury and arsenic for syphilis, silver for gonorrhoea. Doses were meant to be low enough to poison the VD bacteria and not the patients. Dosing continued until testing returned negative results, or until the cure was stopped.

Heavy metals were mostly prepared in injectable fluids. Those for syphilis were introduced into the bloodstream of patients by hypodermic injections. Those for gonorrhoea were directly injected into the urethra using rubber- or glass-tipped urethral syringes or douche nozzles. Mercury, arsenic, and silver were also dispensed in pills, ointments, lotions, and washes, and applied directly to venereal buboes and chancres. The technique of inunction was also used, which was a method of mixing the metals into absorbable substances and rubbing them into the skin.

The consequences of using anti-venereal drugs made from heavy metals were not fully understood during the war. Decades afterwards, it was discovered that even tiny amounts of mercury could be dangerous to humans. Governments banned it in products for human consumption, and its use in medical thermometers and dental fillings became far less common. Governments eventually banned using arsenic as well, after it became known that small amounts could increase the risk of cancers, and cardiovascular and other diseases. In Australia, the advertising of colloidal silver as a medicine was eventually stopped for similar reasons.

Gonorrhoea cures

A drug made from silver was the most common cure for gonorrhoea during the First World War. This was Protargol, developed using colloidal silver by Bayer Chemicals in Germany, and released in 1897. Colloidal silver comprised fine particles of the metal, or its nitrates or salts, suspended in a solution. Numerous copies and variations were made by other European and American manufacturing chemists, using brand names such as Argyrol, Nargol, Melaigen, Albeigen, and Argentamen. During the war, these were usually made up by dispensers in injectable fluids delivered by douche or syringe deep into a soldier's urethra. This might occur several times in a day, and, for it to work properly, the soldier had to hold it in for many minutes. Colloidal silver was also dispensed in ointments and jellies, to be used as prophylactics as well as cures.

Depending on the preference of a doctor, or when Protargol or its alternatives were unavailable, other substances would be used in urethral injections. These included diluted potassium permanganate, or sandalwood oil, obtained from Indian sandalwood trees, or copaiba oil, obtained from South American trees.

In 1917, the standard procedure at the Langwarrin hospital for curing gonorrhoea was to repeatedly do as follows:

1. Soldier to empty his bladder and so wash out the urethra.
2. The penis and all surrounding parts to be washed with soap and water (the soaping to be complete). The parts to be swabbed with perchloride of mercury (1–1000 to 1–4000). Particular attention is to

be paid to the Glans Penis, Meatus, Urinarius and Scrotum, and also any abrasion of skin of Mucous membrane.

3. The injection into the urethra of 2 to 4 c. (1/2 to 1 drachm) of any of the following solutions:

Argyrol	20 per cent
Protargol	10 per cent
Melaigen	10 per cent
Albeigen	10 per cent
Argentamen	5 per cent

The solutions used should be retained in the urethra for 5 to 10 minutes.

If any of the above solutions are unprocurable, Pot. Permanganate (1–1000) may be used as an emergency injection. Care should be exercised that injection is not carried too far back.

4. After solution is injected, the parts mentioned above in Para 2 are to be thoroughly smeared with 20% Calomel Ointment, particular care being paid to parts showing any abrasions. Finally a small amount of ointment is to be inserted into Meatus.[27]

In Australian army hospitals between 1915 and 1919, the typical duration of a short gonorrhoea cure was four or five weeks; however, if syphilis was also present, the treatment time doubled at least.

Syphilis cures

The main syphilis cures used during the war were long courses of intramuscular or intravenous injections by hypodermic needle of solutions containing arsenic or mercury. Mercury was also given to patients in ointments and pills, and the progress of syphilis cures was meant to be monitored by regular Wassermann tests.

The most effective arsenic-based syphilis cure was Salvarsan, synthesised in Germany by a team led by Paul Ehrlich, and released by Hoechst in 1910. It was often just called '606', and, during the war, was copied by manufacturers in other countries. Salvarsan was used in all

Australian army VD hospitals, sometimes as copies with names such as Arsenobenzol, Arsphenamine, Arsenobillon, Silver Arsenobillon, and Kharvasan. These all came from a factory as an unstable crystalline powder that had to be dissolved by army dispensers in distilled, sterile water to make an injectable solution.

Although Salvarsan was meant to be a perfect cure for syphilis, making an injectable solution with the sensitive powder was complicated. It was easy for inexperienced or inattentive dispensers to prepare this solution incorrectly, and unwanted side effects or no effect at all could occur if fluid of poor quality was injected. In 1912, Hoechst released an improved version, called Neo-salvarsan, and this was also copied and eventually used in Australian hospitals as the arsenicals Neoarsenobenzol, Neo-arsphenamine, Novarsan, and Novarsenobillon.

Mercury was also a mainstay of syphilis treatments in Australian hospitals. It was usually called Hydrargyrum, and Hydrargyrum injections with hypodermic needles were routinely given. The mercury was heavily diluted in a solution containing lanolin and oils to make injecting less painful, and was often injected alternately with Arsenobenzol. Another commonly used injection fluid was Grey Oil, a mercury solution containing lanolin and liquid paraffin to reduce injection pain.

Mercury ointments and lotions were also used against syphilis. Mercury-chloride ointment, also called Calomel, was fine mercury particles suspended in lanolin or vaseline. Calomel was applied directly to syphilitic buboes, or rubbed over the whole genitalia, and was also used as a prophylactic against infection. Grey Oil was also used in ointments and lotions to cure syphilitic buboes, as well as chancre. Another cure was Blue Ointment, a mixture of mercurial ointment and petroleum jelly or lard. In the process of inunction, it was applied to a small area of the skin of syphilitic patients at bedtime, and rubbed until absorbed. The skin was wrapped with a cloth overnight, and then washed the next morning to remove any remaining ointment. The procedure was repeated the next night on another small area of skin. Mercury could also be given to soldiers in pills or through the vapour in steam baths.

At the Langwarrin hospital in 1917, the following guidelines were recommended for curing early-stage syphilis:

The treatment is to be carried out at the earliest opportunity and as soon as the Medical Officer diagnoses the case as Syphilis. The treatment is intensive and is set out with the purpose of getting the soldier back to the lines as soon as possible consistent with reasonable chance of permanent cure.

The treatment to be adopted is:

1. Intravenous injection of Arseno-Benzol preparation. There are to be three injections given at two weekly intervals. The amount of each injection is to be 0.3 to 0.6 grams of Arseno-Benzol.

2. Intramuscular injection of Mercury. These are to be alternate with the Arseno-Benzol injections at two weekly intervals, and then weekly afterwards from the 6th to the 10th week inclusive.

3. Inunctions of Mercury. If secondary symptoms or any sign of generalization of the disease are evident, one to two extra doses of Arseno-Benzol should be administered. The mercurial treatment should be carried out for a further period of four or five intramuscular injections, i.e. for a further period of 6 to 8 weeks.

4. Course of Mercury & Iodides also given internally.

5. After above course of treatment. If no obvious lesions are present a Wasserman blood test is made and if Negative the patient is transferred back to his lines non-infective. No man is discharged as non-infective till all induration at site of Primary Chancre has disappeared.[28]

Cures for chancroid and syphilitic lesions

During the war, caustic and toxic chemicals were used to destroy chancres and other kinds of skin-surface venereal lesions, buboes, and sores on the genitals of soldiers. Mercury chloride in the form of Calomel ointment and Black Wash was often used. Black Wash was a lotion containing Calomel diluted in limewater, with the surface of the sore being kept wet with the wash. Mercuric oxide, sometimes called 'corrosive sublimate', was used to make a lotion called Yellow Wash, which was applied in a similar way.

Diluted mercury-nitrate acid was repeatedly applied with a glass rod to chancres and syphilitic buboes until they were destroyed. Zinc and ferric oxide in Calamine Lotion, which was also called Red Lotion and Scarlet Red Lotion, was sometimes tried for venereal sores, as was potassium iodide in Iodine Lotion.

The typical duration of a single course of treatment for chancroid in Australian army hospitals between 1915 and 1919 was about four weeks. If gonorrhoea or syphilis was also present, the treatment time could be more than two months.

Methods of injecting venereal drugs

Two general routes were used to inject mercury, arsenic, and silver solutions into the bodies of infected soldiers. To attack the syphilis bacteria in a man's blood with mercury and arsenic, hypodermic syringes and needles were used. To flood the gonorrhoea bacteria lodged in a man's urethra with toxins, urethral injections were given with hypodermic syringes or gravity-fed douches fitted with urethral nozzles. Whichever method was used, the soldier's usual reaction ranged from discomfort to extreme pain. Between injections, men might be rested in bed, and, after injections of mercury, they might need at least a day to recover.

By the First World War, manufacturing methods for hypodermic syringes and hollow needles had become remarkably sophisticated, but small pre-filled disposable plastic syringes with fine painless needles were still far in the future. The process of preparing an injectable fluid, and assembling and filling the large hypodermic syringes used in military hospitals, was all done manually. Syringes had a glass and plated-steel barrel, a steel plunger, and a thick steel needle screwed to the base. After being used for injections, syringes and needles were washed and disinfected by medical orderlies, to be re-used hundreds of times. The bevelled tips of needles were meant to be regularly ground to ensure sharp penetration of skin and muscle, but, apparently, often were not.

Urethral injections for gonorrhoea patients were often done using a douche. The part inserted into a soldier's urethra was a glass or rubber nozzle. Many different brands and types of urethral nozzles were manufactured by surgical-instrument makers; at Langwarrin, the Valentine's glass nozzle was preferred. This was attached to a rubber irrigator tube, which descended from a glass or ceramic fluid reservoir suspended above the man's bed. When all was ready, a solution of colloidal silver, potassium permanganate, or sandalwood oil was released from the reservoir to run down through the tube and out of the nozzle embedded in the urethra. Soldiers would recoil from the painful sensation of having the nozzle inserted and withdrawn, and having their urethra flooded and distended for up to ten minutes.

Many a suffering soldier could then be grateful for the doctors such as those at Langwarrin, whose research decreased the length of time taken to treat these diseases.

Notes

1   Bean (1915), 'Our Reputation'.
2   Barrett and Deane (1918).
3   *The Singleton Argus*, 20 March 1915.
4   Barrett and Deane (1918).
5   AWM 27/376/200.
6   *The Argus*, 25 January 1915.
7   AWM 3DRL/2222 5/7.
8   AWM MSS453.
9   AWM M1787 3710/201.
10 Butler (1938).
11 NAA CP359/2.
12 *The Argus*, 19 July 1915.
13 *The Argus*, 26 July 1915.
14 *The Sydney Morning Herald*, 4 November 1915.
15 *The Mercury*, 7 August 1915.
16 NAA B539 AIF125/1/1012 409042.
17 *The Argus*, 27 October 1915.
18 NLA MS1454.
19 See Appendix A.
20 The initials 'SRD' marked on the earthenware rum jars stood for the British Admiralty's Supply Reserve Depot, located at Deptford on the River Thames near London. The depot was expanded during the First World War to also supply the British and dominion armies with many items, including the rum.

21 Some of the picturesque AIF slang words associated with drinking and drunkenness that passed into Australian vernacular language included 'blotto', 'canned', 'gay and frisky' (whisky), 'joy juice', 'oiled', 'shick' and 'shickered', 'stung', 'tanked up', and 'vin blank' and 'vin roush', all of which appear in Downing (1990) and the Glossary of Slang website.

22 *The Medical Journal of Australia*, 11 September 1915.

23 Official VD statistics reported in AWM 41/1433 and Butler (1943) were incomplete. Statistics used by the former were those to September 1918, and Butler's were to March 1919; however, the army VD hospital at Bulford operated until November 1919, and, at Langwarrin, the army hospital was still admitting new patients in 1920. As well, identical categories of data were not collected uniformly throughout the war, and there are certain periods and also places when no or little data was apparently collected or reported by AAMC doctors. The official data could not also include estimates of the number of men not treated by army doctors; for example, those who successfully self-treated, or were treated by private physicians. The official data, however, clearly indicates that at least 60,000 men received abortive or hospital treatment for VD between 1914 and 1919. This represents about 14–15 per cent of the 417,000 men enlisted for service in Australia and abroad. The percentage for just the 332,000 AIF men who served overseas was about the same, but higher if an estimate of unrecorded infections is included.

24 *The Canberra Times*, 22 April 1967, an article describing how the Australian defence department intended to give US soldiers coming to Australia for R and R 'thorough medical checks' to prevent introduction of the 'new Asian strains' of VD.

25 The information collated to produce this appendix came especially from wartime articles in *The Medical Journal of Australia*, Langdon-Brown and Murphy (1915), various documents from the Langwarrin isolation hospital contained in NLA MS1454, and other sources, including Butler (1943), listed in the bibliography.

26 Rout (1922).

27 NLA MS1454.

28 *The Medical Journal of Australia*, 9 June 1917.

Bibliography

Abbreviations

AWM   Australian War Memorial
NAA   National Archives of Australia
NLA   National Library of Australia
SLNSW   State Library of NSW
SLV   State Library of Victoria

General archival sources

Australian War Memorial, WW1 Embarkation Rolls, 1914–1918

AWM 1DRL/0428, Australian Red Cross Society Wounded and Missing File, Private William Wilson Crozier

AWM 1DRL/0428, Australian Red Cross Society Wounded and Missing File, Second Lieutenant Reginald Henry Dabb

AWM 1DRL/0428, Australian Red Cross Society Wounded and Missing File, Private Richard Waltham

AWM 3DRL/2222 2/4, correspondence of 28 March 1916 from Governor General to Senator George Pearce, Minister of Defence, and to the Roman Catholic Bishop of Brisbane, *Prostitution in Egypt*

AWM 3DRL/2222 5/7, correspondence of 13 March 1915 from Colonel John Monash to Senator George Pearce, Minister of Defence, *Allegations of misbehaviour by Australian troops in Egypt*

AWM 3DRL/3376, Papers of Lord Birdwood, Series 7 1–2, Correspondence with George Pearce 1915–1918, letter from Cairo, 24 March 1916

AWM 4/23/2/16, War Diary, 2nd Infantry Brigade, August 1916

AWM 4/23/25/20, War Diary, 8th Infantry Battalion, August 1916

AWM 4/23/30, War Diary, 13th Infantry Battalion

AWM 4/23/51, War Diary, 34th Infantry Battalion

AWM 4/23/55, War Diary, 38th Infantry Battalion

AWM 4/26/18/2, War Diary, Assistant Director of Medical Services 1st
    Australian Division, January, February, May 1915

AWM 4/26/69/1, War Diary, 1st Australian Dermatological Hospital AIF

AWM 4/19955, Barrett, James W. *Management of Venereal Diseases in Egypt
    During the War.*

AWM 7 item, 'Wiltshire 3: S.S. Wiltshire Suez to Melbourne, Sept 1915'

AWM 27/371/94, 1st Australian Dermatological Hospital, Daily Average
    Number of Australian Cases Under Treatment for VD, Cairo 1916

AWM 27/371/94, Special Report Upon VD Cases

AWM 27/376/200, Report on the 1st Australian General Hospital, Isolation
    Camp, Egypt

AWM 32/105, Control of Invalids (AIF), Administrative Methods for Special
    Cases, C. Venereal Disease

AWM 38/3DRL606, Records of C. E. W. Bean — Diaries

AWM38, 3DRL606/1/1 — October–December 1914

AWM38, 3DRL606/2/1 — January–March 1915

AWM38, 3DRL606/3/1 — March–April 1915

AWM 41/479, article on the 1st Australian General Hospital

AWM 41/812, Isolation Hospital — Abbassia Detention Barracks — Egypt

AWM 41/1433, Cumpston J. H. L., *Venereal Disease in Australia*,
    Commonwealth of Australia Quarantine Service Publication No. 17, 1919

AWM 224 MSS425, Analysis of 287 venereal cases admitted to B Section, No. 2
    Stationary Hospital, 19 February 1915

AWM 224 MSS425, Letter from the Secretary Venereal Disease Conference to
    the Director of Medical Services AIF

AWM 224 MSS425, Report by Capts. Sawers and Deakin on the histories of
    284 cases in A Section, No. 2 Australian Stationary Hospital

AWM Donor File 93, item 12/5/68 part 14, *Donation of John Dunbar
    Sketchbook*

AWM M1787 3710/201, Conference of Senior Medical Officers at the Palace
    Hotel Heliopolis 17/2/15

AWM MSS453, VD Hospital Abbassia — General File

AWM MSS453, VD Hospital Abbassia — General File, 'Letter dated 27 April
    1915 from Surgeon Major B Pares, ADMS, written on behalf of the

Surgeon General, Egypt, to Lieutenant-Colonel Brady Nash'

AWM Particulars Required for the Roll of Honour — Randolph Dunbar

AWM Particulars Required for the Roll of Honour — Richard Waltham

NAA A471/307, District Court Martial, 20 October 1915, William Costello
and 16 others

NAA A471/316, District Court Martial, 25 October 1915, Albert Neil and 36 others

NAA A471/347, District Court Martial, 19 November 1915, Charles McGhee
and 22 others

NAA A471/7268677, Field General Court Martial, 27–28 December 1915,
William Powell

NAA B73/R21878, Repatriation Case File, John Beech/John Dunbar

NAA B539 AIF125/1/1012 409042, Disposal of Remains of the late Major
General Sir W. T. Bridges

NAA C138/M133626, Repatriation Case File, Harold Ernest Glading

NAA CP359/2, Confidential Report by Miss E. A. Rout to the New Zealand
Government Commissioner, Cairo, 12 March 1916

NAA MP367/1 527/21/101, Venereal Disease in AIF Camps in England

NAA MP367/1 556/44/1473, Venereal Diseases and Venereal Disease
Forfeitures

NLA MS1454, Papers of Walter T. Conder Part 1

NLA MS1454, Papers of Walter T. Conder Part 2

NSW Registrar of Births Deaths and Marriages 1954/016179, death certificate,
Albert Edward Crozier

SLNSW CY4939 (Mitchell Library), 1915 diary of Dr John Brady Nash and
other personal papers 1915–18

State Records Authority of NSW, Inquest 54/1553, death of Albert Edward
Crozier

University of Melbourne Archives, 75/22 Papers of Sir James Barrett

Series 5 Newspaper Cuttings

Series 7 WW1 Lecture Notes, Newspaper Cuttings and Reprints

AIF soldiers, non-A18 *Wiltshire*

NAA B2455/3052653 Keith Barrett (KIA)

NAA B2455/4028768 Charles Bean

NAA B2455/1935325 Robert Beatham, VC

NAA B2455/3068309 Frederick Beech

NAA B2455/3068330 John Beech

NAA B2455/3068333 John Thomas Beech

NAA B2455/4028769 William Birdwood

NAA B2455/1935247 William Bridges
NAA B2455/3162386 Gerald Buckley
NAA B2455/3162819 William Buckley
NAA B2455/3175931 Arthur Graham Butler
NAA B2455/1935343 John Carroll, VC
NAA B2455/1935347 Claud Castleton, VC
NAA B2455/3270777 Herbert Collett
NAA B2455/3473388 Reginald Crozier
NAA B2455/3473439 William Crozier
NAA B2455/3481715 Reginald Dabb (POW DOW)
NAA B2455/3515282 William Doolan (KIA)
NAA B2455/1/3525682 John Dunbar
NAA B2455/3525708 Randolph Dunbar (KIA)
NAA B2455/5099376 Walter Glading (DOW)
NAA B2455/5099374 William Glading
NAA B2455/1935361 Bernard Gordon, VC
NAA B2455/1935364 John Hamilton, VC
NAA B2455/4265834 Michael Hamilton
NAA B2455/4769234 Henry Hayden
NAA B2455/8334256 Albert Jacka, VC
NAA B2455/8334254 Thomas Kenny, VC
NAA B2455/7378889 John Leak, VC
NAA B2455/1935394 Joseph Maxwell, VC, MC and Bar, DCM
NAA B2455/8334259 John Monash
NAA B883/4487930 Harry Murray, VC, DSO and Bar
NAA B2455/8017857 George Platt (KIA)
NAA B2455/8019880 William Powell
NAA B2455/8072246 William Rudolph
NAA B2455/1935373 Edward Ryan, VC
NAA B2455/11973591 Clifford Sadlier, VC
NAA B2455/1935408 Lawrence Weathers, VC
NAA B2455/1935358 Cyril Brudenell White
NAA B2455/1812905 William Williams
NAA B2455/8855072 Michael Willis
NAA B2455/8855073 Michael Richardson Willis

Medical staff, AAMC and Australian hospitals in Egypt (including Abbassia isolation barracks), December 1914–October 1915
NAA B2455/3052620 James Barrett AAMC

NAA B2455/3101184 Isidore Bourke AAMC

NAA B2455/7994190 John Brady Nash AAMC

NAA B2455/3134002 Henry Bryant AAMC

NAA B2455/4703904 William Grigor AAMC

NAA B2455/6994845 Neville Howse AAMC

NAA B2455/3000862 Thomas Morgan Martin AAMC

NAA B2455/8016597 Harold Plant AAMC (KIA)

NAA B2455/1793501 William Ramsay Smith AAMC

NAA B2455/8074093 Charles Ryan AAMC

NAA B2455/1846331 Arthur White AAMC

NAA B2455/1812901 William Williams AAMC

NAA B2455/2015707 Thomas Wilson AAMC

NAA B2455/3457930 Bernhard Zwar AAMC

Military and medical staff, Langwarrin Isolation Hospital, 1915–1921

NAA B2455/3092739 Ivie Blezard (WIA Gallipoli)

NAA B2455/3175751 John Butchart AAMC

NAA B2455 3244015 James Chirnside AAMC

NAA B2455/3281938 Alexander Cook AAMC

NAA B2455/6138247 Walter Conder/VX38735 Walter Tasman Conder
    (WIA Gallipoli)

NAA B2455/4669863 Andrew Robertson Grant AAMC

NAA B2455/4711989 Henry Hunter Griffith AAMC (DOD)

NAA B2455/5476284 Whitfield DeWitt Henty AAMC

NAA B2455/8197744 Archibald Lloyd

NAA B2455/1941800 James McCusker AAMC

NAA B2455/7981794 Arthur Morris AAMC

NAA B2455/7993510 George Gray Nicholls AAMC

Medical staff and escorts on the A18 *Wiltshire*, Suez to Melbourne, August–September 1915

NAA B2455/3032565 Herbert Alsop AAMC

NAA B2455/3507182 William Dilley (WIA Gallipoli)

NAA B2455/3534588 Ernest Edgar

NAA B2455/4362998 Jack Haddon

NAA B2455/7368596 Thomas Keane

NAA B2455/7984497 Laurence Mouldey

NAA B2455/7998478 Terence O'Neill

NAA B2455/8018829 Albert Pritchard

NAA B2455/8390779 Albert Tiegs (WIA Gallipoli)

Medical staff, 1st Australian Dermatological Hospital Bulford and at other hospitals in France and Belgium that treated venereal patients
NAA B2455/4703904 William Grigor AAMC
NAA B2455/7369761 Alan Jolley AAMC

Venereal cases transported from Suez to Melbourne, A18 *Wiltshire*, August–September 1915
NAA B2455/3032693 Lewis Ambrose
NAA B2455/3033983 Kenneth Annear (KIA)
NAA B2455/3035966 Charles Arnold
NAA B2455/3036452 Frederick Arthur
NAA B2455/3038829 Thomas Atkins (WIA Gallipoli)
NAA B2455/3010227 William Baker (DOW)
NAA B2455/3048646 Frederick Banwell (WIA)
NAA 2455/3052801 Rupert Barrie, DCM
NAA B2455/3057042 Esca Bateup (WIA Gallipoli)
NAA B2455/3059010 Herbert Baxter (WIA Gallipoli)
NAA B2455/3095005 James Boase
NAA 2455/3101960 Albert Bowbridge
NAA B2455/3103392 William Bowers
NAA B2455/3105429 John Boyd
NAA B2455/3115130 Cyril Brayshaw
NAA B2455/3118965 Harry Brett
NAA B2455/3128532 Ronald Brook (WIA Gallipoli)
NAA B2455/1798919 John Brown (KIA)
NAA B2455/1804093 William Brown, MM
NAA B2455/3132667 John Bruce
NAA B2455/3133218 Walter Bruton
NAA B2455/1935335 Maurice Buckley (Gerald Sexton), VC, DCM (WIA)
NAA B2455/3168851 Edward Burke
NAA B2455/3168972 John Burke MM (WIA, KIA)
NAA B2455/3171341 William Burn (WIA Gallipoli)
NAA B2455/3176289 Joseph Butler (WIA)
NAA B2455/3179570 James Byrne
NAA B2455/3181299 Tasman Cadee
NAA B2455/3199752 Donald Cameron
NAA B2455/1852453 Charles Campbell

NAA B2455/1853115 Frank Campbell
NAA B2455/3219325 Edric Castle (DOD)
NAA B2455/3235244 Thomas Chappell
NAA B2455/3235935 Alfred Charlton
NAA B2455/3243412 Frederick Chigwidden
NAA B2455/1969980 Leslie Clarke
NAA B2455/3014536 Charles Collins
NAA B2455/3014817 Frederick Collins (KIA)
NAA B2455/3277168 Edward Connell
NAA B2455/3426889 William Costello
NAA B2455/3428807 George Cotton
NAA B2455/3473317 Albert Crozier (Michael Willis) (WIA)
NAA B884/N107844/5688199 Albert Crozier (WW2 records)
NAA B2455/3489297 Albert Davey
NAA B2455/1902491 William Davies
NAA B2455/1902491 George Davis
NAA B2455/3495192 Samuel Dean
NAA B2455/3510206 Charles Dodd
NAA B2455/1/3525683 Ernest Dunbar (John Dunbar, John Beech) (WIA
    Gallipoli & Flanders)
NAA B2455/3531093 Ralph Dyer (WIA Gallipoli)
NAA B2455/3540825 Joseph Ellis
NAA B2455/3543962 John Erikson
NAA B2455/3545253 Leslie Everon (WIA)
NAA B2455/8334119 Thomas Farrell
NAA B2455/3549579 Alfred Farroway (WIA)
NAA B2455/3902010 Hubert Figg
NAA B2455/3909878 Daniel Fitzgerald (DOW)
NAA B2455/4035393 George French
NAA B2455/4035135 John Fretwell
NAA B2455/4035767 Albert Gallafent (Albert Burns)
NAA B2455/4001951 Michael Gallaher (James Collins) (WIA)
NAA B2455/4036585 Thomas Galloway (KIA)
NAA B2455/4028036 Sydenham Gardiner
NAA B2455/5008458 William Giles
NAA B2455/5099378 Harold Glading (WIA)
NAA B2455/4668322 Joseph Gough
NAA B2455/4391036 Charles Grose (WIA)
NAA B2455/4362543 Charles Haberle

NAA B2455/3007816 Ralph Hall
NAA B2455/4265110 Leslie Halls (WIA)
NAA B2455/4932829 John Harman (KIA)
NAA B2455/5476295 Reginald Henwood (WIA Gallipoli)
NAA B2455/5457876 Herbert Hicks
NAA B2455/5454613 Keith Higgs
NAA B2455/3011661 Alfred Hill (KIA)
NAA B2455/52657 William Hocking
NAA B2455/5485270 George Howard
NAA B2455/7017982 Charles Hughes (WIA)
NAA B2455/7031830 William Hull (KIA)
NAA B2455/7031906 Claude Humberstone (WIA Gallipoli)
NAA B2455/6928697 James Hutton
NAA B2455/6928765 Ernest Huxley
NAA B2455/6928726 Ernest Hyland
NAA B2455/7366119 Tom Ingram (WIA)
NAA B2455/7361530 Sydney Jenkins (KIA)
NAA B2455/7369622 Robert Jinnette
NAA B2455/7369636 Percy Job
NAA B2455/1825225 David Johnson
NAA B2455/1831147 William Johnston (WIA)
NAA B2455/1821812 Robert Jones
NAA B2455/7365735 Sidney Judd
NAA B2455/7366389 Percy Jukes (George Ernest Jukes)
NAA B2455/7368879 Robert Keily
NAA B2455/7367514 Leo Kenny
NAA B2455/7364693 Thomas Kenny (WIA Gallipoli)
NAA B2455/7364816 Francis Kerr
NAA B2455/7374234 Frank Kluck (KIA)
NAA B2455/8207728 Rudolph Kolb (Ralph Manner) (WIA)
NAA B2455/7376190 Edward Lakovsky
NAA B2455/7377710 Thaddens Leach (KIA)
NAA B2455/8193325 Edward Leech
NAA B2455/8198550 Duncan Leslie (WIA)
NAA B2455/8193650 George Leunig (DOW)
NAA B2455/8193949 George Lindsay
NAA B2455/8202539 Robert Lindsay
NAA B2455/8195818 Cecil Lines (WIA Gallipoli)
NAA B2455/8202633 Gordon Linsley, MC (DOW)

NAA B2455/8195969 Alfred Liston

NAA B2455/8202982 William Lock (DOW)

NAA B2455/8205753 Reginald Lucas (WIA)

NAA B2455/8212208 Sydney Lucas (WIA Gallipoli & France)

NAA B2455/8214187 Leslie Lye

NAA B2455/11615996 George Mabbott (WIA)

NAA B2455/1993846 Percy Macauley

NAA B2455/1947719 John McIvor (WIA)

NAA B2455/1957741 William McNaughton

NAA B2455/1958513 John McPhee (WIA Gallipoli)

NAA B2455/1958541 Neil McPhee

NAA B2455/8039159 Robert Marshall (WIA)

NAA B2455/2017459 Charles Martin

NAA B2455/8012875 George Mildren

NAA B2455/1905886 Alfred Millar (WIA)

NAA B2455/7983059 Thomas Milne (WIA)

NAA B2455/7980233 Harry Minnie (KIA)

NAA B2455/7984014 Sydney Mitchell

NAA B2455/3006849 Walter Moore, DCM (WIA)

NAA B2455/7984349 Victor Morris (WIA)

NAA B2455/7983454 Charles Mountjoy

NAA B2455/7983751 Frank Mundy (WIA Gallipoli & France)

NAA B2455/7994867 James Neve

NAA B2455/7993601 George Nicholson

NAA B2455/8004065 James Nunn

NAA B2455/7991610 William O'Brien (WIA)

NAA B2455/8000234 Leo O'Toole (James O'Toole) (KIA)

NAA B2455/8000578 Bertram Paget

NAA B2455/8005121 Guy Palmer (WIA Gallipoli)

NAA B2455/8000876 Edward Parer (Edward Schneider) (WIA Gallipoli)

NAA B2455/3132746 Walter Paterson (Walter Bruce)

NAA B2455/8015111 Thomas Pennant (Thomas Bain)

NAA B2455/8018068 William Joseph Platt (William Josiah Platt) (KIA)

NAA B2455/8016750 Thomas Popple, MM (WIA)

NAA B2455/8018829 George Poulson

NAA B2455/8019727 Herbert Powardy

NAA B2455/8019937 Francis Power (DOW)

NAA B2455/8023768 James Quinlan

NAA B2455/8024839 Percy Rawnsley (WIA)

NAA B2455/8027535 Arthur Reed (DOW POW)

NAA B2455/1905791 William Robinson

NAA B2455/8036360 Bertie Rogers

NAA B2455/8037607 John Rose

NAA B2455/8037939 Oliver Rossiter (WIA)

NAA B2455/11974155 John Rowe

NAA B2455/8074400 Thomas Ryan (WIA Gallipoli)

NAA B2455/3002826 Donald Scott (WIA Gallipoli)

NAA B2455/8075849 Frederick Seaman

NAA B2455/8078752 Frank Selleck (WIA)

NAA B2455/4769494 Mervyn Shepherd (WIA Gallipoli)

NAA B2455/8084915 Hugh Sinclair (WIA)

NAA B2455/1781055 Harry Smith

NAA B2455/8087788 William Sorenson

NAA B2455/8093243 Leo Spring

NAA B2455/8086824 Charles Souter (WIA)

NAA B2455/8092014 William Stein, MM (KIA)

NAA B2455/1922451 George Stevens (WIA)

NAA B2455/8070942 Eric Swallow, MM (WIA)

NAA B2455/8098666 William Temple (William Considine)

NAA B2455/8098721 Cecil Terrell

NAA B2455/3001303 Bertram Thomas (KIA)

NAA B2455/3001900 James Thomas

NAA B2455/6493138 William Thomas, MM (WIA)

NAA B2455/1831424 Albert Thompson

NAA B2455/1833951 James Thompson

NAA B2455/8391385 Ivan Tindall

NAA B2455/8393288 John Tracy (WIA Gallipoli, DOD)

NAA B2455/8395979 David Underwood (WIA)

NAA B2455/8397708 Linton Vendy (Gerald Linton Vendy) (WIA)

NAA B2455/8398272 Lucius Vincent (WIA Gallipoli)

NAA B2455/8398877 Daniel Walburn

NAA B2455/8399856 Henry Wallace

NAA B2455/8361749 Richard Waltham (KIA)

NAA B2455/8361686 Henry Warby

NAA B2455/8361286 David Ward

NAA B2455/8193687 Richard Warn (Richard Leslie) (DOW)

NAA B2455/8380678 James Wells (WIA)

NAA B2455/8380893 Alfred West (Arthur West) (WIA)

NAA B2455/8381616 Sydney West (WIA Gallipoli)

NAA B2455/8383504 John Wheeler

NAA B2455/1806309 David Williams (WIA)

NAA B2455/1806830 Francis Williams

NAA B2455/1811473 Rupert Williams

NAA B2455/8855780 George Withers

NAA B2455/8860002 Albert Wolstenholme (DOD)

NAA B2455/1916342 George Wood (WIA Gallipoli)

Journal articles

Arthur, Richard, 'An Address Delivered to the Officers of the Australian Imperial Force by Richard Arthur, MD, MLA', *The Medical Journal of Australia*, 20 May 1916

Barrett, James, 'Management of Venereal Diseases in Egypt During the War', *The British Medical Journal*, 1 (3031), 1 February 1919

——, 'Venereal Prophylaxis', *The Medical Journal of Australia*, 13 April 1918

Beardsley, Edward H., 'Allied Against Sin: American and British responses to venereal disease in World War 1', *Medical History*, 20 (2), April 1976

Curran, James, '"Bonjoor Paree!": the first AIF in Paris, 1916–1918', *Journal of Australian Studies*, 23 (60), 1999

Flecker, H., 'The Prophylaxis of Venereal Disease', *The Medical Journal of Australia*, 5 April 1919

Hughes, James, 'Venereal Infections in Soldiers', *The Medical Journal of Australia*, 11 December 1915

Morris, Arthur E., 'Army Medical Service: prophylaxis and treatment of venereal disease', *The Medical Journal of Australia*, 5 July 1919

Mulder, Audrey, 'The Camp Hospital for Venereal Diseases: Langwarrin, Victoria', *Australian Society of the History of Medicine Conference 1991*, 1992

Pryke, Sam, 'The Control of Sexuality in the Early British Boy Scouts Movement', *Sex Education*, 5 (1), February 2005

Roth, Reuter, 'The Prophylaxis of Venereal Disease', *The Medical Journal of Australia*, 29 March 1919

Thappa, D. M., 'Evolution of Venereology in India', *Indian Journal of Dermatology, Venereology, and Leprology*, 72 (3), 2006

Medical Journal of Australia, The, 'The Abbasian Detention Barracks Isolation Hospital', 11 September 1915

——, 'British Medical Association News: Medico-Political', 29 September 1917

——, 'British Medical Association News: Scientific', 9 June 1917
——, 'British Medical Association News: Scientific', 5 July 1917
——, 'Naval and Military', 8 January 1916
——, 'The Tobacco Fund', 11 September 1915
——, 'The Venereal Compound', 11 December 1915
Tyquin, Michael, 'Sir William "Mo" Williams, KCMG, CB, KStJ, Creator of Australia's Army Medical Services: maligned or misunderstood?', *Journal of the Royal Australian Historical Society*, 1 (84), June 1998
White, Richard, 'Sun, Sand, and Syphilis: Australian soldiers and the Orient, Egypt 1914', *Australian Cultural History*, 9 (60), 1990
Wilson, Graham, 'A Prison of Our Own: the AIF detention barracks 1917–1919 (Australian Imperial Force)', *Sabretache*, 1 June 2005
Wyman, A. G., 'The Decrease of Venereal Disease in the Indian Army', *The British Medical Journal*, 1 (2036), 6 January 1900
Zwar, B. T., 'The Army Medical Service and the Prevention of Venereal Disease', *The Medical Journal of Australia*, 5 July 1919

Newspaper articles
Advertiser, The, Adelaide, 28 December 1914, 'Australian Troops in Egypt, A Message from the King, Christmas Day Events'
——, 22 January 1915, 'Wasters in the Force — Some Not Fit to be Soldiers', and 'Views of Mr. Hughes'
——, 29 September 1915, 'Returning Heroes — To Reach Adelaide To-morrow'
Advocate, The, Burnie, Tasmania, 30 September 1919, 'Our Soldiers and Sailors'
Age, The, Melbourne, 28 January 1921, 'Sergeant Buckley VC, Accident Proves Fatal, Military Funeral Today'
——, 29 January 1921, 'Sergt. Buckley's Funeral, Large Public Attendance'
——, 30 May 2009, 'A Second-chance Soldier, "Bravest of the Brave"'
Al-Ahram Weekly Online, 7–13 June 2001, 'Back Roads'
Argus, The, 5 June 1884, 'Social Purity: deputation to the chief secretary'
——, 5 March 1889, 'Death of Dr. Bromby'
——, 25 January 1915, 'Weeding the Wasters — Minister's Comments'
——, 12 March 1915, 'Arrival of Kyarra — Three Hundred Men Return'
——, 13 March 1915, 'A Cruel Slander'
——, 19 July 1915, 'Deserter's Language — Hope Germans Will Win'
——, 26 July 1915, 'The Kyarra Soldiers — Reception Arrangements — Two Officers Suspended'

——, 2 September 1915, 'Returned Soldiers — 414 Medical Cases'

——, 16 September 1915, 'The Nameless 400'

——, 25 September 1915, 'Transport Arrives' (arrival of HMAT *Wiltshire* at Port Melbourne)

——, 20 October 1915, 'Soldiers Break Camp — Trouble at Langwarrin'

——, 22 October 1915, 'Langwarrin Camp — New Site Selected'

——, 25 October 1915, 'Escapes from Langwarrin — Men Arrested in City'

——, 27 October 1915, 'State Parliament — Legislative Council'

——, 28 October 1915, 'Escape from Langwarrin — Reply to Criticism'

——, 29 October 1915, 'Escape from Langwarrin — Men Sentenced'

——, 25 November 1915, 'Langwarrin Camp Soldiers — Removal to Bendigo Feared'

——, 26 November 1915, 'Langwarrin Camp — Bendigo's Fears Allayed'

——, 17 December 1915, 'Langwarrin Camp — Men Sent to Other States'

——, 25 September 1916, death notice, Richard Waltham

——, 26 December 1916, 'Langwarrin Camp Recreation Hall Opened'

——, 24 July 1918, 'SS Barunga's Heroes'

——, 23 September 1918, 'Tivoli Entertainment at Langwarrin'

——, 17 December 1918, 'Victoria Cross — Australian Heroes'

——, 19 September 1919, 'Venereal Disease — Military Statistics — Defence of Soldiers'

——, 21 October 1919, 'Captain Jacka VC — Return of SS Euripides — Great Reception by Crowds'

——, 16 December 1920, 'Huts at Morwell'

——, 28 January 1921, death notice, Maurice Buckley

——, 29 January 1921, funeral report, Maurice Buckley

——, 11 February 1921, 'Sergeant Buckley's Death, Evidence at Coroner's Inquiry'

——, 8 June 1923, 'Fighting Venereal Disease, Victorian Act Criticised'

——, 6 September 1930, 'Boot Clicker Imprisoned'

——, 3 December 1930, 'Suspects Imprisoned'

——, 18 September 1931, 'Death of Dr. A. E. Morris'

——, 8 January 1938, 'A Great Schoolmaster'

——, 7 April 1945, 'Sir James Barrett Dies at 83'

Barrier Miner, The, 18 March 1920, 'St. Patrick's Procession in Melbourne on Saturday'

Bendigo Advertiser, The, 14 December 1918, 'Infected Men Detained'

Canberra Times, The, 22 April 1967, 'Smallpox, VD Check-up'

——, 12 February 1968, 'Disease Worry in South Vietnam'

——, 11 February 1995, 'Medical Aspects of Wars in Asia'

Brisbane Courier, The, 26 May 1916, 'Badges for Volunteers'

Chronicle, The, Adelaide, 30 January 1915, 'The Other Side — A Chaplain on Australian Soldiers'

——, 12 April 1919, 'A War Disclosure — A Disaster Averted'

Daily News, The, Perth, 14 February 1920, 'New Regulations for Soldiers' Badges'

Examiner, The, Launceston, 16 February 1915, 'Invalided Australians — Matter of Accommodation'

Frankston and Somerville Standard, 28 January 1921, 'Our Langwarrin Letter — A Gala Night at the Langwarrin Camp'

Geelong Advertiser, 25 October 1915, 'Langwarrin Camp Site Unsuitable'

Goulburn Evening Penny Post, 18 May 1939, 'Daring Theft: cheque stolen from police station'

Goulburn Evening Post, 9 June 1953, 'Stole Pajamas: fined £10'

——, 23 February 1954, 'Two Months for Vagrancy'

Great Southern Star, The, 20 April 1915, 'To Our Critic'

Herald, The, Melbourne, 13 June 1918, 'Liquor Law Broken — Many Girls over 14 Years Associating With Soldiers'

Kalgoorlie Miner, The, 20 January 1915, 'Australians in Egypt, General in Command, Description of the General'

London Gazette, The, 5 December 1918, 'Distinguished Conduct Medal — Sjt Gerald Sexton'

——, 14 December 1918, 'Victoria Cross — Sjt Gerald Sexton'

——, 27 June 1919, 'Amendments — Distinguished Conduct Medal — Sjt Maurice Buckley'

——, 8 August 1919, 'Amendments — Victoria Cross — Sergeant Maurice Vincent Buckley'

Maitland Weekly, The, 16 August 1919, 'Venereal Disease'

Mercury, The, Hobart, 2 January 1915, 'The Australian Army, Impressions of British Generals, A Splendid Sight'

——, 7 August 1915, 'Back from the Front — Wounded Men at Melbourne — An Enthusiastic Welcome'

——, 3 October 1944, 'Biology as a School Subject Advocated'

Moorabbin News, 2 November 1918, 'The Langwarrin Camp'

Mornington Standard, 31 May 1919, 'Farewell Social — Major Conder Entertained'

——, 28 May 1920, 'Heard on the Train — Boys of the Langwarrin Camp'

Muswellbrook Chronicle, The, 2 March 1904, 'Local and General News'

——, 28 January 1905, 'Diocese of Newcastle — Sunday School Examinations'

——, 24 June 1924, 'Personal'

——, 11 April 1930, 'Gala Concert and Minstrel Show — Swimming Club Benefits'

——, 4 March 1932, 'Obituary — Mr Charles Dunbar — An Interesting Link with Early Scone'

Nepean Times, The, 2 October 1947, 'Carried away Wine'

Newcastle Morning Herald and Miners' Advocate, 19 March 1947, 'Police Court'

Portland Observer and Normanby Advertiser, 6 September 1917, 'Temperance Meeting'

Port Pirie Recorder and North Western Mail, 18 February 1915, 'Military Offenders Discharged — With Ignominy'

Register, The, Adelaide, 17 February 1915, 'Wasters Return. Men Will Be Closely Guarded'

——, 28 August 1924, 'Venereal Disease'

——, 29 August 1924, 'The Red Plague — Australia's Terrible Scourge — Combating the Disease'

Richmond Guardian, 28 September 1918, 'Tivoli Review Company Entertains Soldiers at Langwarrin Camp'

St Arnaud Mercury, 10 August 1918, 'Strength of Empire — Movement Launched in St Arnaud — Address by Mr Gifford Gordon'

Scone Advocate, The, 11 October 1918, 'Private E. Dunbar'

Singleton Argus, The, 20 March 1915, 'Meant as a Warning — Cairo's Terrible Dangers'

Sydney Morning Herald, The, 27 May 1915, 'Men of the Dardanelles'.

——, 4 November 1915, 'Medically Unfit'.

——, 19 March 1918, 'Appeal for Prohibition — Special Campaign Proposed'

——, 9 August 1919, 'Soldiers Defamed — Dr Cumpston's Report — Strong Comment by Health Minister'

——, 5 June 1925, 'Dr J. B. Nash — Death Announced — A Fine Career'

——, 12 February 1936, 'Shoplifter Sentenced'

——, 20 June 1936, 'Gaol for Shoplifter'

——, 20 January 1938, 'Shoplifting'

——, 4 April 1939, 'Methylated Spirits Not Intoxicating Liquor — Magistrates Decision'

Sunday Times, The, Perth, 30 March 1919, 'Gifford Gordon — Strikes Trouble — And Agrees to Climb Down'

——, 13 April 1919, 'Vile Calumny Repeated — The Strength of Empire Slanderers'

Sunday Times, The, Sydney, 17 August 1919, 'The Red Plague and Returning Soldiers'

Tamworth Daily Observer, The, 26 June 1915, 'Roll of Honour: 44th casualty list'

———, 16 February 1916, 'From Our Correspondent in Scone'

———, 15 October 1918, 'Soldiers of the North'

Times, The, London, 20 July 1918, 'Transport Sunk by U-boat', 'Australian Troops' Bravery', 'A Lesson in Discipline' (report of the sinking of HMAT *Barunga*)

West Australian, The, 17 April 1897, advertisement for Constance Waltham, music teacher

———, 9 June 1914, death notice, Joshua Waltham

———, 15 June 1914, funeral report, Joshua Waltham

———, 8 April 1919, 'Soldiers and Disease — The Gifford Gordon Incident'

———, 23 December 1943, death notice, Constance Waltham

West Gippsland Gazette, 14 November 1916, 'The YMCA on the Sands of the Desert'

Western Mail, The, 15 December 1900, 'Lemyn College — Annual Prize Distribution'

———, 17 December 1936, 'Winners of the Victoria Cross — Sergeant Maurice Buckley VC'

Non-print sources

Australian Film Commission, *Pozieres*, documentary film, written and directed by Wain Fimeri, 2000

Australian War Memorial, *Australians in the Great War*, CD-ROM, 2008

War Collection, The, *Gas Attack: gas and chemical weapons in the First and Second World Wars*, CD-ROM, 2002

References

Adam-Smith, Patsy, *The Anzacs*, Thomas Nelson, Melbourne, 1978

Andrews, Eric M., *The Anzac Illusion: Anglo-Australian relations during World War I*, Cambridge University Press, Cambridge, 1993

Austin, Ronald J., *Cobbers in Khaki: the history of the 8th Battalion, 1914–1919*, Slouch Hat Publications, McCrae, Victoria, 1997

Australian Government Department of Veterans' Affairs, *1916: Fromelles and the Somme*, Canberra, 2006

———, *1917: Bapaume and Bullecourt*, Canberra, 2007

———, *1918: Amiens to the Hindenburg Line*, Canberra, 2009

———, *Advancing to Victory, 1918*, AWM, Canberra, 2008

———, *To Flanders Fields, 1917*, AWM, Canberra, 2007

Barr, Geoff, *Military Discipline: policing the 1st Australian Imperial Force, 1914–1920*, HJ Publications, Canberra, 2008

Barrett, James, and Deane, P. E., *The Australian Army Medical Corps in Egypt: an illustrated and detailed account of the early organisation and work of the Australian Medical Units in Egypt in 1914–15*, HK Lewis, London, 1918

Barrett, James, *The War Work of the YMCA in Egypt*, HK Lewis, London, 1919

Bean, Charles E. W., *The Official History of Australia in the War of 1914–1918*, Angus and Robertson, Sydney, 1941

> *Volume I — The Story of ANZAC from the outbreak of war to the end of the first phase of the Gallipoli Campaign, May 4, 1915*
>> Chapter III, 'The AIF'
>> Chapter VII, 'The Training in the Desert'
>> Chapter X, 'The Corps Leaves Egypt'
> *Volume III — The AIF in France, 1916*

———, *What to Know in Egypt: a guide for Australasian soldiers*, Societe Orientale de Publicite, Cairo, 1915.

Bet-El, Ilana R., *Conscripts: forgotten men of the Great War*, Sutton, Gloucestershire, 2003.

Blackmore, Kate, *The Dark Pocket of Time: war, medicine and the Australian state, 1914–1935*, Lythrum Press, Adelaide, 2008

Butler, A. G., *Official History of the Australian Army Medical Services, 1914–1918*

> *Volume I — Gallipoli, Palestine and New Guinea*, AWM, Canberra, (2nd edition), 1938
>> Chapter VII, 'The Gallipoli Campaign: strategic preparations'
>> Chapter X, 'The Landing: expeditionary base'
> *Volume II — The Western Front*, AWM, Canberra (1st edition), 1940
> *Volume III — Special Problems and Services*, AWM, Canberra, (1st edition), 1943
>> Section I, Chapter III, 'The Venereal Diseases in the War of 1914–18'
>> Section IV, Chapter XIV, 'Sea Transport of Australian Soldiers'

Calder, Winty, *Australian Aldershot: Langwarrin military reserve, Victoria, 1886–1980*, Jimaringle, Melbourne, 1987

Carlyon, Les, *The Great War*, Pan Macmillan, Sydney, 2006

Clark, Manning, *Manning Clark on Gallipoli*, Melbourne University Press, Melbourne, 2005

Collett, H. B., *The 28th: a record of war service with the Australian Imperial Force, 1915–1919. Volume 1 — Egypt, Gallipoli, Lemnos Island, Sinai Peninsula*, Trustees of the Public Library, Museum, and Art Gallery of Western Australia, Perth, 1922

Corfield, Robin S., *Don't Forget Me, Cobber: the battle of Fromelles*, Melbourne University Press, Melbourne, 2009

Downing, W. H., *Digger Dialects*, Oxford University Press, Melbourne, 1990

——, *To the Last Ridge*, Duffy and Snellgrove, Sydney, 1998

Duffy, Christopher, *Through German Eyes: the British and the Somme 1916*, Weidenfeld and Nicolson, London, 2006

Fairey, Eric, *The 38th Battalion AIF*, Bendigo Advertiser and the Cambridge Press, Bendigo, Victoria, 1920

Ferguson, Niall, *The Pity of War 1914–1918*, Penguin Books, London, 1999

Hartnett, H. G., *Over the Top: a digger's story of the Western Front*, Allen and Unwin, Sydney, 2009

Helmi, Nadine, and Fischer, Gerhard, *The Enemy at Home: German internees in World War I Australia*, University of NSW Press, Sydney, 2011

Horner, David, 'Maurice Vincent Buckley' in Nairn, Bede, and Serle, Geoffrey, (eds), *Australian Dictionary of Biography, Volume 7*, Melbourne University Press, Melbourne, 1979

Junger, Ernst, *Storm of Steel*, Penguin Books, London, 2004

Kahan, H. K., *The 28th Battalion, Australian Imperial Force: a record of war service*, HK Kahan, Perth, 1969

Keegan, John, *The First World War*, Vintage Books, New York, 1999

Knyvett, R. Hugh, *Over There with the Australians*, Charles Scribner's Sons, New York, 1918

Langdon-Brown, W., and Murphy, J. K., *The Practitioner's Encyclopaedia of Medical Treatment*, Henry Frowde, London, 1915

Larsson, Marina, *Shattered Anzacs: living with the scars of war*, University of NSW Press, Sydney, 2009

Lewis, Milton, *Thorns on the Rose: the history of sexually transmitted diseases in Australia in international perspective*, AGPS, Canberra, 1998

Lindsay, Patrick, *Fromelles*, Hardie Grant, Melbourne, 2007

Lynch, E. P. F., *Somme Mud: the war experiences of an Australian infantryman in France 1916–1919*, Random House, Sydney, 2006

Malvery, Olive, *The White Slave Market*, Stanley Paul, London, 1912

Mansfield, Peter, *A History of the Middle East*, Penguin, London, (2nd edition), 2003

Martyr, Philippa, *Paradise of Quacks: an alternative history of medicine in*

Australia, Macleay Press, Sydney, 2002

Mason, Tony, and Riedi, Eliza, *Sport and the Military: the British armed forces 1880–1960*, Cambridge University Press, Cambridge, 2010

Maxwell, Joseph, *Hell's Belles and Mademoiselles*, Angus and Robertson, Sydney, 1932

McCoy, Alfred W., *Drug Traffic: narcotics and organized crime in Australia*, Harper and Row, Sydney, 1980

Mitchell, George, *Backs to the Wall: a larrikin on the Western Front*, Allen and Unwin, Sydney, 2007

Mitchell, T. J., and Smith, G. M., *Medical Services, Casualties, and Medical Statistics of the Great War*, HM Stationery Office, London, 1931

Penguin Books, *Poems of the Great War, 1914–1918*, London, 1998

Perry, Roland, *Monash: the outsider who won a war*, Random House, Sydney, 2004

Porter, Roy, *Blood and Guts: a short history of medicine*, WW Norton, New York, 2003

Porter, Roy, *Quacks: fakers and charlatans in English medicine*, Tempus, London, 2003

Ramsay Silver, Lynette, *Marcel Caux: a life unravelled*, John Wiley and Sons, Milton, Queensland, 2006

Rees, Peter, *The Other Anzacs: the extraordinary story of our World War 1 Nurses*, Allen and Unwin, Sydney, 2009

Rout, Ettie, *Safe Sex: a return to sanity*, William Heinemann, London, 1922

Russell, Thomas, *Egyptian Service, 1902–1946*, John Murray, London, 1949

Shalit, Ben, *The Psychology of Conflict and Combat*, Praeger, New York, 1988.

Sim, Norma, *The Sixty Miler*, Pier 9, Sydney, 2008

Smith, Neil, *What's In a Name?: aliases of the Australian Military Forces 1914–1919*, Mostly Unsung Military History Research and Publications, Melbourne, 1995

Stanley, Peter, *Bad Characters: sex, crime, mutiny, murder, and the Australian Imperial Force*, Pier 9, Sydney, 2010

Tolerton, Jane, *Ettie: a life of Ettie Rout*, Penguin, Auckland, 1992

Travers, Richard, *Diggers in France: Australian Soldiers on the Western Front*, ABC Books, Sydney, 2008

Tregarthen, Greville, *Sea Transport of the AIF*, Naval Transport Board, Melbourne, 1920

Walker, Allan S., 'Clinical Problems of War', in Long, Gavin, (ed.), *Australia in the War of 1939-45, Series 5–Medical*, AWM, Canberra, 1952

Willey, Harry, *Scone's Fallen ANZACs*, Harry Willey, Scone, 2005

Theses

Hemming, Lisabeth, *Soldiers, Sex, and Syphilis: venereal disease in the Australian Imperial Force, August 1914 to April 1915*, honours thesis, University of New England, undated

Millar, John, *A Study in the Limitations of Command: General Sir William Birdwood and the AIF, 1914–1918*, University of NSW, 1993

O'Keefe, Brendan, *Venereal Disease and the Military: the case of Australian servicemen in Malaya 1950–1960*, University of New England, 1991

Websites

AIF Project, The, https://www.aif.adfa.edu.au/index.html

Australian Dictionary of Biography, http://adb.anu.edu.au/

    Bate, Weston, *Robert Williams*

    Clark, Chris, *William Bridges*

    Clark, Manning, *John Bromby*

    Horner, David, *Maurice Buckley*

    Hill, A. J., *William Birdwood*

    Inglis, Kenneth, *Charles Bean*

    Inglis, Kenneth, *Edwin Bean*

    Murray-Smith, Stephen, *James Barrett*

    Thomas, Alan, *Walter Conder*

Australian Light Horse Studies Centre, http://alh-research.tripod.com/Light_Horse/index.blog?topic_id=1104120

Digger History, http://www.diggerhistory.info/

Glossary of Slang and Peculiar Terms in Use in the AIF 1921–1924, http://andc.anu.edu.au/australian-words/aif-slang

The Harrower Collection of memorabilia of the 33rd, 34th, 35th, and 36th Australian Infantry Battalions (9th Infantry Brigade), http://www.harrowercollection.com/

Lost Leaders of Anzacs, http://www.anzacs.org/

Index